From the Snows of

Kathmandu

to

The Sands of

Timbuktu

A MEMOIR

Juanita Owen Fleming

with

Robert L. Fleming

TO SOW THE FALLOW SOIL

Winston-Derek Publishers, Inc.
Pennywell Drive—P.O. Box 90883
Nashville, TN 37209

First printing

PUBLISHED BY WINSTON-DEREK PUBLISHERS, INC.
Nashville, Tennessee 37205

Library of Congress Catalog Card No: 88-51483
ISBN: 1-55523-205-1

Printed in the United States of America

My thanks are due to the friends who have helped me: Alletta Owen and Toni Cossaboom for typing the manuscript; my sister, Bernice Fordham and Sam and Mary Esther Burgoyne for reading the script and making helpful suggestions: and, most of all my co-author, Dr. Robert L. Fleming, my husband, who shared many of the experiences and whose love has been my inspiration.

Juanita Owen Fleming

DEDICATED

TO

ALL WHO STRIVE TO MAKE THIS

A BETTER WORLD

Preface

This book carries the name of two authors although one—Dr. Robert L. Fleming—passed away in April, 1987. A few days after Bob died, I went into his office and looked through his desk. There I found a stack of yellow lined papers with a rubber band around them, papers I had seen him working on for several months. I was curious. It was apparently an autobiography, but as I read I knew it was not *his* autobiography. Yet he continuously used the first person. Then I realized it was *my* autobiography he was attempting to write. But why? Why mine?

As I looked back over the previous year, he had been urging me to write my life story. Was this his way of getting me to finally do it? He knew I would change and correct his statements and facts, but then I would have a start and a reason—a very compelling reason— for going ahead with it. There they lay—all thirteen chapters! I couldn't throw them away.

So here you have my story, some of which is seen through Bob's eyes. Since his were the eyes of love, they have perhaps colored the story just a bit. I have endeavored to make it realistic, and as true and authentic as possible. However, if you detect a dichotomy anywhere this may explain it.

Juanita Owen Fleming

Contents

BOOK ONE

KATHMANDU

1952

Chapter I

I Meet the King

The telegram from Chester Bowles, the American ambassador in Delhi, read, "Can you go to Nepal to deliver Mrs. Rose's baby?" It arrived one morning while I was in the midst of my work at our hospital in Fatehgarh, India, and my response was almost immediate: of course, I will go. Since it was time for my summer vacation, the Presbyterian Board readily granted me leave.

(Another telegram had come a few weeks before, asking me to help evacuate Lowell Thomas, who had broken his hip in Tibet, but the telegram had taken three days to arrive and another nurse had been sent.)*

There was no transportation except the king's plane, which the Embassy borrowed. No commercial air lines, no cars or buses and no roads, only foot paths. This was 1952 and Nepal had just seen the downfall of the old Rana regime six months before. The T.C.A.** mission had been established with Paul Rose as the administrator. His wife was expecting her third child after an interval of eight years.

It was a hot and windy day as the plane took off through the haze, and soon we were winging over the Gangetic plain. I had never been to Nepal, nor had many other Americans. Was it a land of mystery as people had made out? I would soon know.

* Emily Bateman. See *Out of This World* by Lowell Thomas.

** Technical Cooperation Administration formed in 1950 by the 81st Congress for aid to developing countries. In 1964 it became the Agency for International Development (AID).

Flat, dry plains gave way to low, rocky foothills. Soon mountains began to rush at us at a fearful rate until we were literally flying between them. It was breathtaking. Suddenly a valley full of golden grain broke into view, exposing several small towns and villages nestled in the sunlight. We circled a grassy field dotted with cattle—the runway. Only after several minutes was it cleared of livestock, allowing us to touch down in Goucher Field.* We taxied through the grass to a small tent containing a wooden table and a single folding chair.

A lone Nepali officer cleared me and I glanced around at the crowd, faces with decidedly Mongolian appearance that pressed against the fence. The women were wearing brown garments and each a blanket, the end of which was thrown over the right shoulder. They appeared to be strong people with weather-beaten faces.

There was no one there to meet me. I looked around and saw a taxi of sorts—a Rolls Royce well past its prime—waiting outside the fence.

"Do you know where Mr. Rose, the T.C.A. director, lives?" I asked in Hindi.

Yes, he knew, and after loading my skimpy luggage we were off. There were no door handles or fixtures on the taxi. Such items were valued for their silver and had long since been removed.

Kathmandu City was some five miles to the west over a winding, bumpy road. We drove past wheat fields heavy with grain, many terra cotta dwellings, often with thatched roofs, and innumerable animals. Gradually, rural farming communities gave way to shops with open fronts and larger places of business. We had reached Kathmandu.

Our car chugged up a short hill into Dilli Bazaar. I saw no other automobiles, only masses of people walking in the streets, along with cows, buffaloes, dogs, goats, and chickens. The taxi's raucous horn kept blaring. At last we came to a halt in front of a white palace, with a porte-cochere draped in long lines of orange trumpet flowers. The extensive lawn was bordered with a low hedge of hundreds of gardenia shrubs in full bloom. This was

* Translation: Cow pasture. A name it still carries.

Rabi Bhawan, the Rose's residence.

The first floor was taken up with offices and storerooms. The family lived on the second floor, reached by a stairway whose carpet was adorned with large roses, one rose on each step. (The builder, Col. Rabi Shamshere Jung Bahadur Rana, never dreamed he would have Americans living here by the name of Rose!)

Paul Rose met me at the landing and introduced Mary, his wife, and Eveline Holmes, whom I knew from India. Eveline had accompanied me to a village where I did a difficult delivery, and was the one, I realized, who had suggested my name to the Embassy.

It had been planned that Eveline and I would occupy the gambling den.* It was a most attractive place, a small round house within a walled compound and a sunken garden laden with colorful flowers. One entered by a small gate, which could be locked. It even had electric lights, but water had to be carried in. It was an ideal place for privacy and quiet.

That first afternoon, Mary and the other ladies of the AID mission were invited to the British Embassy for tea. Since they did not know of my arrival, I was not invited, so Paul asked if I would like to accompany him to a groundbreaking ceremony for a village school.

The road lay over a rough, bumpy road, and in spite of the dust stirred up by the Jeep, I enjoyed the sight of the Persian lilacs, silky oak and bottlebrush trees lining the roadway. The typical dress for men seemed to be peaked caps and long shirts hung over tightly fitting trousers. Rural women appeared in black bodices and long full skirts with red borders. Children wore simple, loose upper shirts and were naked from the waist down. They all covered their faces with scarves against the dust we kicked up.

The school site was bustling with activity. A platform stood in front of the school site and this was thoughtfully topped by a colorful *shamianah* (awning) to protect honored guests from the sun. Folding chairs lined the platform on either side of three armchairs.

---

* It was formerly used for gambling by the maharajas.

We were escorted by the headmaster, past rows of school children seated on the ground, to the platform. I was placed near the center with Paul on my right.

Suddenly, with a great blaring of horns, a pickup drove up, and out jumped liveried men in crimson and gold uniforms. They scurried about, lifting a long, narrow red carpet which they unrolled from the road to the platform. Potted palms were placed on either side of the carpet.

We were surprised by this sudden burst of activity and Paul whispered, "Someone important is coming."

No sooner had he spoken than another jeep, bulging with buglers in red uniforms, screeched to a halt. Then, just as the musicians had taken their positions, a shiny new Rolls Royce drew up, flying the royal flag of Nepal. His Majesty the King had arrived.

King Tribhuban Bir Bikram Shah stepped out of the Rolls Royce and was followed by his entire cabinet.

I leaned over and asked Paul in a whisper, "Shouldn't I take a seat in the second row?"

Overhearing, the headmaster said, "I've placed you just where I want you."

His Majesty was rather large and tall with a smiling, round face. He greeted his foreign visitors and took the middle chair, flanked by the health minister on his left and his commerce minister on his right, next to me.

Once settled, His Majesty leaned over and asked me in excellent English, "What brings you to Nepal?"

"I was asked by the Ambassador in Delhi to come here to deliver Mrs. Rose," I replied.

"Oh, then you are a nurse! We need nurses badly in Nepal."

The King then conferred briefly with the health minister, instructing him to call me to the Health Department office the very next morning.

A blast of bugles announced that the ceremony had begun.

At a signal, the king stepped forward and cut the ribbon. Then the scroll was unfurled, revealing plans for the new school building. Lengthy speeches followed—the headmaster, assembled dignitaries,and local officials all spoke. At the close, the children sang two songs and the king moved to his car, followed by his cabinet, and they swirled away in the dust.

Paul and I returned to our jeep and slowly moved through the assembled crowd. Paul had not expected the king to be present. Thinking he himself was to be the guest of honor, he had nervously been thinking up a short speech for the occasion.

On the way home I kept thinking, "Here I have met the king on my first day in Nepal !"

That evening we recounted the events of the day. Back in my room in the gambling den I lay awake a long time; so much had happened.

Next day, the health minister's Rolls Royce arrived at midmorning to take me to Singha Durbar. The driver drew up beside the most magnificent building in Nepal. Chandra Shumshere Jung Bahadur Rana had seen the palace in Versailles early in the century and had instructed his workers to build him an even larger and more beautiful palace,which was to become the private residence of the maharajahs.

But following the revolution in 1950-51, the reign of hereditary prime ministers* came to an end, and His Royal Highness, King Tribhuban Bir Bikram Shah Dev regained ruling power for the monarchy. He converted the Singha Durbar into the government secretariat, where most of the ministers and their assistants had their offices. The king lived in his own palace a mile away.

The Singha Durbar was four stories high and about a mile around. What a labyrinth of halls and rooms! One could easily get lost among the many winding corridors. Fortunately, a guide was waiting for me at the first gate. He led me up some stairs, around a quadrangle, up more stairs, and along an endless corridor to the office of the health minister. This was the first of a series of meetings with Mr. Gurung, who greeted me in Hindi, as he did not speak English.

"His Majesty tells me you speak Hindi. I am sure we are going to get along well."

Our opening topic of conversation was about the lack of nurs-

---

* For several centuries the ruling power had been held by the Rana family, who handed down the office of prime minister (maharajah) from generation to generation, while keeping the royal family virtual captives in the palace.

ing services in Nepal. Only a few months earlier, the crown prince had lost his wife in childbirth with the arrival of their sixth child. There were no obstetricians and not a single nurse in all Nepal. Nor were there facilities for a major operation, should one be necessary. If the king's family or the more wealthy Ranas needed medical attention, they would fly down to Calcutta. The king, his family, and His Majesty's government were all concerned and wished to know what could be done.

I had come on the scene at the moment when officials were acutely conscious of their need. I felt God had brought me to Nepal not only for a delivery but for some deeper reason. Could it be that I could work with the government in mapping out a workable nursing program?

The health minister suggested that I be commissioned to make a survey of existing facilities. During the next few days, I visited the Military Hospital, the male and female sections of Bir Hospital*, the Cholera Hospital on the west side, Tokha Tuberculosis Hospital up on the northern rim of the valley, as well as a number of private clinics.

I visited and asked questions. Who cared for the patients? Who administered medicines? How many were employed? And not one nurse in all these hospitals!

Frequently, Mr. Gurung and I compared notes. Growing out of this survey was the very obvious need for nurses.

"What would you suggest?" he inquired.

"You might employ British or other foreign nurses to start a training program. Or you might send your girls to England or America to train, which would mean they would have to have a knowledge of English. But I doubt if you could find English-speaking girls who would want to undertake this, and it would be frightfully expensive.

"Or you might send Nepali girls to India for training. That would be cheaper all around," I pointed out.

Mr. Gurung considered this for a while, then said, "I agree with you. We might better send our girls to India."

"We have our hospital in Fatehgarh, in the United Provinces,"

*Named for Maharajah Bir Shamshere who came to power after killing Maharajah Udip Rana in 1885. He ruled Nepal until 1901.

I volunteered, "where we have a training program. We could take either two or four girls and I would be there to supervise them."

"First I want to consult with my government about the program," replied Mr. Gurung, "then I'll see what we can do about recruiting some girls. Beginning tomorrow we have a three-day holiday and all government offices will be closed. Would you kindly return on Monday?"

I consented.

"Thank you for coming," he said. "This peon will show you to your car."

The health minister placed his hands together in a farewell gesture and said, "Namaste," and I, doing the same, turned to go. I would never have gotten out of this place by myself, I thought as we went down some wooden stairs, through a dark passageway to more stairs, and finally out through a side entrance. Back down the dusty road to the Thapatali crossroad, the traffic policeman beckoned us westward along the narrow Tripueshwar bazaar. After another mile or so we were back at Rabi Bhawan Palace.

"Well, how did your conference go?" Mary inquired eagerly.

"Oh, I have been given so much work to do I am sure it will take me all of a month to finish it," I answered. "I have been commissioned to make a survey of existing nursing facilities.

"And what about you, Mary? Do you feel all right? Let us go into the bedroom so I may examine you. When are you due?"

"In about two weeks, I should think," she replied.

Then I pointed out, "In that case we should do a little planning. From what I gathered from the health minister, there are very few facilities available, should you need them. I think your delivery will be quite normal, but after an eight-year interval, there are factors we should consider. As I have been thinking it over, I would be much happier if I could take you to Landour to Dr. Bethel Fleming. She is a skilled obstetrician on the staff at Landour Hospital."

Mary's eyes brightened. "Then I could see our two girls in Woodstock School!* They have been very eager about the coming

---

*Woodstock School was founded in 1854 by the London Society for Promoting Christian Education for Females in the East. It later became co-educational and interdenominational.

of the new baby. As soon as Paul comes home, I'll talk to him about it."

Paul's jeep pulled into the driveway and he came bounding up the stairs with his hands full of invitations from the palace.

"The whole American community [about a dozen of us] has been invited to the *Tundikhel* * to witness the military show celebrating a rather special festival," enthused Paul.

"I'm afraid I can't go," said Mary. "Juanita feels we should get ready to go to Landour for my delivery. If you would request the use of the king's plane for day after tomorrow I could get there the same day.

"Juanita says it would be safer to have the delivery in Landour Community Hospital under the supervision of Dr. Bethel Fleming."

"It sounds like an excellent plan," replied Paul. "I'll see what I can do. One can't get hold of the plane all that easily, but I shall go to the palace to see what can be arranged. Then I'll contact Delhi."

As the jeep left, Mary turned to me and said, "But Juanita, you needn't go with me; it will only take an hour to Delhi. The Embassy car will be waiting for me and I can go right on by car to Landour, Mussoorie, and be there by afternoon. My time is not due for a couple of weeks."

"That is true," I replied. "If there were the slightest risk I would come with you."

"Juanita, I have a feeling His Majesty's government needs you right now and that you should stay here in Kathmandu."

"Maybe you're right, especially since the health minister had made a rather important request. I'll help you get ready," I volunteered.

The bearer rang the bell for lunch just as Paul drove in. His Majesty had offered his private plane, day after tomorrow, to take Mary to Delhi. A wire to the Indian Embassy in Delhi got through and they would be ready for Mary. We sat down to lunch. So much had taken place in the last hour or two.

Immediately after lunch a car pulled into the porte-cochere— a Rolls Royce bearing the royal flag.

---

* Parade ground.

"Oh, it's someone from the palace!" exclaimed Mary. "I had better change my dress."

A servant came up the stairs bearing a gilded card with the names of the second and third princesses. Mary took the card, thinking it was for her. But with a look of surprise she handed it to me.

"Bearer, show the guests up," she ordered.

Princess Princep Shah was impressive in a beautiful pink Benarsi silk sari. Her slighter sister-in-law, Princess Helen, wore one of mauve.

"When we heard that you speak Hindi we wanted to come over and meet you," said Princess Princep Shah.

Later I learned that I was the first American visitor the princesses had been able to talk with. What an animated conversation! We talked of many things—the flowers in the gardens, the customs of women in Nepal, the things one should buy in Kathmandu and some of the upcoming holidays.

Almost an hour later the guests rose to take their leave.

"We hope we shall meet with you often," said Princess Helen. It had been a happy time together.

I had come to a crossroads and needed to pray about things. I had thought I would be returning to India with Mary, but she felt so sure she did not need me. The health minister had given me quite an assignment. What should I do, go or stay? I knew the Lord would make it plain to me. Here I was *in* Nepal where very few Christians had ever been. Had God led me to this moment? What an opportunity! It did seem I should remain a few more weeks and suggest possibilities to His Majesty's government regarding a nursing program. I was glad to be here with something to do.

Next morning, Paul and I and two or three others from the palace drove out to the airport to see Mary off. The wind was fairly strong and the air was filled with dust as we watched the plane glide over the grass and slowly rise at the end of the runway. Instead of clearing the rim of hills surrounding the valley, the plane headed for a cut between the hills, along the Bagmati River, a tributary of the Ganges.

"Mary will be in good hands as soon as she reaches Dr. Bethel," I remarked.

We returned to our Jeeps and drove back to Rabi Bhawan.

* * * * *

Mary wrote us about her trip. A blast of hot air like a furnace hit her as she descended from the plane at Delhi. She had never experienced the Indian *loo* before: the strong southern air currents which were a prelude to the monsoon season.

Mary hurried into the airport, where she was met by a man from the American Embassy. He explained that an Indian driver was waiting to take them cross country to Dehra Dun and Mussoorie, and escorted her to a fairly new Chevrolet after she freshened up a bit.

The Delhi streets were crowded with trucks, bicycles, two-wheeled tongas, ox carts, and people. The Chevrolet was only partially air-conditioned, so Mary dampened a kerchief and tied it around her head.

Soon they were on a broad dusty road lined with trees, many of which were mangoes. Fields of sugarcane, pulses and mustard stretched out between groves of trees. Thatched huts clustered around ponds, where people were bathing, washing clothes and immersing their water buffaloes to escape the heat.

Low-lying hills ranged ahead. Soon they were driving through lush green, jungle vegetation backed by rocky outcrops. The road wound upward to a 3,000-foot pass, descending again until it reached the edge of a broad valley bounded on the north by still higher ranges. Dehra Dun was quite a thriving city.

From there the road began to weave in switchbacks as it rapidly gained altitude. The dust was less, the air cooler, and oak and pine trees began to appear. At the tollgate, two little urchins were selling freshly-picked yellow raspberries, while others offered cookies, sweets, and peeled hard-boiled eggs.

The road ended at Kincraig, and Mary's escort engaged a dandy* to take her the rest of the way and porters to carry her bags. Bidding goodbye to her escort and driver, Mary took her place in the dandy and was soon swinging up the last few miles

---

* A sort of sedan chair, quite comfortable, carried on the shoulders of four coolies.

to Landour. From time to time a coolie would shift the weight of his load to the other shoulder but kept trudging on and upward without missing a step.

The sun was nearing the horizon of the dim plains below when they reached the main road at the Picture Palace, and the coolies set the dandy down for a few minutes' rest. Ladies in colorful saris and well-dressed men strolled by.

Two European ladies approached and Mary found out from them that she was about twenty minutes from Landour Community Hospital. As it turned out, they were teachers at Woodstock School, which stood about a mile beyond the hospital.

"Could you do me a great favor?" she asked them, explaining that she had just come from Kathmandu, Nepal, and that her two daughters, Betsy and Carol Rose, were students at Woodstock School. She asked the teachers if they could tell the girls that their mother was at the hospital and would like to see them. The teachers, who knew the girls, promised to give them the message.

After a simple supper served in her hospital room, Mary lay down gratefully. On the gentle breeze floating through the window there came a sound of distant bells. Nearer and nearer they came, evidently a train of pack animals passing on the road below.

From a distant minaret, a muezzin called the faithful to prayer.

"What a clear, strong voice he has," Mary thought drowsily. The clock tower in the bazaar struck nine as she closed her eyes in sleep.

Chapter II

Evening at the Cloud Club

Back in Kathmandu, a momentous event was about to take place. At the time, the hand of God was invisible, but in retrospect, His plan was obvious.

Paul had wanted for some time to go to the exclusive Cloud Club and invited us ladies to go along.

"We'd love to go, Paul, but I didn't bring any evening clothes along," I responded. "However, perhaps I can find some material in the bazaar to make a simple dress. I have seen some lovely fabrics, even though there are no ready-made clothes available."

I found a cloth shop in the bazaar and told the shopkeeper what I wanted.

"Come with me upstairs, where I keep the finer materials," he said.

So we climbed up a dark, narrow staircase, and the array of silks, brocades, and satins that met my eyes outdid anything I had ever seen in London, Paris, or America. It was definitely a shop for royalty. I purchased a piece of soft pink silk and hurried home to make my dress for the Club.

It was a dreary, foggy night as we drove the Jeep up the steep hill, round and round, until we arrived at a spot close to the summit. There, in a bungalow lit with petromax lights, blared a loud, raucous juke box.

The main room was large, with benches and seats arranged around the edge. Women were at a premium. Few of the Rana ladies accompanied their husbands to places like this. After a short time, a well-dressed gentleman came up and asked whether we might sit and talk a bit. We found a corner as far away from the jukebox as possible. At once he introduced himself as Crown Prince Mahendra Bir Bikram Shah.

"My father told me about you after you met at the school ground-breaking ceremony."

"Yes," I answered, "I was highly honored to meet His Majesty, your father."

I told him that I had been sent by the American Embassy in Delhi to deliver Mrs. Rose.

"Yes, I know," replied the crown prince. "That is why I want to talk with you. My wife, Indira, died only four months ago in child-birth. It was all so useless. If we only had had someone like you, Indira need not have died."

There was a moment of silence, then I said, "Yes, Nepal needs nurses and obstetricians who can treat the women. Health Minister Gurung and I have talked at some length about this problem. He has asked me to make recommendations after I have made a survey of the existing facilities."

The two of us talked on and on about many things, including religious topics, in which the crown prince was much interested. Had he not sent his own children to Catholic schools in Darjeeling soon after the revolution* the year before?

At one point we were interrupted by a man who asked me for a dance. Looking up I saw a youngish Nepali individual with a wilted collar, shirt open, tie askew, and wet with perspiration. He was breathing heavily. I declined the invitation and, after he had gone, turned to the crown prince.

"I don't think that man is in fit condition to ask a lady to dance," I remarked.

"That is true. My brother drinks too much," he volunteered.

It was after twelve when we decided it was time to leave. We three Americans had been cordially received and had greatly enjoyed ourselves. Eveline had danced the whole evening.

---

* His Majesty, King Tribhuban and his family had been held prisoner in his palace by the Nepal prime ministers, as had his predecessors, until escaping to India in November, 1950. When they returned in February, 1951, the prime minister, Mohan Shumshere Jung Bhadur Rana, never again locked up the royal family in their palace. And he soon felt it wise to retire permanently to South India, where he hoped to spend the rest of his life.

To me, it was the opening I had been waiting for. My talk with Prince Mahendra promised much in the way of medical advance for Nepal. I hoped that I would be able to follow through with my survey and make some suggestions.

As we made our way down the winding road, Paul remarked, "At last I have seen the Cloud Club."

The following morning I was driven to Singha Durbar. We drove ten miles an hour or less, for the road was crowded with people, dogs, cattle, a few bicycles and an occasional Jeep. At one place there lazed a bunch of rough-looking hill men.

Most of the Nepalis appeared to be Aryans of varied hues of brown. Men often wore tight, white trousers and a dark coat, below which drooped a long white shirt tail. Nepali topis of various materials adorned their heads. Some wore shoes, while others had open sandals, tennis shoes or went barefoot. Women, of which there were few, were clothed in tight bodices, flowing skirts, and light shawls thrown over one shoulder. Some had their hair in buns decorated with red hibiscus, while younger girls, their hair in single braids, wore long jackets and flowing white trousers. Most of the populace was quite oblivious to the Jeep and walked across the road at will. The driver explained later that should he injure anyone, he would be clapped in jail. The people had the right-of-way and any accident was considered the fault of the driver. So he merely crept along the street.

At the Singha Durbar, I was guided to the health minister's office.

"*Namaste*, Miss Owen," said Mr. Gurung, rising with the palms of his hands clasped together in the traditional Nepali greeting. "We would like to have you visit our Cholera Hospital at Teku today, if you will."

The telephone rang, and as he answered it, I happened to glance at a letter on his desk. Though it was upside down, I recognized the letterhead of our hospital in Fatehgarh. I knew that Dr. Carl Fredericks, who had accompanied the Drs. Fleming to western Nepal, had been planning to send a letter to His majesty's government asking whether they would be interested in a more permanent arrangement for medical work by the team who had worked in Tansen that past winter.

Yes, this must be Carl's letter, I thought.

Finishing his phone conversation, Mr. Gurung returned to his desk and looked down at the letter.

"I have been instructed by my government," he said, "to refuse the offer from a Dr. Fredericks to come to Nepal for medical work. Nepal has its own medical department and good doctors. We have never allowed foreign doctors to come into the country."

"I can understand the hesitation on the government's part," I suggested, "but His Majesty would very much like to have help for the women of Nepal. I had a long conversation with the crown prince on this subject only last night, and I suggest you check with His Majesty before you write your refusal letter.

Laying the letter aside, Mr. Gurung agreed that he did represent the king but that it would be better to consult with His Majesty on the matter. He then gave me information about the Cholera Hospital, set up several years before to deal with the regularly occurring, four-year cholera epidemics. Afterwards, he called his peon, and with the usual farewell, sent me through the labyrinth of corridors to a driver waiting in the courtyard.

The Cholera Hospital was much like the health minister had described it. He had failed, however, to mention anything about the approach to the place. It was the city dump, with rubbish above the road and along the narrow lane, the area where night soil was collected. There were few flush toilets in the city, so sweepers brought their buckets of night soil to this central place, where the contents were sold to distributors and carried to gardeners, who used it to enrich their vegetable gardens.

Apparently there were no hospitalized cholera cases at the moment, but three patients were evidently suffering from small pox. Since there were other patients as well, and no cholera, I assumed the hospital was being used for assorted contagious diseases. Two orderlies were in evidence. The doctor had not yet been around that day. I made note of various things, then returned to the car and was driven back to write my report.

That afternoon as I went on my usual walk, my *hawa khana**, a Nepali lady in a colorful *sari* stepped through the moon gate from the adjoining compound. Accompanying her was a bevy of ladies in waiting, clad in brilliant silks. With them was a white,

*Literally, "eating the air."

pint-sized dog.

Obviously someone of importance, I thought. I addressed her in Hindustani, much to her delight.

"I am Madhuri and we live in Kalamati Durbar, just over the wall," she explained and expressed her surprise that I used the Hindi language.

I noticed that only the princess wore shoes, while the others had their bare feet dyed with henna. The group of young women strolled along the extensive walk bordered by a gardenia hedge while the two of us chatted. Princess Madhuri seemed hungry for outside contacts, and many more happy walks were to follow. The acquaintance begun that day became a friendship that lasted many years.

Paul explained later that "Marjorie," as the Americans called her, was one of the numerous daughters of Maharajah Judha Shumshere Jung Bahadur Rana and that Kalamati Durbar Palace had been a wedding gift to the chief wife of the Maharajah.

Rabi Bhawan compound, through which the party strolled, was a quadrangle with an inner border of gardenias and an outer border of tall silky oaks, eucalyptus and chinaberry trees. The inner lawn boasted of a central pool flanked by a couple of magnolia and cypress trees. The porte-cochere of Rabi Bhawan Palace was festooned with an orange trumpet vine. Banks of petunias and other annuals had been planted around the moon gate. This was a delightful place to walk in the cool of the evening when the air was heavy with the scent of gardenias.

I accompanied the group back to the moon gate, but just as Princess Madhuri was about to step through, she turned, picked up the tiny white Nepalese Apso, which I had admired, and presented it to me. I was taken aback, but thanked her profusely as she made her way to her Kalamati Palace. I turned and walked up the rose-carpeted stairs to the Rose's suite.

"What have you here?" exclaimed Eveline when she saw the tiny head peering out of my coat pocket.

"Oh, the rani who lives in the neighboring palace, just gave her to me. Let's find a place for her. We'll call her Rani."

We settled down for the night.

Next morning the door was ajar and the dog was gone. Evidently a maid servant had come by and opened the door and the dog had run out and disappeared. She must have gone home, we thought. Sure enough, while we were having our breakfast the watchman from next door arrived with Rani.

A messenger then came bounding up the stairs with a telegram in his hand. He passed it to Paul, who opened it and read: "Baby girl arrived last night. Weight: 8 lbs. 12 oz. Normal delivery. Mother and child doing well. Signed, Bethel Fleming, M.D."

"Oh, congratulations, Paul," Eveline and I cried.

Paul blushed and rung the outstretched hands. "I think Mary will be back soon," he said with a feeling of anticipation.

As predicted, Mary and her new baby flew in on Friday of the following week, both looking fine. It was so good to have her home again.

I had feelings of anticipation and achievement when the driver took me on my morning trips to Singha Durbar. Mr. Gurung was a jovial person and always met me with a beaming smile. Following the usual *namaste* greeting, I drew up my chair to plan for the day.

"I have been working on the problem of making selections for nurse's training in your hospital down in India," said Mr. Gurung. "It is a more difficult task than you would imagine. You see, girls in Nepal have only recently been admitted to school. That was about four years ago. And so the level of achievement is not very high; there are no high school graduates among our girls. What is more, to be a nurse is not the custom among Nepali families, and they feel it is a lowering of their moral standards to allow their girls to take up nursing. That is one reason for the lack of nurses in Nepal. To try to change social customs is almost impossible. I have talked with a dozen or more families and only two have given partial consent. For one thing, they do not want their girls to go so far away from home. And for another, none of the ones I interviewed can speak Hindi, let alone English. I understand the nurse's courses at Fatehgarh hospital are in Hindi."

"Yes, that is correct," I replied. "We mostly use Hindi and Urdu and a bit of English."

"Well," continued Mr. Gurung, "our government can set aside a sum which will largely cover expenses."

"It may be possible to supplement costs with a mission stipend," I answered. "I think I can arrange it. My hope is that the girls can go with me shortly when I return to my work in India."

"We would like that," replied Mr. Gurung, "as anyone we select is likely never to have been out of Nepal before. And in regard to these possibilities, the families of two girls have said they would allow their daughters to take up training if they are in Fatehgarh and if *you* would look after them."

"Yes, I would be more than glad to do this, for I see how badly nurses are needed in Nepal. We will help them with their language and get them settled so they will be happy there."

"One of the girls is named Uma Devi Das," continued Mr. Gurung. "She comes from a high caste family, but she has had very little formal schooling. She seems quite capable, and we would like to send her with you. The other is Rukhmani Charan, who is a year or two younger. She is also quite bright, and her family is also high caste Hindu. Rukhmani expressed quite a lot of interest in my proposal. I think we could have them ready to go by the time you leave."

I hurried to Rabi Bhawan with news of the latest developments.

"The government will send two girls to Fatehgarh where I can look after them," I announced to Eveline and Mary. "That will take a lot of doing, since the girls have never been out of Nepal and they only know Nepali and Newari. They will have to pick up Hindi right away, but I think we can manage it.

"They have not been in school, but both of them were tutored at home and are very intelligent. It is a heavy responsibility, but Nepal needs nurses so badly, I shall gladly do all I can to keep the girls happy and to help them make progress in their training. This will take three years, of course, and they may not get home in all that time."

The bearer rang the bell for lunch. As Paul came in, his jovial smile indicated that something was up. It was always pleasant to hear his Virginia drawl.

"We are invited to the British Embassy to tea this afternoon, in honor of Col. John Hunt* who is leading the British Recon-

---

* Col. John Hunt became Sir John Hunt, after the successful expedition on Everest the following year.

naissance Expedition to Mount Everest. It will be a big affair and most of the elite of Nepal will be there, but the dress is informal."

Although that was only a three-hour notice, there was an eager response. To meet Ambassador and Mrs. Summerhays, in itself, was an honor. The ambassador had come from a missionary family and was much liked by the Nepalis.

The Rose party squeezed into the Jeep shortly before four. There were not a great number of cars beyond the Rolls Royce of the palace people. Cars of the same make, but of older vintage, were being used as taxis. Many of the Nepalis, not having transportation, had to walk and came a bit late. Paul was very much at the center of things and introduced his party. Ambassador and Mrs. Summerhays were most gracious, and, in turn, introduced the Americans to all the members of the expedition.

"You will come to see us off tomorrow morning at Bhaktapur?" urged Col. Hunt cordially.

"Yes, we shall be there," replied Paul.

There were many important Nepalis present. I greeted various members of the King's family, as well as ministers and others. General Kaiser Shumshere was present, wearing his little iron-rimmed spectacles, as was Mr. Dixit, who invited us to take a conducted tour of Singa Durbar the next week. Also present were Colonel and Mrs. Richard Proud. He was the first secretary of the British Embassy, and Mrs. Proud was a well-known ornithologist. These and other contacts at the tea led to further social events in the coming weeks.

Next morning, Mary felt she should stay home, but Paul, Eveline and I crowded into the Jeep and drove down through town and eastward through Dilli Bazaar, toward Bhaktapur, to see the expedition off. The broad, rolling fields along the eight-mile route were full of people gathering the last of the wheat harvest. Willow trees lined the streams, mostly dry beds this time of year, and as we drove up into the town, we passed through a grove of pines in which resided a colony of noisy fruit bats.

The military installations bordered the road, and soon we saw the open parade ground, where all the gear of the expedition had been assembled. There were hundreds of porters around, some in Sherpa costumes and many in Tamang attire. The loading-up process took quite a while. Each load had to be about sixty pounds, on top of which porters placed their personal belongings. It was fully an hour before the first porters were ready to take off. Meanwhile, the British climbers assembled in a circle, drinking their lemonade and barley water and eating the sandwiches we had prepared. Their hiking outfits were quite attractive and their heavy shoes had been made for mountain climbing.

Then with shouts of "Hip, hip, hurray!" the group started down the eastern road toward Everest. It would be at least six weeks before they returned. The crowd of spectators wished them well.

On the way back to Kathmandu, Paul told us about the Swiss Expedition that had left three months earlier to climb Everest. If successful, they would be the first to make it. In fact, they should have been somewhere near the top by then, but there had been a lot of rain and bad weather of late, which certainly must have hindered them. The British were scheduled to make the climb the following year, leaving in February and attaining the summit, hopefully, by late May, in time for the coronation of Queen Elizabeth.

Nepal had only opened up a year or two before and no one yet had tried to ascend Everest from the southern side. All the earlier attempts had been from the northern Tibetan side, including the famous 1926 attempt in which Mallory and Irvine were last seen very near the summit. A British reconnaissance trip had been made in 1950 and possible routes to the top were charted. There was real competition between mountaineers of several countries to be the first to the top. Thus, Nepal had suddenly become a center of intense interest as far as alpine climbers were concerned.

Evening was always a delightful time. A slight breeze rustled through pine branches and disturbed the eucalyptus leaves, and the air was heavy with the scent of gardenias. As a robin dayal raised his evening song, I saw Princess Madhuri coming through the moon gate. She was followed by her usual ladies-in-waiting, and she greeted her little white dog, which by this time was very content with Eveline and me. Hands with palms held together were raised with the usual greeting and nod of the head.

"I would like to have you come over for tea tomorrow afternoon," invited Madhuri. "About five o'clock we shall look for you.

I am not asking the other American ladies, as none of them speak Hindi and they might not feel at home."

As the party strolled towards the entrance to a neighboring palace grounds beyond the southern wall, the little dog suddenly dashed forward and began to bark furiously. What was causing the disturbance was obvious. Two large snakes were closely entwined and stood up about three feet from the ground. They were performing a mating dance prior to copulation.

"Oh," gasped the princess and several of her ladies, who shielded their eyes, turned, and beat a hasty retreat.

When Rani saw the party leaving abruptly, she came running back. I stood there astonished at the sudden drama and wondered what it was all about. Not a great friend of snakes, I returned to Rabi Bhawan and climbed the rose-carpeted stairs more rapidly than usual. Hurriedly, I told what I had seen and asked what it all meant.

"Oh, we have several rat snakes in the compound," Mary informed me. "They are non-poisonous and, although quite large, they are very beneficial. If it weren't for them, we would be overrun by rats, mice, shrews and toads. We do not harm them. In fact, we seldom see them, for they are largely nocturnal."

"Then should I carry a flashlight at night?" I asked. "We always do down in the plains of India, for some very poisonous species roam around at night and seem to enjoy the warm dust of a footpath. Most of our snake-bite victims come to the hospital at night. Usually, they have been walking barefoot along their usual path and accidentally have stepped on one. Not many die from their bites, but some of them do, unfortunately."

"Nepalis feel it is very bad luck just to see a snake," Mary said. "If one should step across a path of a snake, they say someone in their family will die. The same is true when driving a car and a snake crosses the road ahead of you. One must either turn back or wait until someone else crosses the path first. Quite a few Nepalis have strong feelings in this matter."

"Now I understand," I said, "why the party broke up so suddenly."

"That little dog was the first to see the reptiles, and I imagine they looked strange to her, entwined the way they were. I shall keep a lookout for them from now on."

It so happened that in the next two months not a single snake was reported in the Rabi Bhawan area.

The nights were largely peaceful, but were punctuated at intervals by the howling of numerous dogs. After a quiet interval, first one then another and another would join in a wild chorus which would gradually die down again for a time. There were also the regular sounds of the faithful *chaukidar*, the night watchman who called out to let all know that he was on the job. Then there was some kind of bird which kept up an incessant call, "koel, koel, koel," and another with a four syllable "kaiful packyo," and still another with a plaintive "cuck-oo, cuck-oo" that sounded like a Bavarian cuckoo clock. Except for an occasional rattle of the tin pail in the bathroom, silence reigned. It wasn't until the morning bell sounded that one knew the world was astir again.

Breakfast time was a happy occasion for the Roses and their guests. Paul would outline any unusual events likely to take place that day, and I would see my Rolls Royce waiting for me as I left the compound by ten o'clock. Summer hours at government offices were from ten until four, with tea breaks. Nepalis usually had their first main meal about nine o'clock and the second one after work in the evening. Upper classes often dined around ten p.m. and, of course, got a late start the next day.

The next morning when I visited the health minister's office, two Nepali girls were there, standing to one side. One was small with a lock of hair dangling over her shoulder. She looked uncomfortable. The other, a little taller and well filled out, appeared to be more self-confident. Both demurely hung their heads.

"The parents of these two girls have consented for them to become nursing sisters. This is Uma Devi," Mr. Gurung introduced, "and this is Rukhmani Charan. Both are willing to train in your hospital as you suggested."

I turned to the girls and greeted them warmly in Hindustani, a language they were yet to learn. They smiled a bit and said, "Namaste."

"They will be ready to go with you when you return to India in July," said Mr. Gurung. "Meanwhile, they will get their wardrobes ready.

"By the way, would you lend me some of the papers relating to nursing which you showed me last week, especially those relating to entrance requirements?"

"Oh, certainly," I replied. "I shall bring the material tomorrow."

Thus began new Nepali contacts which would grow into friendships lasting for the next thirty years. Little did I know then what fortunate choices Mr. Gurung had made.

Several times that morning I thought about Madhuri's tea. "What does one wear and how long should one stay?" I was wondering when I returned to Rabi Bhawan.

That morning Paul had received an invitation from the district magistrate of Bhaktapur, Badri Prasad Thapaliya, to come and witness a very special local festival. So, leaving a note for Eveline and me, the Roses had departed for the Newari city in the eastern part of Kathmandu Valley. Nepali festivals continue during the day and far into the night. Sometimes they go on for days.

When it was time for me to go to tea, I elected to pass through the large main entrance rather than the moon gate to Kalamati Durbar. It was only a two-minute walk from Rabi Bhawan. As I entered, I saw a large white palace similar to the one in which the Roses resided. An oval park of green grass was surrounded by roses. At the porte-cochere, Madhuri and her retinue were waiting. With clasped hands and bowing heads, we greeted each other.

"It is so good of you to come," announced our hostess. "Let us go upstairs to the reception room for tea. After that, I would like to show you around."

I had learned that Princess Madhuri was the only daughter of the eighth wife of Maharajah Judha Shumshere J. B. Rana. Her father had retired as prime minister nine years before and was now living as an ascetic in Dehra Dun.

"Would you take me sometime to see my father?" begged Madhuri.

"Why, of course," I replied. "I shall be glad to. We hold our annual mission meeting in Mussoorie, only a few miles above Dehra Dun. I expect to be over there in just about a month and will gladly accompany you to see your father."

Upon entering the palace, I had noted that the layout, like Rabi Bhawan, was around a quadrangle. As I peered into this large open space, I noted a series of rooms on all four sides. Two or three were apparently used as offices, but the remaining ten or twelve rooms were heavily padlocked, and an armed guard squatted on the floor in front of one of them. Later I learned that money, jewels and other valuables, as well as gowns for state and special occasions, were kept there.

The party ascended a broad flight of carpeted stairs to the second floor, where there were two large ballrooms with life-size portraits of Ranas dating back several generations, all in official regalia and finery. Each had a massive gold frame. Largest of these was the portrait of Madhuri's father himself, Maharajah Judha, in royal robes of red and gold.

In one ballroom there was a grand piano in one corner and colorful, overstuffed furniture around the sides of the room. Elaborate chandeliers had been imported from Europe, and large vases of gold and silver held artificial paper and wax floral arrangements. In a large, glass-faced breakfront were gold and silver cups, vases, and *pan** boxes.

As I entered, a large, pleasant lady came in from an adjoining room.

"This is my mother," explained Princess Madhuri. "We live together here. Formerly, I was married to the Maharajah of Jaipur. I went down there to live for a while, but later we separated and I returned to Kathmandu. I am at home here."

The Maharani seated herself and the ladies-in-waiting stood nearby, while the hostess waved me to a large sofa and two elaborately-carved Kashmiri chairs, where she seated herself and me.

What a beautiful tea set and solid silver plates! I was surprised to see that there was only one cup and that none of the others in the room, including Madhuri, were having tea.

"We serve only the honored guest," pointed out the Rani. "We shall have our tea later. This is our Nepali custom."

Curried vegetable *tarkari, samosas,* and *puris* appeared, as well as platters of finger food and bowls of fruit. It was really a meal. I felt a bit self-conscious, eating alone. After a second cup of tea came sweetmeats: *rusagulas, jalebis,* and *gulab jamuns,* flavored with pistachio nuts.

As the tea concluded, Madhuri wished to show me something

---

*Betel nut.

very special. I had noticed four large breakfronts in the dining hall and was directed to one of them. The silver pieces gleamed across the room. Upon closer inspection, I was astonished to see among the silver bowls tiny Post Toasties boxes, as well as various miniature trinkets from Crackerjack boxes.

"These are from America," she informed me. "My father collected them years ago."

Then thanking our hostess profusely, the party descended to the main entrance, where *namastes* were said and I walked toward the moon gate and home.

What a palace, and what an experience!

As it turned out, this was only the first of several such occasions, for Madhuri was lonesome and enjoyed my company, as I did hers.

Some days later, the health minister announced that he wished to take me over to the Bir Female Hospital (named after Bir Shumshere Jung Bahadur Rana, a former maharajah) to see a patient. We descended to the side entrance, entered the private car and were driven out through the massive entrance, along a road bordered with cultivated fields, around an oval of buildings that included shrines, shops, and the post office, and onto the parade ground. At the corner stood a beautiful equestrian statue of Jung Bahadur (1866), festooned with numerous electric lights.

We turned right along the parade ground, past Judha Road and the Military Hospital to the Women's Hospital. At that time it was felt that men and women should not be housed in the same building, thus the "male" and "female" hospitals.

A number of people bowed and *namasteed* the health minister as our party ascended to semi-private rooms on the second floor. We turned into one where a doctor was hovering over a patient. She looked very pale and drawn.

"Two months ago," I was told, "the Rani gave birth to a child which died the second day. Since then she has run a constant fever. We have given her a minimum amount of food and liquid."

Knowing that the practice in India was to starve a patient with fever, I suspected such was the case in Nepal as well.

"The patient is the fifth wife of the general and is very much loved. We wish she would recover her health," confided Mr. Gurung.

"I am not a doctor," I reminded them, "and hesitate to make any suggestions, but in our country we would encourage liquids. I do wish the patient well."

The haunting eyes of the rani followed us to the door as we left.

Downstairs, ward patients had just been served their ten o'clock meal of rice, *dal* and a bit of cooked vegetable, along with sweetened tea. When finished, they placed their white enamel plates under their beds. In passing, I saw several street dogs licking the plates clean. The health minister noticed my astonishment and informed me that this was the Nepali custom. Dogs were sacred, and to give them something to eat brought merit.

"If you have been kind to dogs in this life, the two big mastiffs chained one either side of the gate to the next world will let you through. Otherwise, they will keep you out. Everyone wishes to pass through those gates.

"Of course, I realize this is an unsanitary custom, but traditions are so strong we find it very difficult to change them."

During my visit, I had noticed the absolute lack of nurses. There were some compounders and sweepers besides the doctors, but not one nurse! I realized again how essential was my work of drawing up a nurse's training program for Nepal.

Chapter III

General Kaiser Takes a Bride

What were those emerald green patches of gardens I saw as I came past the fields near Singha Durbar this morning?" I asked at luncheon.

"They must have been seeding beds of rice," Paul replied. "They're prepared a few weeks before the monsoon rains begin, which is usually about the middle of June.

"That electrical storm we had night before last was only a cyclonic disturbance; the wind blew from the west. When the monsoon season begins, winds blow strongly from the southeast, bringing with them a canopy of thick clouds. Then the wind continues to blow from that direction, bringing rain for the next three months. Here we have about forty-five inches a year."

"Does it rain day and night for several days in a stretch as it does in Mussoorie in the northwestern Himalayas?" I asked.

"Oh, no," replied Paul. "It rains for about an hour, mostly at night, then clears up for a while. As soon as the fields are flooded, you will see long lines of women in colorful costumes, planting those seedlings. Then you will want your camera. They don't mind your taking their pictures," added Paul.

"What did I see in that little English newspaper you get, about a cow being milked in the dry Bagmati river bed to bring rain?" inquired Eveline.

"Oh, that actually occurred just before the cyclonic storm," Paul replied. "It has been so dry that the city's reserve water tanks were almost empty. So many people depend on this water for drinking.

"Brahmin priests took their sacred cow into the river bed and milked her there. And within an hour, rain came pouring down. Call it coincidence, if you wish, but the people believe the practice actually works."

Rice is the staple crop for the Nepalis. They eat rice at both of their main meals each day. Most of the two hundred square miles in Kathmandu Valley is farm land. In a country where everything is done by hand, the task is tremendous.

Most of May had been spent whisking off the winter wheat crop from the fields so they would be ready for their rice planting. Potatoes, often only the size of large marbles, had also been removed from the ground, for every bit of soil would be given over to rice. Fields paralleling rivers were vacant for soon the streams, now only a few inches deep, would rise several feet after the heavy downpours and would flood these areas. No more wading across the river then; pedestrians would have to take the bridges. Back in the hills, travelers would have to wait maybe several days until the water level lowered before they could cross.

"By the way," announced Paul, "We have all been invited to General Kaiser Shumshere's palace this afternoon to see his new baby. He is very proud of his attractive wife and their child. Kaiser Mahal is directly opposite the king's palace and is one of the most impressive homes in Kathmandu.

"The General is a very unusual man, the most brilliant in the king's cabinet. His library has over 15,000 volumes and he knows where each book is. He has a photographic memory."

Nepalis have interesting customs, and the story of the general's wife bears this out. It seems that the time came to make the marriage arrangements for his son, so the general sent a search party to Helumbu, a hill district directly north of Kathmandu reputed to have very beautiful girls. They found a young girl of good family who was rather tall and very attractive. Negotiations continued for some days until an arrangement was reached, and she and the party returned to Kathmandu.

The son was not permitted to see his prospective bride until their wedding day, so she was placed in the care of the general himself. When the father saw her, he was smitten with her figure and her beauty. What followed is widely known. General Kaiser arranged for his own wife to be placed in a house farther along the street and he himself married the bride from Helumbu. It was she whom we were going to visit.

At the appointed time, the Jeep turned into the outer entrance to Kaiser Mahal. We drove past magnolias and high eucalyptus trees to the porte-cochere where the general was waiting. He greeted us enthusiastically and led the way up the steps to the foyer. The ladies drew back in astonishment at the magnificent tiger which greeted them. It was a trophy of one of the general's numerous hunts.

"I shot that tiger when King George VI visited Nepal some years ago," he explained.*

Tiger and other skins adorned the room. The general beckoned us to the next room. Lined with tiers and tiers of books, this was obviously the famous library.

"I am always searching for new books about this day and age," he explained. "I have read about a third of these books and browsed through another third.

"Now come upstairs with me to our private rooms."

The walls of the broad stairway were hung with pictures of prominent European personalities the general had met while Nepalese Ambassador in London. The British Royal Family scored heavily, as did Kaiser Wilhelm of Germany. Toward the top of the stairs was an engraving in copper. It was of some Hindu deities which seemed to have a hundred arms and legs.

"That is Shiva and his consort in sexual embrace," explained the general. "We all do it, you know. It's a frequent pastime of the maharajahs, at least. One Nepalese maharajah had over 100 offspring."

We turned to the left and proceeded down a long hallway flanked with steel book cases. Asked about a certain flower seen in hedges along byways of Kathmandu, General Kaiser stopped in front of one of the cases, opened the door, and reached to take a book from the top shelf.

"Here on page nineteen is the species about which you ask." A most remarkable memory!

The party reached the dining room, and the general beckoned to a tall, beautiful lady.

"This is my wife, Rani Kaiser," he proudly announced, "and

---

* *National Geographic Magazine,* October 1910, contains an account of the hunt.

these are my son and daughter. I want you to come into the next room to see our new baby."

It was a spacious room with a large four-poster bed at one side and a little nursery bed just opposite. The general had the nurse pull back the mosquito net and the blue covering so that we could see the baby's dark hair and fair skin. The child was beautiful, and much adored by both parents.

Turning back toward the royal bed, our host explained that the two pallets, one on either side of the bed, were for female attendants who assisted them in intercourse.

"One on each side of my wife," he said.

We had not known that making sexual contact was quite such a community affair, nor one requiring the assistance of servants.

We returned to the dining room, where tea was served.

"I would like to show you my garden," urged the general after we had finished refreshments.

We all followed him downstairs and outside. Many tall trees covered the area, one of which was entwined with a giant bougainvillea vine. On the very top branches hung a colony of large fruit bats, while most of the remainder of the tree was full of nesting cattle egrets. Quite a sight!

Several wild ducks arose from the water as we approached. It was a spacious pool dotted with water lilies.

"Those three blue gum trees are from Australia. They are exceedingly fragrant in wet weather. On the other side of our grounds we have a series of six pagodas representing the six seasons of the Nepali year."

There were six small stone pavilions of varying designs. They seemed to be ornamental and little used.

"That one over next to the wall represents our warm season, which begins the 15th of April and ends on the 15th of June. Our Nepali new year is the 14th of April, so you could call this our first season.

"Next, is the pavilion for summer, and this one opposite represents the monsoon season. There is one for our dewy season, followed by fall. Then near the back wall is the one for winter. Each of our seasons is just two months' duration," explained the general, while overhead came the clatter of breeding night herons.

The party walked back toward the entrance where Paul enthusiastically thanked General Kaiser for the tea, for meeting his family, and for the tour of his extensive gardens. Our Jeep drove onto the King's Highway, past the Royal Hotel grounds and on through the city.

"General Kaiser is one of the few class 'A' ranas. I know the country would have prospered had he ever become prime minister," stated Paul.

The Jeep had just drawn up in front of Rabi Bhawan when a man appeared from around the corner. He had come to call on Mr. Rose, who had the status of chief of missions, close to that of American ambassador.

The tall visitor had graying hair and was somewhat shabbily dressed. In rather broken English, he introduced himself as Peter Aufschnaiter, an Austrian, who had recently come from Tibet. He and Heinrich Harrer had gone there as escapees from the camp in Dehra Dun for prisoners of war.

They had become very useful to the Tibetans while in that country. At the request of the Dalai Lama, Peter had planned and built irrigation systems and Harrer had taught the young Dalai Lama English, history, geography, science, and photography.

Paul invited Aufschnaiter to bring his friend Harrer to dinner that night.

"He looks as though he could benefit from a good meal," Paul remarked to us.

That evening at dinner they recounted the story of their escape from prison camp and the arduous struggle over the high mountains, with encounters of wild beasts, avalanches, and brigands. They were often in need of food and water, which was nonexistent.

Peter related stories that were electrifying.

"One night," he said, "I was not able to make it back to camp, which was located near some nomadic tents in western Tibet. I had walked a long way—through mountainous country. As dusk drew on, I decided to seek shelter under a boulder.

"I had no sooner spread my sleeping bag on the ground when a huge wolf appeared, then another and another. There must have been fifteen or twenty of them. They acted like tame Alsatians and soon lay down in company not fifteen yards away. When I woke up next morning, the wolves had departed. I had no fear of them at all."

The government of India had invited him to Delhi to work on a series of maps of Tibet, as the Austrian exile had kept copious notes and made accurate sketches of many areas he had visited.

Aufschnaiter wanted to settle in Kathmandu after his Delhi stint and had come to ask Mr. Rose of possible places to settle. The logical place seemed to be Ekanta Kuna in Patan, where the Swiss were. There he could freely use his German language.

After he had gone, Eveline exclaimed, "What a man and what experiences! I hope he is going to write a book about all this."

But it was Harrer who wrote the book, *Seven Years in Tibet,* which was published the following year (1953).* How stimulating life in Kathmandu was!

On a bright June day, with the sky unusually clear of clouds, Eveline and I emerged from our den to go to breakfast at the Roses' and climbed the stairs to the second floor. We could almost feel the rana maharajahs looking down on us as we passed on up through the reception room to the spacious dining room. Paul was already there, and in his southern drawl, bid us welcome.

"Today is very important for the people of Kathmandu, Patan, and the outlying villages. It is the Machendranath festival in Patan City," he announced. "The king and queen will arrive in state and then the jeweled vest will be shown. Let me call one of our English-speaking Nepalis to explain something about Machendranath. I understand this is one of the major festivals of the year."

In a few minutes, Kiran arrived and, in excellent English, told about the king of snakes which lived under a small lake about five miles south of the city. It was a long, complicated tale of how a farmer with special power had been summoned to the underground abode at Tanda Lake to attend the snake king's ailing wife. After some time, she was cured and, as a reward, the snake king gave the peasant a black, jeweled vest. The farmer emerged from under the water with the magnificent gift. He took it home and would not leave it out of his sight. When he went to work in the fields each day, he took the garment with him.

One day he placed it at the edge of a furrow and went behind a shrub to defecate. A thief, at this unguarded moment, seized the garment and made off with it. As soon as he could, the farmer raced after him; they kept going for several miles and all the while the owner gradually closed in on the thief.

At the last moment they ran past the idol Machendranath. In desperation, the thief threw the vest into the lap of the idol. The owner couldn't retrieve it because now it belonged to the god.

Thus, every year a chosen man balances on the rails of the structure in which the idol rests, to show the public that the garment had been in safe keeping for another year.

The entire population of the city seemed to be drawn, as if by magnet, across the same bridge. It was narrow, with one-way traffic, and the police officer directed the flow using green and red flags—green for stop and red for go. We moved forward at a snail's pace with the hundreds of people crossing the bridge. The cars could go no farther, so we got out and walked the rest of the way.

In the open space were hundreds of family groups sitting on the ground. Nearby was a bamboo tower almost a hundred feet high, tapered at the apex. It looked very top heavy and we marveled that it had not toppled over. It had been pulled on ropes through the streets of Patan by many straining devotees and now stood in place next to a little enclosed platform where sat the living personification of the goddess of Patan. A gaudy costume shrouded the 14-year-old girl, who surely looked like the goddess she portrayed, so solemn with her downcast eyes. She had graceful black lines around and over her eyes, and her forehead was covered with bright vermillion.

Our party was waved on to seats on a raised, covered platform. A priest sitting there rose to greet us. He and Paul Rose shook hands, and then he greeted the rest of us.

Father Moran, who was sitting nearby, was a Jesuit priest from Chicago, the only Christian missionary in Nepal at that time. He had been invited to come to Nepal to set up a boys' school. Fluent in Hindi and Nepali, he was already well known in Kathmandu Valley. His school at Godaveri, some eight or nine miles southeast of Kathmandu, already had forms sixth to tenth, standard instruction. There had been a rush by well-educated Nepalis to enter their sons in the Jesuit school, for their superior education was well known and appreciated. Father Moran had heard that I was setting up a nursing education program for Nepali girls and remarked that such was greatly needed.

There was a sudden hush and everyone stood up.

"Their Majesties, the king and queen," whispered Father Moran.

They got out of their Rolls Royce and came over to our raised platform. When all were seated, a man clad in black mounted the front rail of the Machendranath chariot, assisted by a man on either side to help him keep his balance. He produced a small black garment studded with "diamonds." Holding it firmly by the top corners, he stretched out his hands and showed it to the audience. Then he moved with uncertain steps to the other three sides of the chariot displaying the vest to everyone.

After that, His Majesty, King Tribhuvan, stepped down from his seat and moved towards the chariot and threw coins into the lap of the god. A murmur of approval arose from the crowd.

Thereupon, the rest of the royal party joined His Majesty, re-entered their vehicles and slowly drove through the crowd. The Rain God, Indra, had now been properly informed that it was time to send rain into the many rice fields to insure a good crop in October.

On one of my frequent visits to Health Minister Gurung at Singha Durbar, he announced that he was scheduled to visit the Tokha Sanatorium the next morning and invited me to go along.

"Tokha is upon the northern slope of the valley," Gurung explained. "We have a doctor in charge, with a number of assistants. There are several buildings, a doctor's residence and barracks, but only a limited number of patients can be accommodated."

The next morning we drove by Sita Nirwas, the Indian Embassy. It was here about eighteen months before that their Majesties sought the protection of neutral ground where the prime minister could not get at them. A great crowd escorted them to the airport when they made their escape to India. The prime minister's men were helpless in their attempts to seize His Majesty.

We were soon twisting and turning up a steep road through a pine forest. Higher and higher we went until we had a glorious view of the winding streams and clusters of villages of Kathmandu valley. The farther hills surrounding the valley were blue in the distance.

The driver gradually approached the T. B. barracks and stopped his car. The sanatorium building and the doctor's quarters were within walking distance. Tokha Sanatorium on the whole was rather bleak except for the doctor's house, which commanded a delightful view of the valley below.

The hillside above was newly planted with young pines, which were thriving, while terraces were covered with shrubs. The air was cold and the vistas beautiful. Little wonder patients wanted to linger on.

June was almost over and my vacation time was near its end. All told, I had pretty well finished the work I had been asked to do. I had proposed to the health minister a detailed plan, which had been forwarded to His Majesty's government for approval. The first Nepali girls were being sent to our hospital at Fatehgarh for training. A lot had been accomplished in the eight conferences with Mr. Gurung.

Back at Rabi Bhawan, on one of our last evening strolls, Rani Madhuri spoke to me again about escorting her to see her father, in exile in Dehra Dun. We formed a plan whereby I would meet her at the railway station in Dehra Dun on July fifth, following my annual mission meeting in Mussoorie, and accompany her to her father's abode.

That noon I had a letter from Mr. Dixit, foreign secretary in His Majesty's government. He did not want me to leave Kathmandu before seeing Singha Durbar and asked me to come there at three that afternoon, when he would be free to show me around.

I replied that I was very much interested in accepting the invitation and asked if the other American ladies could come with me. Of course, was the reply, so the three of us crowded into our Jeep and were off to Singha Durbar.

As we arrived, a long row of colorfully clad Nepali women were bent over planting rice seedlings in a field nearby. One could hear snatches of songs as they worked.

"To think that every blade of rice in the whole valley is put in by hand," exclaimed Eveline. "It must be back-breaking work."

Armed guards stood at the massive gates and waved us in. As

the Jeep wheeled around to the left, we caught the fragrance of *magnolia grandiflora*, of which there were several large trees originally brought from the U.S. Just ahead glittered the huge white columns of the Singha Durbar, reputed to have more than a thousand rooms. Mr. Dixit was waiting for us at the main porte-cochere.

"I was anxious for you to see the showrooms of this palace before you left to return to India. How are you traveling?"

"We have ordered horses from the bazaar and will ride over the Chandragiri Trail to the railhead," I replied.

"That will never do," he declared. "I'll order two of the king's horses for you. Cancel your request for those bazaar horses, please."

And the party moved up to the broad marble steps into the main entrance of the palace.

Packing day finally arrived. Eveline and I had our suitcases spread out on the floor. Little Rani ran about excitedly, for she knew something was going to happen.

"How will you take the dog?" Eveline inquired.

"I plan to carry her in my pocket. She will be no trouble," I replied.

Bright and early the next morning, Paul had the driver load up his Jeep with our belongings, while we rode in the other Jeep. The eight-mile road westward to Thankot, where the horse trail began, was grueling. Most of the stones on the way were turned on end and it was like driving over a seemingly endless corduroy road. The vibration set one's teeth on edge. There was only one paved road in the whole kingdom, and that was in front of the king's palace.

At Thankot, syces waited with two beautiful palace horses complete with spanking new saddles. The two porters requested were squatting there, ready to carry our loads. We would arrive at Bhimpedi, on the other side of the mountain range, some time the next day.

We bade farewell to Paul Rose as the syces helped us mount our horses. Paul tucked little Rani in my pocket. But in a moment or two we were back on the ground. Those new saddles needed a lot of padding, so the porters had to open our packs and extract sweaters.

We mounted again and Paul helped tuck in the sweaters where most needed. Even then, it was most uncomfortable riding; new saddles do not give and certain spots of the anatomy were soon chafing. But we had to endure it for the next four hours to Chisagarhi rest house.

Waving to Paul for the last time, we took off up the trail. The northern slopes of Chandragiri were well wooded with oak, chestnut and rhododendron forests. Not a single dwelling did we come across all the two thousand feet to the top. From there, as we reined in our horses, we had a great panoramic view of the valley. Even little Rani gave a squeak of delight. Meanwhile, the accompanying porters let out mighty screams and cast rocks on a six-foot pile of boulders. This, we were told, warded off the evil spirits which inhabit the passes of Nepal.

The road on the southern sunny side zigzagged sharply through more oak forests, down to the village of Chitlang. Several little tea shops lined the way, and I suggested we dismount and give our nether regions a rest.

"How about a glass of tea?" I said. "It will be hot and fairly safe."

Eveline assented and we watched the dark brown liquid, boiled for several hours, being strained into the glasses. Sugar and milk followed; here was tea as the Nepalis know it! We both stood to drink even though the shopkeeper offered us a couple of battered chairs. About this time Rani made herself known, so she got a drink of water.

We learned we were halfway to our destination. The porters drank a couple of glasses of tea each and were soon ready to go. Their regular eating place was a couple of hours down the valley.

It was interesting to see travelers passing to and fro along the trail. Quite a group were resting in the mile-long Chitlang bazaar. This was the main trail into Kathmandu Valley as there was nothing like a motor road. The only way to get to the capital city was either to walk, be carried in a dandy, ride a horse, or fly in the king's plane. Most people had to walk.

Then, coming towards us was a bevy of men carrying an automobile, of all things! It had been divided into two parts, the upper half and the chassis. Each half was firmly lashed to long bamboo poles which extended beyond the length of the automobile. Sixteen men, four on each end of the bamboo frame, carried the auto on their shoulders for about a hundred yards, then set down their burden. Soon a second group of sixteen men shouldered the vehicle and slowly proceeded another hundred yards; then a third group took over, and so on up the mountain. What a sight! Little did we know that 600 other vehicles had already been carried up over the 7100-foot Chandragiri Pass down into Kathmandu Valley.*

Now rested and refreshed, we continued down the trail, past cultivated fields and frequent houses. Ahead we could see another mountain range almost as high as the one we had just come over. Meanwhile, at the bottom of the descent, ran a stream clustered with huts. Here the porters announced they would eat their evening meal while the horses and syces began their climb upward. The place was called *Kulikhanna*.**

This road was quite barren in contrast to Chandragiri. It twisted this way and that, finally arriving at a sort of bungalow, which was to be our resting place for the night.

We were surprised to find a cook on duty, offering to prepare us a curry dinner. The water, from a well, was deliciously cool. The building even boasted electric lights that went on at the push of a switch. Such luxury!

We immediately used the rest room for there were none along our entire trail. We washed and soothed our bruised anatomies. And then it was time for dinner. The quality and quantity of food was surprisingly good.

We then decided to stretch out and rest our weary bones. Horseback riding was much more strenuous than we had anticipated. Rani had her snack of food and was comfortably curled up in a corner of the room. We heard the calls of the scops owl and the jungle nightjar. We began to think of sleep. But where were the porters with our bedding?

"Still down the trail eating their *khana*,"*** syce told us.

It was getting chilly by this time at 6500 feet, so we decided to go to the nearby bazaar and buy some blankets. All we could find

---

* See *National Geographic Magazine,* Oct., 1910.
** meaning place of the porters
*** food

were dark horse blankets with a musty odor.

"These will have to do," exclaimed Eveline. "There is no other choice."

So back to the bungalow with them we went. There were two four-legged beds strung with jute cord. We decided to use only one bed, place the first blanket under us, put on all the warm clothing we had, and cover up with the second blanket. We were uncomfortably crowded, but fairly warm. When one turned, the other had to do the same. After a restless night, we were up at dawn when the porters appeared, with our bedding but without a word of explanation!

After a breakfast of cooked wheat and bananas, which we had brought with us, we were ready for the trail. It was only a short two hours down to Bhimpedi, we were told. The horsemen need not hang onto the tails of their animals any longer, as they had when climbing upward. Then buildings appeared ahead. We had arrived at the end of the horse trail.

Over in a small square were two or three dilapidated buses, one of which was already partially loaded with passengers. The seats were so narrow and close together we had to pay for three of them in order to have enough room for our legs.

After a faulty start, the engine warmed up and we were off. It was a zigzag course, with two stops at villages, when a few got off but more got on, until there were six or eight riding up on the roof.

It was an uncomfortable ride, and at the sight of Amalekganj, we drew breaths of relief. The bus stopped about a hundred yards from a tiny engine and train, which would take us to the Indian border. We bought first class tickets for $1.10 for our 25-mile ride.

The train was divided into compartments. No one else was in first class, but third class was jammed, with a few extras hanging out the door and on top of the train. The whistle blew and the engine chugged off into the *tarai* forest. It was the wrong time of day to see any of the big carnivores, but they were around. Hadn't an engineer recently wounded a panther that had charged him, wrestling until he could reach for his knife and plunge it in the animal's throat?

Yes, it was an exciting place. The forest on either side was so green, for now the rains had begun. We ate snacks and enjoyed the rest of the way to Birganj. This was the end of the narrow-gauge railroad. Across the international border, reached by horsecart, we sighted a broad-gauge railroad. After an hour wait, we were moving again, into the Gangetic plain of North India toward Lucknow.

"What were you going to do with Rani?" inquired Eveline.

"I plan to take her with me to the mission meeting in Mussoorie," I answered, "and after that, probably to Fatehgarh."

"But how can you keep her in the heat? She is accustomed only to the mountains. Why don't you let me take her to Delhi where she could enjoy a cool house?" Eveline implored.

"Well, I just might do that," I answered. Rani was easy to take care of and knew Eveline. "I'll be coming through Delhi in about a week and I could pick her up then."

At Lucknow we parted, and Rani going to Delhi and I to Dehra Dun, where there were numerous taxi men clamoring to be engaged. But on a missionary's salary, one travels by bus when one can, and there was one going to Mussoorie in fifteen minutes. What a comfortable seat after the Nepal experience!

The city of Dehra Dun lay in a low plateau between the outer and inner Himalayan ranges. It was a thriving city with many vehicles, bazaars and higher class homes surrounded by spacious grounds. The route led over a ten-mile paved road bordered by tall trees. Ahead the Himalayas loomed higher and higher. At Rajpur, we began to climb, making over a hundred right angle turns from 3000 feet to 6500 feet.

Kincraig was the end of the motor vehicle road. The rain had slackened, and I engaged porters who put tarpaulins over the suitcases. I beckoned for a rickshaw, and when I was buttoned in securely, I felt quite protected against the rain. My five rickshaw men were fairly damp, but they coaxed the vehicle up the steep incline to Landour bazaar. Such familiar smells! Since it was Saturday, groups of foreign school children passed by with their gaily-colored umbrellas.

The final quarter mile of Landour bazaar was very steep and the rickshaw men zigzagged to gain altitude. At Mullingar, they pulled up under a shed and asked for their pay. It was still five or six hundred feet higher to Landour cantonments where I would be staying.

Under the shelter were several dandies and their attendants, all of whom wanted to be hired. The transfer was made directly up to Hazlewood, where my sister lived. Soon the dandy reached the *chakkar*.*

"Firs cottage," I directed and was carried along the path where one could look back over the town of Mussoorie.

Then it was on to my final destination, where I was warmly greeted by Sammy and Fishy, my friends of the American Presbyterian Mission. I was ushered to my room, which was rather dull and clammy, for in the monsoons, with the humidity at about 100%, shoes soon sported green mould, and everything else is appropriately saturated with moisture.

Mission meeting began in an hour, which gave me time to settle in and get a bite to eat, after which I left for the community center where the sessions were held. The rain had ceased temporarily, and the road was a series of puddles, but the fragrance of the deodar forest through which we passed was exhilarating.

Quite a group had already gathered and greetings were being exchanged. The agenda seemed quite full as the sessions were to last through Sunday. Many heated discussions took place during the sessions. Whenever they ended in a draw, someone would move that the matter be referred to the Executive Committee. This occurred so often one began to feel as if the Presbyterians needed a bishop!

It was a time for renewal of friendships among the missionaries of North India and the Punjab. At prayer time, calls on God for divine guidance were frequent. Devotional periods were inspiring and helped ready the participants for the difficulties of the coming year. I was looking forward to Monday, when I was to meet Madhuri Rana in Dehra Dun.

The bus down from Mussoorie to Dehra Dun was half filled with mission members returning to their respective stations. I sat with a lady who was also going to my station, Fatehgarh.

I told her of my few weeks in Kathmandu, where I worked on a nurses' training program for the Kingdom of Nepal, and how the government had selected two young girls to train as nurses. I

* The main road around the top of the hill.

noted how they should have arrived at the Fatehgarh hospital by
now.

The folks seemed pleased that Fatehgarh hospital had been
selected for such pioneering work, for everyone knew how closed
Nepal had been for so many years.

At Dehra Dun I took my luggage and went to the first class
waiting room to look for Madhuri. She was waiting for me, and
we had an emotional meeting. Leaving our luggage in charge of
the woman caretaker there, we engaged one of the numerous
*tongas** in front of the station to take us to the place where Madhuri's father stayed.

The driver climbed up into the front seat while we passengers
scrambled into the second one and faced backward as we rode
along through the city. There were no sidewalks, so all the people
and vehicles were in the road. One had to drive carefully and
what few cars there were constantly honked their horns.

After some time, the driver turned to the left up a smaller
street and drew up at an open space near a Hindu temple. There
we saw the lonely figure of the once mighty Maharajah Judha
Shumshere Jung Bahadur Rana of Nepal, Madhuri's father. He
sat on a small piece of gunny sack, quite naked except for a loin-
cloth, counting his beads in meditation. He did not look up at the
approach of the *tonga,* and Madhuri remained silent and began
to weep quietly.

After his prayer was finished, he nodded and Madhuri went
forward and sat on the ground near her father. The two engaged
in quiet conversation for a while, and the daughter could not
suppress her tears. At the end, she rose, clasped the palms of her
hands together in a final *namaste,* and climbed back into the
tonga. Later, Madhuri left on the train to Lucknow and the Nepal
border, while I went to the platform for the train to Delhi and
Fatehgarh.

I followed my porter as he wove his way through the crowd of
squatting women and children with their boxes and bundles,
men sitting cross-legged smoking their *hookas**,* sweetmeat and
curry vendors, and a couple of voracious dogs hoping for a

---

* A two-wheeled, horse-drawn vehicle with double seats, back to back, covered
with a canopy.
** A pipe, the base of which is filled with water.

dropped tidbit.

As the train whistled around the bend, there was a sudden movement of the waiting crowd, each traveller shoving and pushing to be in position to find a place in the train. My porter took me to the third class Zenana compartment, reserved for women (which always meant their young children and babies as well). It is usually full and every foot of space is packed with bundles and pottery jars, but I was able to climb up onto the upper berth. This was merely a wooden shelf with no hint of upholstery. It gave me a great vantage point, however, from which to look down on the crowd of women and listen to their conversations. In fact some of the comments were about me.

"She is different," one woman said. "She must be from some other place."

"Yes," said another, "I think she is a half-caste. Don't you see her face and arms are white, but her legs are brown. [I was wearing brown hose.] I've heard of these people. That comes from marrying a foreigner."

I wanted at this point to get into the conversation and explain, and also to use this opportunity to tell them about why I was in India, and about the Lord who asked me to come, and how he loved them and that we were all his children. But I was so tired. I had had an exhausting day, and I knew that starting a conversation would mean a whole night of it.

The babies, irritable from the heat, were crying and mothers were singing or chanting dirges to try to quiet them. Again, I lost an opportunity to tell the Christ story. I said a prayer, asking God to bring His light and salvation to them, but here was I, His ambassador, failing him when the opportunity was given to me.

I was restless. I planned to see the two Nepali girls as soon as I reached Fatehgarh in the morning. They were beginning careers and a new life. I was still surprised how the way had opened for the first two Nepali girls to begin their nurses' training. I could see God's hand making the seemingly impossible possible.

Then, while I was thinking of new beginnings, I went back to my own beginnings and to all the many ways God had led me to my present stage of life.

The entrance to the Singha Durbar Palace, Kathmandu, Nepal.

The Singha Durbar: home of the Maharajas prior to 1951.

Side view of the Singha Durbar, the part that was burned in the fire of 1972.

The throne room. The throne at the far end is flanked by bigger than lifesize portraits—the king on one side and the prime minister on the other.

Their Majesties King Mahendra and Queen Ratna.

Eveline Holmes and Juanita on an outing with Foreign Secretary N.A. Dixit and his lovely wife.

General Kaisar with his young wife and baby and his son and daughter by his former wife.

Princess Mahadhuri shows Don the portrait of her father, Maharaja Judha.

Devil dancers celebrating
the spring festival while
His Majesty looks on.

Nyatapola
Temple,
Bhadgaon.

Palace of the pre-
sent king.

Level land is scarce, so hillsides are terraced to provide space for rice planting.

Bodhnath, the largest Buddhist shrine in Kathmandu Valley. The eyes of this temple are electrified and may be seen over the entire valley at night.

Nepali women planting rice. Plowing is done by the men, but planting is always done by the women.

Pitching camp in sight of such beauty lifts the spirit and refreshes the body and soul.

Machhupuchari (Fish's Tail), Anna- purna range, 23,000 feet.

Amadablam with Thangboche Monastery in the foreground.

A Tibetan woman
and her little dog.

Nepali hill boy.

Village home built of mud with a thatch roof.

A group of Tibetan refugees living in Mussoorie, India.

Uma Das and Rukhmani Charan, the two Nepali girls who came to our hospital in Fatehgarh for training.

A Nepali home near Kathmandu.

BOOK TWO

GROWING UP

1906 - 1926

Chapter IV

The Fountain Spring House

I had my own beginning on April 1, 1906 in Indianapolis, Indiana, where my father had brought his bride three years before and where my older sister, Bernice, was born.

The Owen family originally came from Wales. One story which my father liked to tell was that he was descended from a Robert Owen who was present at the birth of Queen Victoria and the first person to hold the royal baby. Another story was of an ancestral officer in Cornwallis' army who came to America, eventually marrying an American girl. He accepted a plot of land in North Carolina and a commission in the American Army. And still another story was about a Robert Owen, a prosperous mill owner who had introduced humane reforms in his own mill in Wales and, according to Allistir Cooke*, conceived the idea of setting up a commune of like-minded persons in the New World. He purchased 30,000 acres and formed a commune of some 1,000 persons on the banks of the Wabash at New Harmony, Indiana. (It was his son who was instrumental in establishing the Smithsonian Institute in Washington, D.C.)

The Owen family later moved to Decatur, Illinois. Grandfather Owen had one girl and seven boys, two of whom were my father, Roy Pearl Owen, and his twin, Ralph Earl Owen. When the twins were very young their father died, leaving Grandmother to support the family by sewing shirts cut out at a local factory. She was paid ten cents a shirt and had to make all the buttonholes

* See *America* by Allistir Cooke, page 377.

by hand.

None of the younger Owen children ever had any money to spend. Each year they would attend the church Christmas program, but there was never a present on the tree for them. When they were seven years old, an older brother gave Roy and Ralph each a nickel to spend for Christmas. The boys decided they would each buy a little tin horn, wrap it and put it on the tree so they would also have a present for Christmas. Later on in the summer while playing with his Christmas toy, Ralph fell with the horn in his mouth, piercing his throat. He died a short time later.

Mother's family were long residents of Decatur. The Gebharts were of Pennsylvania Dutch background whose forebears had been in America for a number of generations. As a lad, Grand-father Gebhart pushed a cart along Water Street, selling shoe-strings, pins, buttons and the like. As his modest business prospered, he purchased a small space in a building fronting the street. In time, he bought the whole building and then the one next to it and on down the street, until he owned the entire block, which became known as the Gebhart Block. Then he went into real estate, buying houses. This led to his purchasing land in Florida during a boom, wheat fields in Canada, and oil fields in Texas. He eventually became a millionaire and provided well for his four sons and three daughters.

Father and Mother were high school sweethearts. They would pass love notes to each other when they met briefly in corridors. After high school, Father went to Brown's Business College (which later became Millikin University) for two years. He found employment with Bell Telephone and was sent to Indianapolis. This was too far away for the two young lovers. Thus, two years later, Father returned to Decatur, married mother and took his bride to Indianapolis, where they lived for six years. During this period, the first three girls were born. I was the second.

The Company brought Father back to Decatur for a couple of years and then sent him to Chicago. I do not recall much about the Chicago house in North Ravenswood, except that it was a bleak dwelling, without the yard and flowers we'd had in Decatur.

I do remember, however, being sent with my sister on the interurban down to the loop to meet Father with our names and addresses tied around our necks. Father would pick us up and take us to the beach or the zoo on Saturday afternoon when he was not working. The conductors were always helpful in keeping an eye on us when we traveled on their trains.

I also remember Dad swimming in Lake Michigan once, with me on his chest. One time I fell off and when my feet felt the gritty sand, I had a strong feeling I was going to drown. Of course, I was quickly pulled from the water, but for many years afterwards, whenever I felt any grit in a bathtub, I suddenly was seized with fear and anger. Much later, I knew those powerful reactions stemmed from that Lake Michigan experience.

An event which changed the direction of our family history was the visit of two ladies to our home in Chicago. They knocked on the door and Mother let them in. They were dressed alike in long gray wool dresses with high collars edged in a narrow white band of handkerchief linen. On their heads were small gray wool hats, no larger than a pancake, held in place by two long, white silk sashes tied into a large bow under their chins.

They introduced themselves as Ava Ball and Flora Lucas, missionaries from the Metropolitan Mission on Federal Street down in the heart of Chicago, a mission newly formed by members of the Metropolitan Methodist Church in the Loop. Two of these were men of means who had experienced an encounter with Christ and were anxious to use their money to train and send missionaries to all parts of the world with the Gospel. They sold Christian literature door to door and used the proceeds to support the mission. Mother liked the ladies. They were warm and friendly, and their faces glowed with a happiness expressive of inner joy and peace. This impressed Mother greatly. They left a copy of the *Burning Bush* as they said goodbye.

When Father came home that evening, he saw the publication and scolded Mother for subscribing to yet another magazine.

"But the ladies left it this afternoon; it didn't cost anything," protested Mother.

Glancing at the editorial page, he noted the names of the two founders.

"Why, I have seen these names on a bank in the Loop on my way to work," he commented. Later, he was angry when he heard these bankers were a part of the group who professed to have given up everything to the cause of missions.

"How could they do so and be in the banking business?" he blustered and resolved to track down these men and get an explanation.

One day as he was passing the bank, he turned in and found the men. He discovered they were, indeed, giving up material gains to sponsor the group. Greatly impressed, Father hurried back home to Mother to tell her that the original report of the two ladies was indeed true.

There followed many visits when the ladies brought their guitars and sang and talked of God's claim on their lives, and the joy that came from total surrender of property, family, time and money. They sang songs with happy rhythms that we children enjoyed and learned to sing, Ava carrying the soprano and Flora the alto part. We children tapped our feet and clapped our hands to "Climbing Up the Golden Stairs," or "When They Ring Those Golden Bells." Mother liked "In The Garden" and "Shall We Gather at the River." She would often sing softly as she rocked the baby to sleep:

> "Trust and obey
> For there's no other way
> To be happy in Jesus
> But to trust and obey."

Her voice was soft and sweet, and it carried into our bedroom as a soothing benediction.

> "Beautiful Isle of Somewhere,
> Land of the true
> Where we live anew,
> Beautiful Isle of Somewhere."

We children always knelt at Mother's knees to say our bedtime prayers. (It was only after the coming of the missionaries that we began family prayers.)

The teachings of the group were centered around those of the early Christian Church where the Christians sold all their possessions and laid the money at the apostles' feet. They shared everything in common, and "no man called ought that he had his own." They decried the ministers who lived in fine houses on fat salaries and spoke of them as the "hireling ministry." Living should be frugal and dress plain with no adornments, even to wedding rings. Women should wear their hair long as St. Paul admonished his early churches, and there were no places for curling irons or "crisping pins."

The ladies had won a place in the hearts of our family and they were invited for Thanksgiving dinner. They had told us about the Fountain House in Waukesha, Wisconsin, and how they sang a hymn before the meal—often "Come and Dine, the Master Calleth" — then turned up their plates, which were kept turned downward between meals.

Father had a twinkle in his eyes this Thanksgiving, for he had done the same thing. When our plates were upturned for dinner, there was a gold watch under each of the ladies' plates. That was his way of telling them how much he appreciated them.

Most of the talk at the table was about Waukesha; we kids asking questions and wondering how different life was going to be if we moved there.

Should we move to Waukesha, it would mean leaving our dogs. We had two lovely collies whom we played with constantly and who were always taking care of us and seeing to it that we didn't wander. Mother had made Dorothy and me soft white coats of imitation fur with large mother-of-pearl buttons. (I still have the buttons!) The dogs loved to cuddle in the soft fur.

Among my recollections of our days in Chicago was the Aviation Meet where my father and Uncle Tom, his older brother, took us to see the "flying machines." I was too small to see anything from the ground, so Father let me ride on his shoulder as I held my gas-filled balloon and waved a red pennant with an airplane imprinted on it. How little could I then envision the air traffic of today or the many thousands of miles I, myself, would ride in airplanes.

Waukesha, which became our new home, had long been known as one of the nation's most popular health resorts. There were many springs yielding naturally medicated water, which was bottled and sold as far away as Calcutta, India. The palatial Fountain Spring House had been the vision of Matthew Laflin, a well-known millionaire of Chicago. It is said he was cured of a "painful and dangerous malady" by the famous Waukesha mineral waters and determined to make them available to the public.

He built his hotel for $160,000, and it was first opened for the 1874 season. In 1878, fire destroyed much of it, but none of the 200 guests was harmed. With astonishing rapidity, it was rebuilt and enlarged, with accommodations for 800 guests. The new building cost $250,000 and was ready for the 1879 season. For years, wealthy people from all over the U.S.A. flocked to Waukesha to escape the heat and the dreaded malaria of the south at that time.

The Fountain Spring House—"Queen of the Northwest" — covered three acres and was situated on a rise of land surrounded by 120 acres of parks, gardens, and the Fountain Spring. There was also a barn with thoroughbred racing horses and room for many carriages, as well as a golf course on the west side and a horseracing track. Guests could promenade for a quarter of a mile on the wide, open verandas. The Fountain Spring House proved a mecca for many distinguished guests. Service was excellent and the highest-priced suite was $28 a week. The first full-dress ball took place in 1888. Later they staged concerts and Shakespearian plays.

Notable for that time was the system of electric bells and telephones to all rooms from the central switchboard, which had direct telephone service to Milwaukee and Chicago. Each room also had electric buttons to call for service. The very large closets allowed storage of the then-popular wardrobe trunks and suitcases, and left plenty of room for clothes.

It was this place that had been purchased to house the new Bible School and which would be our new home.

Each family or unit cared for its own apartment, with help available for those with small children or for the elderly who were unable to do housekeeping chores. Work assignments were made by the housekeepers and matrons, of whom there was one to each floor and each wing. Young people were usually assigned to the dining rooms, and as soon as we were oriented to the place and had settled in, we were given chores and tables to wait on. Prior to meals, a piano near the door sounded out the hymn which all joined in singing while still standing. The blessing followed then, and all were seated and the door closed, making the rare latecomer's appearance conspicuous.

The grounds around the Fountain Spring House were delightful. The rolling lawns of two parks across Grand Avenue were kept neatly trimmed and bordered with maples and oak trees, which cast lights and shadows on the green grass. In between the two parks was the latticed summer house, where band concerts were held in the early evening while children played "Drop The Handkerchief" or "My Fair Lady" on the grass nearby. A third park, across Laflin Avenue, was more wooded and had wrought-iron benches where the older residents could sit in the shade and read or talk.

Then there was a fourth park on the north side of the building and at a slightly lower level. It was a paradise of fir trees and pine, especially in the winter when each limb would be so covered with snow that the lower branches touched the ground. This was named "the ladies park," but I never knew why. It was a grand place to hide when we played "Run, My Good Sheep, Run" or "Arrow Hunt."

At the south end of the Fountain House was the Fountain Spring, a unique circular structure thirty feet in diameter and encased in white marble, with a fountain spurting up in the middle. Around it circled a marble staircase with an ornate wrought-iron railing. Above the spring, a pergola housed a bandstand that offered music while the residents wandered down to enjoy the cool, refreshing water. It was a favorite focal point of thirsty school children on hot summer days.

Just above the spring, south of the main building, was a garden where strawberries, asparagus, peas, and other vegetables were grown. This was the scene of many happy evenings when volunteers gathered the crop, often accompanied by singing.

But it was in February, on a bleak cloudy day, when the Owen family arrived. We weren't impressed at the time with the surroundings, just awed and a bit frightened by the enormous size of the building and the wide dark halls where no sunlight ever entered and dim light emitted from drop-type electric fixtures. Our rooms were on the ground floor at the extreme south end of the long hall, on the southwest corner. There were plenty of tall, draped windows and the steam heat was on, but still the rooms felt cold and clammy.

I wanted to cry. If I only had my dolls with me for comfort! But they were packed and our baggage had not arrived yet. Mother suggested we girls climb into bed and take a nap—her favorite solution to such problems.

On Sundays, we weren't allowed to play or to read anything except the Bible or other religious literature. We *could* go walking; in fact, most everybody took walks—strictly girls with girls and boys with boys. We seldom had any money, so we couldn't buy anything, although there was one exception: my closest girl friend, Lois, occasionally would buy me an ice cream cone.

The schoolhouse was a couple of blocks to the west of the main building and had two classrooms on each of the three floors. The principal's office was under the gable on the fourth.

The street by the school sloped just enough to make an excellent slide in the winter. We had a bobsled—a wide plank fastened on each end to a sled—large enough for six or eight youngsters. We would whiz down hill, past the spring house on the left and the cow pasture on the right to the schoolhouse.

Gradually we overcame our homesickness and made friends. I was in first grade and already had a boyfriend, Melville Green, whose family lived on the third floor. He had some Noah's Ark toys which floated on the water. We would fill the bathtub and, with splashes, propel the toys around the tub. We were friends until he became too shy to play with girls. At one point the Greens wanted to adopt me, as we now had five girls in our family and they had lost five of their seven children in a boating accident. Only the youngest and the oldest survived, both boys. However, my parents would not agree to the adoption.

Life was pretty much regimented, but I didn't mind it as a child. Parents acted as a police force to see that the boys and girls behaved. There was plenty of time for prayers: each morning right after breakfast, twice on Sundays, and a long prayer meeting on Tuesday and Friday evenings. Saturday there was band practice (boys) and string band (girls). I played in the string band, but music was not my forte. I still cringe when I think of my piano teacher's knitting needles striking my knuckles.

As children, we were obliged to attend all services, except the weeknight meetings when we were doing our homework. Much of the preaching was of the hell-fire type. Sermons on the Old Testament told of how the wrath of God was poured out on the enemies of the children of Israel and how they were ordered to "kill every man, woman, and child," especially the uncircumcised.

I would shake with fear at such times, and one day, when I was deeply disturbed, I went to my father telling him I wanted to be circumcised. Mother sat by while Father explained that that did not mean little girls—but he missed a good opportunity to explain the *difference* between little girls and little boys. We were seven girls before we had a brother, and I was still in the dark about the difference.

There were sermons about the "secret rapture" when the Lord would come and take away the true Christians and those that were left would suffer damnation. After a sleepless night, I would go down to breakfast the next morning and look the crowd over. I would relax only after I saw people there who I thought would have been those taken away.

I have often wished I had been taught more of the love of God, that He was a good God and loved me and that I could love Him in return. How much heartache and anxiety would have been eliminated had love, rather than fear, motivated me.

In his capacity as buyer for the institution, Father went up to Wautoma to purchase a flock of sheep that he had seen advertised for sale. In order to save money, he decided to drive the sheep back rather than pay to have them shipped—one hundred miles as the crow flies! He was not used to walking all day, nor had he ever driven animals before. But he made it, and in the days following, we had not only mutton and lamb to eat, but we had the wool, which was shorn and washed.

Old Mr. Wolf taught me to card and spin the wool on an old-fashioned spinning wheel, to which he had added a switch hooked up to his electric light. I later used some of the wool to crochet a little coat and cap for my baby sister, Mildred.

Chapter V

Life on a Texas Communal Farm

When I was eight, Father was assigned to the farm in Texas, which the commune had purchased to provide the food supply for Waukesha and to provide another outlet for spreading the gospel. Mother assented, thinking the change in climate might alleviate my tendency toward recurrent respiratory diseases.

Dad packed our few possessions (we had given up all household furniture and equipment when we left Chicago) and helped plan provisions for the three-day journey to Bullard, Texas, by train. There were about 300 members to provide for, and we filled three coaches on the special train. Dad was in charge of the coach in which we, and other families, rode.

It was exciting to speed along the countryside flying our white flag, and to watch the astonished faces of the disappointed people waiting at the stations as we roared, nonstop, through their towns and cities—Milwaukee, Chicago, St. Louis, Fort Worth, and finally, Bullard, Texas.

Carriages from the farm picked us up at a siding near the station and took us to the "Big House" of the farm, where the first person I saw was my friend, Gladys Smith, in a Texas sunbonnet and a calico dress. Her father was among the members who had gone down the year before to purchase the farm and get the work started.

The "Big House" was a typical southern mansion, with tall white pillars holding up a spacious veranda covered with trumpet vines and passion fruit. This housed the offices and residences of the leader and members of the executive board. Numerous tents were pitched here and there, as temporary quarters for the 300 newcomers, until more houses could be built. There were acres of woodland where lumber could be obtained and a large sawmill to cut the lumber. This gave employment to 200 blacks who worked in the mill, along with a number of members of the commune.

On my birthday, April 1, while we were still living in tents, I was sick with fever and a sore throat. (The policy of the church did not allow doctors or medicines.) I was to have a birthday party, but I was sleeping so, Mother did not want to waken me. When I did wake up, I found the party was over. I cried and cried.

It was hot in the tent, but in spring with the flap open, I could see acres of pretty pink peach blossoms surrounding our tent. On cold nights, fires in smudge pots lit up the orchard like a pink fairyland.

In just a few weeks, three "long houses" had been built with freshly-cut lumber and we moved into one of them. At one end was a large room for the school where Gladys Clark taught us our "readin', 'ritin', and 'rithmetic." She was young, pretty, and kind—I still think of her as my favorite teacher. She had left her fiance, Duke Farson, in Waukesha, and we kids liked to see her blush as we put the word "duke" into the sentences she would ask us to diagram.

"The Duke of York is very rich," we might suggest.

"And what is the subject of the sentence?" she would ask.

"Duke!" we'd all shout in unison.

The other end of the "long house" held the dining room and the common kitchen, where all meals were prepared. (Heavy meals they were, for the men were hauling lumber, working the fields and building houses.) Two four-hole outhouses were provided at each end of the long house, marked MEN and WOMEN. Corn husks and Montgomery Ward catalogues served as toilet paper, and candles lit the place at night, as copperheads and other snakes had been found in the area.

Crops were so different in Texas. There was a very large asparagus field which our geography book said was the largest in the world. They raised sugar cane, cotton, tomatoes and sweet potatoes, some of which we would roast and eat in the field. There were orchards of peach trees, as well as pecans and almonds. In the cannery, we put up thousands of cans of tomatoes and peaches, and all that was not needed by the local group and by Waukesha was sold by the carload.

Living on a farm in the hot summer had its compensations. Each morning, a wagon loaded with watermelons would stop at each house and hand out one melon for each member of the family. We rated the best and choicest because Bernice worked on the watermelon crew and had agreed to carefully save the seeds from the finest melons for the following year's planting.

When crops were being harvested, school would be dismissed so we could help. In the spring, we would be digging around the fruit trees, or cutting asparagus. With one student at each end of a row of this huge asparagus field, it would take us four hours to meet. In the summer, we cut okra (wearing stockings on our arms) or picked tomatoes or peas or corn. By late summer, we were picking peaches (also with stockings on our arms!) or digging sweet potatoes, and then, come fall, we cut sugar cane. At the end of the cutting, we would put a huge kettle of the juice (sorghum) on a bonfire, boil it down, and have a taffy-pull out in the field in the moonlight.

Weekends, when we were free, we loved to roam the woods, picking wild flowers, berries or gathering nuts. Or just climbing trees. A favorite pastime was a hayride, when we would sing rounds and harmonize—songs like "In The Evening by the Moonlight," "Old Black Joe," and "Let Me Call You Sweetheart"—but the boys and girls still had to maintain proper deportment and no smooching was allowed. We had to romanticize in our minds and hearts only.

The group in Texas followed the Waukesha pattern of a Camp Meeting each year and, during the rest of the year, religious meetings were held in neighboring towns and villages. Dad's itinerary took him to Red Lawn and two other small towns where he used the local one-room schoolhouse for the gathering. On Sunday morning, he would hitch up the team to the wagon, while Mother would make a dutch oven of a large wooden lard tub. It was first packed with straw, followed by one hot lid from the stove, then a pot roast in a pan, one more hot stove lid, a pan of potatoes and vegetables, and another hot lid on top of that. Then the whole thing was covered and put under the seat of the wagon. A bed of straw was placed in the back, where we kids—all six of us—would ride.

We would stop first at Red Lawn, twenty miles away, for an early Sunday service, and then Father would hitch up the team and move on another ten miles for a late morning meeting, after which we would stop in a grove and Mother would get out the dutch oven with our noon meal piping hot and deliciously cooked. Then everything was put back in the wagon, and we drove another twelve miles for an evening meeting, followed by a supper of cold sliced meat and potatoes in a nearby grove.

When the weather was cold, Mother carried along bricks, which she would put under the pot-bellied stove during the service, and then at our feet in the back of the wagon. On the way home she would cover us with blankets and we'd sleep all the way while she rode up front with Father to keep him awake.

What a day for a preacher! Fortunately, he only had to prepare one sermon, but that one sermon Mother had to hear three times.

It was in Bullard that I had my first ride in an automobile. Uncle Frank (Mother's sister's husband) came to visit us in his new Model T Ford. He piled all of us kids in and took us for a ride on roads never designed for motorized traffic. We bounced along, eating dust and enjoying every minute of it. That was the only car ride I had until we returned to Wisconsin at the end of the War (1914-1918).

Winters were very cold in Texas, especially when we had a "norther." I recall the snow blowing through the cracks and covering the quilt on my bed as I lay suffering from tonsillitis. This was in a small temporary house built by Mr. Blinn and Dad while we waited for the new "big house" to be completed. It had been built in the summer with newly-cut lumber from our sawmill, and as the Texas sun dried the planks of wood, wide gaps developed, through which rain and snow drifted in.

Mother, always resourceful, found narrow slats left over from the construction and, taking a hammer and nails in hand, was out in the snow nailing the slats over the cracks and stuffing in paper when she ran out of slats. Her hands were red and sore when she came in. She put some more wood on the homemade tin stove and smiled at me, saying, "You'll be warm now."

These are some of the memories of a wonderful mother I shall never forget.

Another visitor who used to turn up at Camp Meeting time was a woman I knew only as Patty. She drove a small covered wagon crammed with canned food, her personal belongings, and a chicken that rode up on the seat beside her. Her wagon was pulled by a team of burros, and when we heard the burros bray, we knew Patty was in town. We children would crowd around her. She would pull out a stool and her antique harmonica and tap her feet to the tune of "Turkey in the Straw," "My Darling Clementine," or "The Baggage Coach Ahead." One song that always made me sad went like this:

> "Father come home, O Father come home
> The clock in the steeple strikes three.
> . . . .
> Mother's been waiting since tea
> With poor little Bennie so sick in her arms
> And no one to help her but me."

Another song often brought tears to my eyes. During the Camp Meeting, a family of four, who had lost their mother during the year, sang:

> "I will meet you in the morning
> Just inside the easter gate over there.
> I will meet you, I will meet you.
> I will meet you in the morning over there."

The young boy, with his high tenor voice, blended with his sisters' soprano and alto, and his father's deep base swelled out as if they just knew they would see Mother again.

Annie Hofnagel lived alone down the road on the outskirts of Bullard in a small shack with her one cow tethered at the back. Mother wanted to do something for her, so she volunteered my services on Saturday morning to help Annie with her churning. She would save her surplus milk through the week until I would arrive on Saturday. Her shack was one room about eight by ten feet, with trunks and boxes piled on one side and her mattress on top of them. There, she slept. The other side of the room had a similar stack of boxes and trunks and the chickens roosted on them. Newspapers were scattered on the floor and over her bed to keep them "clean."

She had no fans or refrigeration. There was the churn on the back step with flies gathering around, and the summer heat already turning the milk rancid. I managed to churn with an outstretched arm, and then, announcing, "It's done!" I'd run off before she could ask me to clean up.

One of the important crops on the farm was sweet potatoes, and these were stored in two root houses placed side by side, with windows opening at various levels between. We had had damp weather and the potatoes in one of the root houses were beginning to rot, so an emergency was called and, as usual, school was dismissed so we students could help out.

There we sat in the root house on top of several tons of sweet potatoes, our teacher in the middle, throwing bad potatoes out one window and the good ones through a chute into the second root house. In the midst of all this, a boy came up with a package addressed to Grace Eaton, our teacher.

"Oh, it's from Mother in Boston—my birthday present," she said as she opened it.

Inside, there were six sweet potatoes wrapped in tissue paper and a card which read, "Darling Grace, I know how much you like sweet potatoes. With love, from Mother."

We all roared with laughter until we saw tears in her eyes. One of life's more poignant jokes.

Although we celebrated holidays, we had no money to spend for gifts or new clothes. Somehow, Mother had managed to order some material from Sears Roebuck to make us girls dresses for the 1917 Christmas program. (I surmised Uncle Frank had slipped her some money.) It was blue wool serge for Bernice and red serge for me, and both had white silk trim. Mother, in her ninth month with my brother Bob, was unable to finish our dresses, so Dad jumped in and did a beautiful job of stitching up the dresses to make them ready in time for Christmas.

So, we had brand new dresses for Christmas, but our only

shoes were ones Mother had made for us. Always resourceful, she had taken canvas from the fly awning over our tent and cut out tennis shoes to our size, using several thicknesses of canvas for soles. She used bright calico for binding the edges and made laces to match. They were very pretty and we were proud of them, when they were new; but now they were no longer new. Besides, it was winter, not the season for tennis shoes, and a light snow had fallen. (Remember, Mother was the daughter of a millionaire, but never once do I remember her complaining about her lot or her lack of money!)

In summer, the sand was very hot and walking barefoot was painful, so we would dash from one grassy spot to another to cool our feet. It was also painful when what appeared to be grass turned out to be burr clover, or "sand burrs," as we called them. There were many of these surrounding the well, making it difficult to run with a full bucket of water. (The line from "The Old Oaken Bucket" that says, "How dear to my heart are the scenes of my childhood" did not tell the whole story of our aching backs, the salty perspiration dripping down our faces, or the blistered red hands that strained at the heavy rope. That job was not meant for ten- and eleven-year-old girls.)

A family of eight, as we were, took a good many buckets of water each day, especially on washdays and bath day (which was each Saturday). A large oval tin tub would be placed in the family room in front of the free-standing, wood-burning stove, while buckets of water were heated on the stove, one at a time. The youngest child was always bathed first—using one bucket of water as the second bucket heated. Then, the second child would get in as more water heated, and so on, until all had bathed, even Mother and Father. We relied on the good old-fashioned soap to do its duty and ward off any infections.

Mother and the other ladies made the soap with the tallow from the cast-off kitchen fat. After heating it to the right temperature, they would throw in ashes from the stove, discarding larger pieces of charcoal and sifting the ashes. When the kettle cooled and the soap solidified, it was cut into bars and useable pieces.

Wash day was always a community affair. Long before daylight in the summer months, a large tin boiler was put on an open fire and, after rubbing the white clothes, they were put into the big boiler and poked as they were boiling. Then they were placed into tubs of rinse water and, lastly, a bluing bath—all except the blouses, corset covers, skirts, and petticoats that had to be starched. Long clotheslines flapped in the breeze, leaving the sun to complete the bleaching process.

The war was on and quite a number of our menfolk had been called up for the draft, which left the field workers shorthanded, and it was necessary to bring families who lived far away into the central area. We moved to our new house, which had been built of new pine lumber and was very spacious. The downstairs was the big dining room and kitchen for the surrounding houses, and our family, by now nine in number, lived upstairs. I can remember waking up in the morning to the smell of bacon and baking powder biscuits, which were always on the breakfast menu. The house was up on stilts about four and one-half feet off the ground, creating an area that we used for a playground.

It was while we lived here that a group of leaders had disciplined one of the boys who, in turn, reported his punishment to the authorities. The police came out to the house to arrest Father, and I was alone with Mother when they arrived.

She said, "You talk to them; I'm leaving for a while. Be nice to them, but don't tell them where I am."

Then she hid under the house.

They asked for Father and, of course, I did not know where he was. It seems he had anticipated this situation and had left for Waukesha, telling us children nothing.

It was not long after he arrived in Waukesha that his name came up for the draft. When he told the draft board his wife and family were in Texas, he was told he would either have to return to Texas, or bring his family north. Mother received his telegram and, taking the baby Robert (Bobby), left immediately. We were told that they would send for us when they had the money. Six tickets to Wisconsin were not a small item.

After our parents left, we felt like orphans. It was late summer and the crops, chiefly cotton, had to be harvested. We were each given a long canvas bag, the width of the space between the rows of cotton. Putting the bag over a shoulder, we picked the cotton as we drew the bag along behind us. This meant crawling on our knees, and before long, I had developed boils and bruises on my knees, which were swollen and sore. I complained to the matron, but they would not release me from the field work. (I was 12 years old.) I got worse day by day. With Bernice covering for me, I would go to the field and then lie on the stack of cotton until time to come home, and Bernice would fill my bag.

I got very ill and dear old Grandma Johnston felt sorry for me. She made poultices and bandaged my knees and nursed me back to health. We all loved her.

In her distinct southern accent, she would say, "Honey child, you're going to be well in no time smart." She cared for her own grandchild, Bartow, always admonishing him with, "Bartow, if you don't, you better!"

Going about the room while she straightened up my bed and nightstand, she would hum or sing in her clipped Southern way.

> "Bye 'n bye, oh when the morning comes,
> All the saints of God are gathered home;
> We'll tell the story how we overcome,
> And we'll understand it better bye 'n bye."

She was old and wrinkled and plain, but to me, she was a saint. She saved my life.

When the cotton was sold at the gin, it provided money for our tickets back up north. All six of us (Bernice the oldest at fourteen) were given new hats (all alike) and a new dress, and we were booked for Waukesha. This meant four changes of trains, at Jacksonville, St. Louis, Chicago and Milwaukee. We had packed a lunch and arrangements had been made to have Travelers Aides meet us at the stations, which helped, but with no refrigeration, our lunch was spoiled and Mary Elizabeth, the youngest, took sick.

It was good, at last, to be back in familiar surroundings and have our parents to look after us again.

Chapter VI

School Days
in Waukesha

Back in Waukesha, we started school again. In my class were about thirty students, among them Haven Franklin and Howard Bitzer. And school life went on, full of work interspersed with play—softball, sledding, hikes, and swimming at the lake.

During these years, I was attracted to Howard. He was the smartest boy in my class, and we would vie for first place in grades and distinctions. He became a very special friend, though we had no contact except that in which others joined in. No hand holding or touching was allowed. But always in my girlish dreams he was the man I would one day marry.

Each Sunday at the church service, I would look up at the band platform and Howard would look back—eye contact was our *only* contact, but what a thrill it gave me! On very few occasions, we disobeyed the rules. One Sunday afternoon, Lois and I arranged to meet Howard and her boyfriend at Bethesda Spring. She and I started out together and then met our boyfriends, and after a delightful afternoon, we came home with our original partners—rather later than our usual walks.

Dad glanced at his watch and said, "Where have you been so long?"

"Oh, Lois and I went for a walk," I said, trying to be casual.

"Mind, you don't stay out so late after this," he cautioned gruffly.

Next morning, Dad had to catch an early train for Chicago. I couldn't sleep that night, but as soon as I heard him leave, I ran into Mother's room, got in bed with her and burst out crying.

"Whatever is the matter?" Mother queried.

"I told Father a lie last night," I wailed. "I said I had been on a long walk with Lois, but most of the time I was with Howard."

"Well, now that you have told me, go try to get some sleep."

I didn't dare tell my father or he would have punished me severely.

The Fountain House had added a farm about ten miles away, not far from Pewaukee Lake where they raised vegetables, chickens, eggs, and cows for the table, and this farm gave the boys plenty of work over the summer vacations. Being near the lake, it was a very popular spot for boating and swimming.

During the summer vacation I would catch a ride on the truck and go out to the farm. It was then that I saw Howard more frequently. We both loved to ride horses and there was plenty of riding space on the farm. One day the boys gave me a spirited horse, but did not tell me he was so feisty. One of the boys switched the legs of the animal as I started off, and he went at a gallop, running some two miles before stopping. I managed to stay on, and when we came to the South Farm, I dismounted to rest. They asked me to lunch and I lingered a good long time.

Meanwhile, the boys were becoming more and more alarmed because I had not returned. When I finally got back, I greeted them pleasantly.

"But where have you been all this time?" they asked. "We were afraid you had fallen into the roadside ditch."

"Oh, no, I rode over to the South Farm. They invited me to lunch and I had a pleasant afternoon, thanks to you both!"

That shut up the boys.

One afternoon our botany teacher wanted to row out to the island in the lake for some specimens. Several of us went over and we girls decided to have a swim. I was having a good time when I discovered I had gone out beyond my depth. I went down and felt weeds. I went down again and I knew I was drowning.

Just then, a boat came by and I was pulled from the water. I took a while to recover, but later that afternoon, Howard came down to the cottage pier and we sat there a long time. We talked about the future, and I told him that I felt God wanted me to go to India. Howard had no inclination to do the same, and when we finally parted, I was a bit sad, for I had hoped he might want to go also.

We had been in the same grade school and graduated from high school together. We had been friends for a long time, but the mission frowned on dating and, on occasion, went to extremes to prevent marriages.

One evening, Lois and I were down in the kindergarten room when Howard and a friend appeared. We talked about our futures again, about mission work and the possibility of going to some foreign field. Then we heard the heavy tread of someone coming down the stairs. The boys fled out the back door and hid in the coal bin until the coast was clear.

These talks always left me in a quandary. I felt God was leading me one way and Howard and my heart were pulling me another—toward a little home together, someplace where we could raise a family and live a comfortable, happy life.

During these school days, I engaged in several extra-curricular activities. Church authorities had been talking of sending me to India where my older sister had gone the year before. I felt I should get some medical knowledge, of which our group did not approve, so I quietly went over to the the city hospital and spent all my spare time observing patients with Dr. Davies, who helped me a great deal.

Whenever I found extra hours on Saturday, I would also go over to O'Brian's studio to learn something about photography. Certainly this would be needed in the foreign mission where there was a printing press and illustrated reports to be sent back home. Several months later, when I became more experienced, the studio manager had me help him a bit, and with the small amount of money he paid me I bought film and supplies. The hospital and photography experiences helped me a great deal when I wrote a book about the India mission. Still another thing I did was to go down to the mission press. I learned to set type and to run off sheets for *The Burning Bush.* This also came in handy later, when I had to prepare some of our mission reports. In all these years were quite fruitful.

Each August, a big circus tent was hauled into the south half of the park across the street, and all the able-bodied men would be corralled into erecting it. One end of the tent would be taken up with a platform, which held 150 chairs. Fifty were to the cen-

ter, back behind the pulpit, for the band, and fifty on either side,
one side for men—preachers and laymen—and the other side for
ladies and the missionaries or deaconesses with their gray uniforms and bonnets.

The big tent with its canvas sign, "Revival Meetings," attracted attention from passersby, and cars would stop and line the
streets long before meeting time. The brass band would start
playing at seven, and the tent would be filled by seven-thirty. The
singing was vivacious and exuberant, and the audience would
give expression to their feelings of joy by jumping, running in the
aisles, and shouting—giving rise to the name which the townspeople called them, "holy jumpers." The scene was often that of a
wild hoopla (though mild compared with the rock and rollers of
today).

After several songs were sung and prayers said, the preacher
would exhort and admonish the audience to come to Christ to
find life's true meaning.

"The wages of sin is death, but the gift of God is eternal life,"
he would warn, pointing out the shortness of life and the uncer-
tainty of tomorrow, and that to die with unconfessed sin meant
an eternity in hellfire. Come and be saved and spend eternity in
Heaven with God and His holy angels.

People were smitten with the preaching and exhortations, and
when the invitation hymn was sung, they would flock to the altar,
often crying and weeping. One hymn of exhortation often sung
was:

> "Just as I am without one plea,
> But that thy blood was shed for me.
> And that Thou bidst me come to Thee,
> O Lamb of God, I come, I come.
>
> "Just as I am! Thou wilt receive,
> Wilt welcome, pardon, cleanse, relieve;
> Because Thy promise I believe,
> O Lamb of God, I come, I come!"

Many came away from the altar changed people. By confess-
ing their sins, they felt a load fall from them and they left with a

newness of life and a committal to live for Christ for the rest of their days.

Those standing around the tent who had merely come out of curiosity were often jeering and laughing and smoking cigarettes, creating a circus atmosphere that was quite foreign to most of the residents, as we seldom smelled tobacco smoke. That, combined with the fumes of the cars starting up and the noise of the traffic, was left in the memories of those attending the camp meeting. Farther reaching, however, was the spiritual impact and renewal of vows.

After the Camp Meeting of 1924, we were all anxious to know what station, or job, we would be assigned, as all appointments were made for a year, from one camp meeting to the next. We crowded around the mail room bulletin board full of excitement and curiosity —where were we going and who else was assigned to our post? Where were our friends going? Would we be together or separated by many miles?

I was listed for Pittsburgh, and the Bob Hitchcocks were to be in charge. I was to pack my things and leave with them the next day, along with two other single ladies whom I hardly knew. All my friends were scattered over the forty-eight states, with Howard going to Storm Lake, Iowa. My heart was heavy, not knowing if our interest in each other would last over a long separation or if we would even be allowed to say goodbye. A year seemed a long, long time.

Pittsburgh was an interesting city, situated among Pennsylvania's hills and valleys, with the Allegheny and Monongahela Rivers meeting in the center of town to form the Ohio River. In the year I spent there, I canvassed almost the entire city and spent much time in North Allegheny, among the poorer families, where we began a Sunday school and a visiting center. I wanted to visit the sick and take clothing and food to the poor families. This was my first contact with homes of the poor and, while I found them depressing, I felt a bond with them and a great desire to help where I could.

We travelled by streetcar, and after the long ride home to the suburb of Elliott, we still had to trudge 97 steps up the hill to our house. After washing up in the kitchen, our evenings were spent in family prayers and reading. It was during the long evenings of the winter of 1924-25 that I read a large number of the missionary biographies—including Hudson Taylor of China, Livingstone and Robert Moffat of Africa, and Ann of Ava (the wife of Adoniram Judson of Burma*)—which influenced me greatly. I was moved by their compassion and sacrifice for God and their fellow men.

Soon after coming to Pittsburgh, I met Gertrude Moffat who, with her children, attended our Sunday school. She was a friend I could talk to about my missionary interest and one who encouraged me to prepare myself for the calling.

She was not a long-faced Christian in somber clothes like so many I had seen in Waukesha, but wore attractive clothes, a jaunty hat (she was a milliner who said she sold "handmade hats, not homemade ones"), and she had a radiant face and a warm smile. Her Christian love was infectious; I wanted to be like her.

The year finally ended. No word had come from Howard directly, but I had frequent letters from his sister and my friend, Lois, and I was getting anxious to see him again. The flame within me had not died down.

The camp meeting that year was somewhat different from the year before. There were several missionaries returned from India, Africa, and the Virgin Islands, and through their stories, I got a clearer picture of what a missionary's life would be. It would be anything God asked of one, a daily giving of one's self in whatever task was there to be done. Renounced was the glamour, the self-glorification, the fame and notoriety. Once one arrived, it was just like the Christian life is here at home—obeying God from day to day and doing the job in hand. And there was no promise of a salary or any furlough down the way.

I was not without some qualms. I had always wanted to travel and see the world, but it now seemed I would be out in a small Indian village for life. I'd never see anything of the world, I thought. Moreover, I loved to read and found books stimulating. In the field, I would be far from a public library and magazines, and the only books I would have would be my own small collection. In addition, I wanted to go on with my education and delve

---

* I later met his grandson, Mr. Hanah, in Burma.

into science, the classics, and philosophy, and meet and converse with cultured peoples. None of this would be available in an Indian village so small its name was not even on the map.

I loved my Lord. He had become a close Friend to whom I went with all my loneliness and troubles, but could He fill all these other desires and satisfy me? I longed for love, but would Howard come and would we ever find happiness together if I now went out alone?

Yet, I felt that was exactly what God was asking me to do. Standing in front of my open window overlooking the pine trees in the Ladies' Park, with a big full moon sparkling on the foliage, I felt a divine peace come over me. God was with me, and he would be in India with me just the same. Yes, I would go.

There was still a year of proving myself ahead. I was sent to Detroit to help with the mission there—canvassing, teaching in Sunday school, helping the mission families in their problems and decisions, etc.

Before the year was up, I was called back to Waukesha to prepare to go to India. There was a passport to get, clothing to buy, and the packing of books and articles I could not purchase over there, and farewells to be said to family and friends.

My folks had moved in the time I was away; Dad had been asked to leave the Bible school, as his family was too big to be an asset to the community any longer. So he had taken a large farm house in Sussex and had to start a new life and provide for his wife and his children. He was bitter, for he had hoped to become a preacher and serve the Lord in that profession. He had already given one daughter to the mission field and now God was asking for another?

During these days at Sussex, I had an opportunity to see my mother as a homemaker for the first time since I was six years old. I saw her buy a thick slice of round steak for fifty cents and make Swiss steak and gravy which, along with bread, was our supper. She would bake strawberry shortcake in a large pan and it was a feast. I also have a picture of my mother making lemon pies in the big wood stove. I cherish these memories, for those few months are the only time I can remember ever having lived in a normal home.

Dr. Davies, of Waukesha Hospital, who had been kind and

understanding, and who helped me a great deal, called me in to deliver one of our women residents. I knew that some knowledge of obstetrics would be most valuable in India, and when Dr. Davies suggested I come to the hospital whenever a delivery case was in progress, I jumped at the chance. Of course I did not tell anyone in the Mission what I was doing, for I knew it was against policy to engage in anything like modern medicine. But I had my own car, which I got from Dad, so I could move about easily. I began spending a lot of time with the doctors, who were very helpful and who knew I was soon to go to India.

The practical experience I was getting proved invaluable, for there was no doctor in our India Mission, and I would have to do everything myself.

"When you get to India," Dr. Davies said, "you won't find things like we have them here. Your patient will be lying on a bed of straw and you will be down on the floor doing the delivery." How right he was!

Finally the day of departure arrived. Miss Katherine Workman and Miss Clara Louise Huntington were to go with me. Both were returning to India, and it was thought wise that a younger person should go with older, experienced ones. Father drove us to Chicago, the two ladies sitting in the back seat with Mother while I was in the front seat with Father.

"Why do you want to go to India when there is so much to do here in America?" Father asked gruffly.

"Because I think it is what the Lord wants me to do," I answered. "You have told us all along that we should follow the Lord."

He had brought us up with the idea that serving God on the mission field was the greatest goal we could have in life, and now he was having second thoughts.

At Union Station in Chicago, Father never said a word. (It was to be sixteen years before we met again, at the same station, upon my return from India. And in all that time, Father did not write once, though Mother did. His was a long, long silence.) The ladies and Mother cheered me up, but I felt an underlying unhappiness about the way my own Father treated me.

Before I left, Mother gave me some money. I don't know where she got it, for we never had money.

She said, "This is for some sightseeing on your way. Go to Washington. You need to know your country."

That made me feel good. And there was still another reason for happiness. In our last long talk together, Howard had said he had been thinking much about going to India, and if the Lord so directed, he would go. I felt God was answering my prayers and I could wait.

We continued on to Washington D.C. where we visited the White House, the Capitol Building and Mount Vernon. I was glad to see something of America before leaving it—it would be a long time before I would see my country again.

Then it was on to New York, where we boarded the Cunard Liner *S.S. California*. We crossed from New York to Glasgow, where we stopped at our sister mission for a number of meetings; then we continued by train to Liverpool, where we picked up the *California* once more and headed for Bombay.

Howard was ever in my heart and thoughts, and there was pain as I stood near the rail, watching the rolling sea taking me farther and farther away with each hour that passed.

Roy Pearl Owen, circa 1889   Pearl Irene Gebhart, circa 1901

The family in 1920. Three more children were born after this: Ralph, William, and Jean. Reading clockwise from left: Naomi, Dorothy, Bernice, Juanita, Muriel, Mary Elizabeth, Robert seated between Mom and Dad, and Mildred in Mother's arms.

The schoolhouse which housed all the grades up through the eighth. The old cow pasture in the rear we turned into our softball field.

An aerial view of the Fountain House surrounded by its spacious parks and grounds.

Where the band played on summer evenings. Marble steps wound down to the spring which supplied the Fountain Spring House with water and also gave it its name.

The main dining room of the Fountain house.

The Fountain Spring House, 200 South Grand Avenue, Waukesha, Wisconsin.

The crowd of well-wishers and friends that gathered to farewell Juanita and Misses Workman and Huntington on their departure for India.

BOOK THREE

INDIA

1926-1933

Chapter VII

A Dream Fulfilled

Our ship stopped at Port Said. We got off and took a bus to Cairo to see the pyramids and the Sphinx. They were most impressive—to think that these had been erected thousands of years earlier. There were camels, the owners of which begged us to ride. But we refused; it was a long way up on the beast's back and, besides, the fee was too much.

Back safely on the ship, we glided through the rather narrow Suez Canal. On the left was barren, sandy country; on the right it looked like a garden trimmed with palms. Then we sailed through the Red Sea towards Bombay. The last evening out we stood at the railing, as the sun sank into a crimson sea.

Next morning, we steamed past the imposing Gateway to India which fronted the teeming city of Bombay. When we had docked, what utter confusion as the coolies ran up and down the gangplank with loads on their heads. They kept spitting what I thought was blood, but later found was their saliva, turned red by the betelenut they chewed.

Cranes unloaded heavier pieces while our baggage was put in a heap on the dock. The two ladies were there, sorting out our things. Not an article was lost! One of the *miss-sahibs* (as the unmarried ladies in India are called) hailed coolies who moved our belongings over to the customs counter on the dock. Meanwhile, I looked up to see innumerable crows, kites and gulls circling around in the air. Birds seemed to be everywhere.

On railroad tracks I noticed a line of sawed-off boxcars, only half the size of the familiar American ones. And I noted that vehicles drove on the opposite side of the road. The sights, sounds and smells of India were rather overpowering!

The baggage went through customs in a surprisingly short time. Miss Workman hailed three *tongas*, distributed the loads and one of us got in each of the vehicles.

"To the GIP," called out Miss Workman in the first *tonga*.

The Great Indian Peninsular Railroad was one of the two main lines running north from Bombay. The other was the B.B & C.I. (Bombay, Baroda and Central India) line. It took fully half an hour to drive through streets crowded with bullocks, buffaloes and horse-drawn vehicles. There were also some carts being pushed by men. Open-front shops lined the streets and large signs were mostly in English. One large banner strung across the street read, "Welcome to the Governor and Governess."

At the railroad, our tickets were issued to Siwait, via Allahabad, in a *zenana** compartment on the Bombay Mail. It was a bit more expensive to travel by mail train, but it was much less crowded and it was faster. Actually, we found ourselves quite comfortably situated, in spite of the hard wooden benches. (We had extracted blankets from our footlockers at customs, and these were spread out over the benches.) There was enough room so all three of us could sit down and later stretch out and try to sleep.

Hawkers called loudly as they walked up and down the platform.

"Pan,** beeri, cigarettes.

"Jalebis, gulab jamuns, halwa.***

"Cha, garam cha****

"Oh, we must get some of those long, green bananas," exclaimed Miss Huntington. "They are called *hari chals*, and they are the world's best."

We bought a dozen of them for about twenty-five cents, and they proved to be delicious.

"I'll go out to the tap and fill our water bottle," said Miss Workman. "I'll add several drops of iodine to make it perfectly safe to drink."

---

* For ladies only
**betelnut
***Indian sweets
**** tea, hot tea

While this was being done, a loud whistle blew and passengers scurried back to their compartments.

"Well, our water bottle is almost full," announced Miss Workman as she settled into her seat.

Now we were to ride over a thousand miles, and the ticket was only a piece of cardboard two inches by three inches, costing less than ten dollars. It was thanks to the British Government that travel was so convenient and cheap.

The train started on the minute, and gradually gained speed as it passed through suburb after suburb of Bombay. Thirty minutes later, we were among cultivated fields situated between low-lying hills. On into the night we rode, with the clickety-clap rhythm mile after mile. At each station stop, there was the usual hubbub of confusing noises, dominated by hawkers selling their wares.

Finally, dawn began to push up over the eastern horizon. By now the train had roared past some hundreds of Indian villages. Looking out over the horizon, one could see scantily dressed men carrying little brass jugs while others squatted in the fields.

"If they are going out to water their fields, why don't they carry buckets with more water?" I queried.

"They are going to the bathroom," Miss Workman informed me, "and for cleansing, they use water instead of toilet paper."

"What do the women do?"

"Well, they are out before it gets light so they won't be seen."

Such is life in a land where the houses have no bathrooms nor running water.

There were sugar cane fields with tall stalks of cane in tassel and ready for harvest. In other fields, water still flooded the ground and water buffaloes lay languidly, with cattle egrets sitting on their backs waiting for the insects that are startled by the buffalo. I was told, then, that water buffaloes have no sweat glands and have to depend on bathing their bodies to cool themselves.

It was Friday when we approached Allahabad—a large city where one could see temple shrines as well as minarets, indicating the heterogeneous population of the city. In front of one mosque, a throng of worshippers had gathered. Most of them wore white garments and knelt in long lines, prostrating themselves toward Mecca in the west. It was a moving sight.

Further along through the city, bells clattered and the wail of a conch shell sounded, as several Hindu devotees sacrificed a goat in front of a blood-stained image of Kali. India was certainly a religious country.

At Allahabad, we transferred to the East India Railway and faced an hour's delay. Flies and pigeons were everywhere. A troupe of rhesus monkeys invaded the station looking for food. One hungry monkey dropped down the side of the train, grabbed a fistful of unleavened bread right out of the hand of a passenger, bounced up over the train and scrambled up a *pipal* tree. Several other monkeys saw the incident and chased the thief, hoping to get a bite to eat, but the first monkey crammed the whole thing into his mouth until his jaws stood out like a pocket gopher's.

Then along came a wandering *sadhu** dressed in saffron, asking for alms. He carried half of a large coconut in which he placed his gifts. Another, behind him, wore nothing but beads, a g-string, and his body rubbed with ashes. A rather gruesome sight, I thought.

I had landed in the heart of North India. *Ganga Mai*, the Ganges River, flowed only a few miles away. The Ganges is sacred to the Hindus, as is the earth itself, which they revere as "Mother Earth."

Clustered around the Siwait railroad station was the town, largely made up of Muslims. A short distance in the other three directions were still other villages, whose populations were predominately Hindu. Members of both communities got along reasonably well together.

The *zamindar*** of that area lived in a well-constructed house with white walls; he was less than a mile away. And to think there were 700,000 other villages like these in India!

For the next sixteen years this was to be my home. Yet I was happy, for I was fulfilling my dream of serving the needs of rural India.

As I looked out over the mission compound on that day in November of 1926, I saw the long building with its concrete floor

---

* An aescetic Hindu holy man.
** Headman.

and walls made of mud and crowned with a thatched roof. At one end was attached a small cook house. The big *mahuwa* tree was directly in front, offering shade to passers-by. Off to the right were three smaller houses, one for the print shop, the second a laundry and coal shed and the third an orphanage. Directly behind the laundry was a deep well with a slope to it, so that oxen could be driven up and down, carrying water in goatskin bags. Beyond stretched the fields, the nearer ones for vegetables. In front of the long house was a row of *neem* trees, cousins of the chinaberry tree of southern U.S.A. Nearer the well was a fine guava orchard, as well as papaya trees, where flocks of rose-ringed parakeets and common mynas babbled incessantly. The mission aimed to be as self-supporting as possible with their garden and orchards.

My sister Bernice took me to her room in the long house. She and I would live with Miss Swenson. With three cots in that small room, the situation was rather crowded. There were no chairs or desks; we ladies wrote our letters on our laps. The back quarter of the room was a dressing room and the fourth quarter, a veranda. This had a concrete tank into which the *bhisti** poured water. One drew a curtain when taking a bath.

On the outer edge was a tiny curtained room with a bucket used to collect night soil. This was emptied each morning and evening by a lowly sweeper. It was a matter of very simple living, with all things held in common.

November was an ideal time to arrive in India; blistering southern winds had given place to cool northern ones, making the days quite pleasant and the nights chilly enough to use blankets.

The first Friday afternoon, Bernice, who taught the mission children, came into the room where I was writing a letter and complained, "I could hardly get through my classes today, I felt so bad. I know I have a fever."

"Yes, you do have a fever," I remarked as I felt her forehead.

The next afternoon, Bernice's temperature was up even more, as it was the following day. Typhoid!

"What will I do about my school work?" asked Bernice. "You

* Water carrier

had better take over Monday morning, Juanita."

And so it was that my schoolteaching began and continued for more than six months, as Bernice took a long time to recover. There were only eight or nine pupils, children of missionaries in the station ranging from two in first grade to one at high school level. Actually there was not much grading, as everyone went along at his own speed.

My activities were not confined to the classroom. One day there was a commotion in the yard, and, looking through the open window, I saw several men carrying another man in a hammock. School had to be suspended for the time being while the teacher went out to examine the patient.

The man had been standing at the edge of the Ganges River when a turtle attacked him and bit off the top of his foot. I removed the dirty bandage, cleaned out the wound with warm sterile water, and put in antiseptic powder. Then I covered it with a sterile cotton bandage. He would not be able to walk for several days, and we needed a place to put him. The coal shed was really the only place available, so a corner of it was swept out and a mat put down for the injured man. After a week, he was able to hobble back to his village.

At night it was a relief to roll into bed and relax. I slept on an average village bed, a *charpai*,* made of a frame of rough wooden three-by-threes, four feet wide and six feet long, with four thin wooden legs. The upper two-thirds was woven with thin jute rope, which was inclined to sag when one sat or lay on it. With a pad, however, plus blankets and sheets, it was fairly comfortable.

Once we three ladies settled down and it was quiet, night sounds penetrated one's consciousness. Among these were those of the night watchman who made his hourly rounds, calling out to warn away any potential marauders. He continually thumped his staff on the ground, as the vibrations were supposed to drive off snakes. Then there was the whistle of the midnight train, as well as the one at six a.m.

One of the first jobs to be done was learning the language. Usually there was no one around to act as interpreter. On the

---

* Literally, "four legs."

ship coming out, my two companions worked with me on a number of key sentences.

One word I kept hearing was *"sunno,"* which I thought meant "good morning." I used it frequently those first few days, only to discover later that it meant, "listen to me." My other sentences got mixed up, too, until it was evident there was a need for a language teacher. A man from the village was hired, but his usage of language was of a limited quality.

When villagers learned that someone in the mission could help them medically, they began to come as outpatients. Eventually there came the day when a woman had to be kept two or three days for treatment, which led to the decision that the coal house should be cleaned out for an occasional patient. Though the mission never gave permission for this extra-curricular activity, the patient load continued to grow.

Bernice had finally recovered from typhoid and could resume teaching her classes. This left me free to study language and take care of patients.

Summer was especially trying, with the temperature running between 110-120°. Even though we had a well, no vegetables would grow except summer squash and onions. The cook would serve squash and onions one day and onions and squash the next. Fortunately, there were a few fruits in season. Especially plentiful were the mangoes that grew around every village. Goat was the only meat available, and that was usually tough. What few hen's eggs there were, were small—slightly larger than marbles.

And there was no refrigeration. Milk had to be boiled three times a day just to keep it from spoiling, while such things as coffee were unheard of. Each year, my mother would send a can of coffee for Christmas, which was shared around on Christmas morning, so that one had no more than a single cup. As for the other drinks, we always had a fine quality of Lopchu tea from Darjeeling. This was served each afternoon along with bits of toasted unleavened bread and an occasional cookie. (They looked like cookies, at least, but the flour was coarse and the sugar was crystalline and rather dirty.) Salt came in large pink chunks and had to be crushed, but even then, one often bit into little salt nuggets in the food.

Meals were not exciting. The only time we had a "spread" was on a birthday, at Thanksgiving, or on Christmas. If we couldn't get a chicken, villagers might have guinea fowl. Once in a while, the men would go out hunting for peafowl, or wild peacock. These were like turkeys with plenty of white meat. Then, we had a feast. Dressing was made of bread with coarse flour and never tasted anything like what we had at home.

The first hot season, I was always hungry. Our cucumber vines produced tiny fruit two or three inches long. With a craving for pickles, I got out a cookbook and found the recipe for them called for lining a large crock with grape leaves. There were no grape vines around where we lived, but I did remember seeing a vine climbing over the Nehru home in Allahabad. The next time I went into the city, I stopped the car outside the palatial residence, intending to ask the gardener for a few of the leaves hanging outside the wall.

Surprised to see a white face, the gardener invited me in while he collected the leaves. At that moment, Moti Lal Nehru, patriarch of the family and solicitor of the High Court, came out of the house and greeted me. He had removed his official robe and was clad entirely in white homespun cloth which matched the color of his hair. He invited me to sit on a garden bench and ordered tea. Then he wanted to know who I was and where I worked. We chatted, covering many subjects, until sundown, when I rose to go.

"Do stop whenever you are passing this way. I enjoyed talking with you," insisted Moti Lal.

This was the beginning of an enduring friendship with the Nehru family. The gardener brought the grape leaves, well washed, and I was on my way.

When I got home, I learned that Bhaktini, one of our servants, was ill over in a neighboring village, and I was asked to go and check on her. Barhaiya was a village of *chamars**, and her house was made of mud walls with rough-hewn door frames. The floors had been washed with cow dung, which was the usual cleanser in the village. A cow was tied outside. Some villagers owned a buffalo and others had no livestock at all.

---

* A low caste of leather workers.

Bhaktini's house boasted one window, high up and small, so no one could crawl through. Meanwhile, other houses nearby were windowless. There were several earthen pots containing *bajara** gathered recently from the fields. They had given anywhere from one-third to one-half to the landowner, and this was what they had left. Bhaktini was feeling much better and insisted on making a fire and preparing a millet cake for me. Bhaktini brought it to me when it was cooked through—and was it hard!

She said, "I have something special for you today," and placed two small pieces of prized rock salt on the cake and handed it to me. I broke off a small piece of the cake and took one bite of salt; such food fills one up in a hurry.

How generous these very poor people were. And she seemed serene and happy.

Making my way back along the narrow path, I came to the village pond. In the middle of it lay several water buffaloes with only their heads and upper backs visible. On the far edge, a number of women were cleaning their cooking vessels. Nearby, a mother scrubbed her young child's head with clay, then rinsed head and body as the child cried lustily. The water itself was darkish with green scum at one end of the pond. Several ducks prodded the debris for food, while the crows and mynas in the *neem* trees above them left their droppings in the water. None of this fazed the man standing nearby, cleaning his teeth with the shredded end of a *neem* twig.

On Saturday, we would go out to neighboring villages to sell gospel tracts. They cost one *pice* apiece, or about half a cent. They were printed mostly in Hindi and Urdu, but we also had some in Bengali and Gujarati. At full moon, there was a *mela*** on the banks of the Ganges near the junction of the Jamuna River. Here, devout Hindus say, is a third underground river, the sacred Sarasvati. It was considered especially auspicious to bathe at the confluence of these rivers during the full moon period. A team of six or eight of us from the mission would put up a tent near the Ganges and spend the day selling Bibles, gospel portions and Christian literature. The tent itself would serve as a

* The poorest of millets.
** A fair.

rest room and bathroom.

During the day, men poled dugouts and rafts up and down the Ganges. Bathing occurred at all hours, especially just before sunup. Men clad in g-strings and women in saris waded into the water up to their waists. Facing the rising sun, they would cup their hands and throw water in an arc above their heads. They would then immerse themselves, one time for each member of their family, to free them of their sins.

On down the river two or three miles were the burning ghats where the wood funeral pyres were constantly burning. A certain number of people, especially the old and decrepit, would die at the river's edge at this time. Their remains would be cremated and their ashes scattered on the surface of Ganga Mai (Mother Ganges). Bodies, wrapped in red or white sheets depending on the sex of the individual, would be placed on the pyres. The oldest male of the family would light the fire, which would then burn for hours. If the family was poor, they burned only the ends of fingers, and toes and also the lips, and the body was cast into the holy waters to be swept away downstream.

Instead of lamenting their departing, the relatives rejoiced that they died in the waters of the sacred Ganges.

At the banks of the river were great green turtles three or four feet in diameter. Crocodiles also lurked here, waiting for a meal. A friend who hunted crocodiles for their hides showed me a string of silver, brass and glass bangles which were recovered from the stomach of a single crocodile. (Dead bodies never have jewelry on them when placed in the river, so these victims had been seized and dragged alive under the water.)

In the Hindu holy month of Magh (January), hundreds of thousands of pilgrims gather at the confluence of the three rivers. Several million devotees will gather at the *Khumbh Mela*, which occurs once in twelve years. At times, there is such a rush for the water that scores of pilgrims are trampled to death. On days such as these, the missionaries sell a great number of pamphlets.

Come evening, our tent would be struck and loaded onto the buffalo cart. It was roughly six miles back to the mission station, so we took turns riding on the cart while the others plodded on foot through the evening dust. When we passed a village, we would see a small circle of men sitting on the ground, warming themselves around a small fire. Over the whole village would hang a canopy of scented blue smoke as the women prepared the evening meal. Here and there, one heard an occasional tinkle of the bells that were fastened around the necks of livestock, or the grunt of a buffalo. In the near distance, jackals gave their long drawn out calls: "ooooooooooo, ooooooooooo, ooooooooooo," each one a little higher, until suddenly they concluded with a "yap yap yap, yap yap yap." Two or three calling together sounded like at least a dozen. Sometimes one heard the barking of the Indian fox or the piercing "meauuuu" of a peacock perched in a distant tree.

Life in a community such as ours at Siwait demanded that each person do his part. On wash day, everybody helped. One person, usually a man, got up at 4 a.m. to light the fires under the boilers and heat the water. Then, after breakfast and prayer, the rest would appear, the men to work the homemade wooden washing machines back and forth while the ladies rubbed the more delicate clothes on old fashioned washboards. Then they were boiled rinsed and blued, and hung out to dry.

The next day the wash shed was turned into an ironing shed and three or four ladies would iron, taking flatirons off the fire in rotation. Fortunately, the shed was open on three sides, so if there was a bit of a breeze, we would get it.

The mission had taken in a number of orphans and there were always a couple of small babies around. Besides washing and ironing for them, there was always the feeding, bathing, dressing, and changing them, which we also handled in turn. When I arrived in Siwait, the youngest was Niwa Mangi (Skipper), a Nepalese baby from the Darjeeling side, and just a few months older was Phul Maya (Love Flower). She was brought to the missionaries in Tung (a hill station near Darjeeling) the previous summer—her father depositing her at the mission house in a basket, saying he could no longer care for her *and* her sick brother, and it was against his religion to give up a *sick* child.

Other orphans came and went, but several grew into adulthood at the mission and served God in their unique capacity. One such was Herbert Hyratt, who had come with his sister. He was musical and became an accomplished pianist and organist. He kept the piano tuned and handled many other jobs, including printing and keeping the printing presses in shape. The villagers loved to listen to his music when we went to the surrounding villages for evening meetings.

Sixteen months had passed since my arrival, and I was still unable to speak the language. I went to Mission director, asking to be sent to the language school in Landour, Mussoorie, where most of the new arrivals went. Here in Siwait, there were so many interruptions with more and more patients coming all the time, and there was no time to study the language as I should. And the servants were not much help.

"No one from our mission has gone to Landour, and we have had to get the language as best we could," replied Mr. Whipple. That no one in the mission had done it before was not a valid reason, I thought. Why, the same could be said about the medical work. No one in the mission had ever worked in the medical field before, but I did not see why I shouldn't, when the need was so evident on every hand. It took a little persuading, but Mr. Whipple finally consented, also allotting a small sum for tuition and living quarters.

This success made me feel a bit bolder. I also told him I felt his son, Norman, should be in Woodstock school, as he was not being challenged by studying alone.

It was a happy April day for me when I took the train for Lucknow and points beyond. I looked for the names of stations as we passed. The signs were both in English and Hindi, and sometimes in Urdu as well. We first came to Partabgarh, then Rae Bareilly, and Lucknow an hour later.

Such a mass of people, sights and sounds and smells! When a conductor blew his whistle, passengers scrambled for their seats. Some of the passengers hung on the outside, as the compartments were crowded. I rode in the *zenana,* which was overcrowded, as usual, but this time contained three other missionary ladies. It did not take long to get acquainted. Two of them were teaching at Isabella Thoburn College in Lucknow and the other was with the Methodist Mission in Cawnpore. All of them were going to Landour to attend language school. None of us knew very much Hindi or Urdu, so we would be in the beginning classes together.

I was intrigued by the names of the cities we passed through: Hardoi, Shajahanpur, Bareilly, Moradabad and on to Lakhsar, the latter evidently a place of pilgrimage, for I never saw so many monkeys and *sadhus* on one station platform before. It was still a half hour before dawn, but what a bustle of activity!

Finally daylight came, and with it flocks of birds in the air, in the trees and on the ponds. Through the window on the right, I could see low-lying blue hills. The Himalayas! How exciting and majestic they looked, and to think I was to live in them for the next five months! What a change from hot dusty Siwait!

Dehra Dun was at the end of the line. To the south lay a wooded ridge of hills, the Siwaliks or Outer Himalayan Range. To the north rose the higher Mahabharata Range where Mussoorie was located.

Dehra Dun was a large, thriving city lying on the plateau between the two ranges. Red-turbaned porters crowded into compartments begging to be engaged to carry baggage. Four of them loaded all our luggage onto their heads and started for the ticket gate. Numbers of *tongas*, cars and bus drivers also vied for our patronage. We learned that a bus was going in a few moments to Rajpur at the foot of the hills. We could ride that far, then proceed on foot or be carried in a *dandy* chair. Or we could ride horseback the final ten miles to Landour. It would take all day to get there, the road was so steep.

We decided to have breakfast at Chapman's Hotel at Rajpur, where we cleaned up and washed, after which we felt much better. Here they served *suji** and bacon and eggs. Not knowing when we would get something more to eat, we decided on this hearty breakfast. As we looked around the room, we saw several Europeans, evidently bound for Mussoorie, too.

Outside, the porters were ready to go. We supplied each with the name of our particular destination. Mine was Parade View, Landour, while the others were going to Rokeby, Landour. These places were within easy walking distance from Landour Language School at Kellogg Church. All of us decided to ride horses and settled on the price. What a pint size these hill ponies were! Fortunately, the saddles were well worn and caused us no trouble.

We started up the steep hill, zigzagging endlessly. I noticed that the horsemen had hold of the tails of the animals, and

* Sort of cream of wheat.

learned that this helped them up the hill.

The country below us began to spread out in a wonderful panorama. The higher we went, the more beautiful it became. The air was so fresh now, compared to that of the plains, and the sky was very blue up above Mussoorie.

Along about one o'clock we arrived at the Halfway House. How glad we were to dismount and to find a place to freshen up and eat. They served us mutton, peas and cauliflower. Oranges and bananas were the dessert. We felt better.

After resting a bit, we called for the horsemen, who were just finishing their rice and curried vegetables, and continued on and on up the mountain. By now, low shrubs had given way to oak trees, pines and Himalayan cedars or *deodars.** The sun was warm, but the air was nippy. How exhilarating!

We reached the Picture Palace in Landour bazaar where the horsemen said they went no further. But another group of porters were waiting to carry our loads to our final destinations.

We finally arrived shortly before dark. It was getting really chilly. I hadn't worn a sweater for weeks.

I took another deep breath—a load seemed to drop off my shoulders.

Landour Cantonment, the eastern section of Mussoorie, where I would spend my next four months, was opened in 1825 for British soldiers. Two officers came up from Saharanpur to set up a shooting range, and a place for convalescent military personnel. These men often went into the hills for pheasant, red deer, goat, antelope and, occasionally, a Himalayan bear. It was a healthy place and business boomed.

Tea planters came to these hills to build summer estates in Landour, and maharajahs to Mussoorie to build palaces. Woodstock School was founded in 1854, and most of the small places on Landour hillside were put up by Protestant mission groups. Parents could come up to these cool hills during the summer and take their children out of the school to stay with them as day scholars—a very convenient arrangement.

My mission had little money for renting quarters. We finally settled on a little row of four servant's quarters next to the ram-

---

* *Cedrus deodara,* meaning "trees of God."

bling Landour Villa, on a level road encircling Landour hill.

There was little space between our quarters and the stone hillside behind it, while in front, there was a sheer drop of several hundred feet. We brought in *namdas** and hung curtains over the few windows there were, and made it cheery and private.It was primitive, but we were used to privations.

I was given an end room, while Tyrrell Fordham, who was expected in a few days, was given the other end. The Freymiller family had the two rooms in between.

Early that first morning, I was rudely awakened by a loud thump, thump, thump on the roof above my head. When I peered up into the neighboring tree, I saw large gray monkeys with black faces chewing away on horsechestnut flowers. The only monkeys I had seen in America were caged in zoos.

I went for an early morning walk about the *chakkar* and found that from that road above our quarters one could see the bazaar and Mussoorie. Houses and shops were scattered for several miles to the west. Beyond, rose the tree-covered peaks of Benog and Badraj. On down the path at a right angle curve, was Childer's Lodge. Beyond which were ridge after ridge of rolling, wooded hills. Nag Tiba looked dark against the distant forests.

The horizon was lined with snowcapped mountains. Bunderpunch (Monkey's tail) was some forty miles distant, as the crow flies, and over 20,000 feet high. The northern face of the chakkar was shaded with a great many tall, graceful *deodars*.

A little farther, a cemetery extended above and below the road. Turning right at Kellogg Church, where our language school was held I passed Ellengowan and Rokeby, where other language students lived. The hillside fell off steeply on the left and one could look way down to the plains, miles and miles to the south and west. A right angle turn took me past military buildings on one side and St. Paul's Church on the other. That sanctuary was pleasantly shaded with cedars.

Beyond Childers Lodge were ridge upon ridge of rolling hills. Down below the *chakkar,* I could hear the spaced barks of an animal, but it didn't sound like a dog. (Later, my neighbors, the Taylors at Landour Villa, told me it was a barking deer.)

---

* Goat-hair rugs.

I stood there breathing in the cool, fresh air. How fragrant it was!

Back at our quarters, a series of *wallas** had brought all sorts of food for sale. There were milk wallas, fruit wallas, meat wallas and box wallas who sold fresh cakes, macaroons, biscuits, wintergreen and peppermint candies. At Sister's Bazaar one could buy sardines, evaporated milk, Jacob's Cream Crackers, and one or two kinds of jam. This was a far cry from our fare at Siwait, where nothing grew on the plains in summer except squash and onions.

Mrs. Freymiller found the air too cool to give her baby a bath, so she set a charcoal fire inside her room. She soon called out, "Something is wrong with my baby."

I hurried over and found the baby was no longer breathing and was quite white. I started artificial respiration and the child began to come around and get pink again.

"Those charcoal fumes!" I warned. "Keep the window or door open after this, for charcoal fumes are deadly."

Mr. Freymiller and I walked around to Kellogg Church and the Language School where we found a number of well-qualified teachers and tutors. The principal was an American, Mr. Cornuelle. There seemed to be about fifty or sixty students, about half to study Hindi and the others, Urdu. A bell rang for morning prayers, then each was assigned to a class according to how much of the language was already acquired. I was put in D section of Hindi, the lowest grade. Although I had been in the country for a year and a half, I had spent much of my time teaching mission children in English.

I was determined to learn Hindi well. We gathered for daily classes throughout the week and in the afternoon we had our *pundits.*** When I got home about three-thirty, I would want to review what we had covered that day. But it was too noisy in our cramped quarters with two small children running in and out, so I would walk down the main steep road to an empty house about a quarter of a mile away. The place was called Hazelwood and was shaded by lovely deodar trees. Here I worked undisturbed.

* Delivery men.
** Tutors.

By mid-term, I was promoted from D to B class, and by the end of those four months, was in group A.

We did not study all the time. On Fridays, Mary Esther Badley in group A would announce plans for a Saturday hike into the hills. She had been born in India, the daughter of a Methodist missionary, Bishop Badley. Mary Esther would talk up the trip until we could scarcely wait to get started. Throughout the week, a tidy little sum would have been collected from fines for using English instead of Hindi (one pice for each word!) and this would be spent on the picnic.

"Tomorrow we are going to Bear Hill on Jabarkhet," Mary Esther announced one day. "It is two or three miles, so wear comfortable shoes. Bring your sandwiches and water bottle. Fruit and cookies will be purchased with the fine money.

"Please stay fairly close together for there is a possibility of getting separated. We shall walk along the *chakkar*, then take the road down to the left past Fairy Glen to the Toll Gate onto Tehri Road. From there, it will be about half an hour to our picnic spot.

"Bring cameras and binoculars, if you have them. Also, adhesive tape might ward off a blister or two. See you all here tomorrow at nine," she concluded.

It sounded exciting and it was. Mary Esther was a botanist and also well versed in natural history. Some twenty of us made up the group—Commonwealth, Scandinavians, Americans.

"Do you hear that 'cuck--oo, cuck--oo'?"

"Oh, yes," called out one of the men. "It sounds just like the one we have in England." And of course it was. "It makes me a bit homesick," he confided.

"You can also hear the *kaiphal pukka* bird," said Mary Esther, "which is an Indian cuckoo."

The group passed a horsechestnut tree in bloom, a host to myriads of white Pierid butterflies.

"Here is a poplar tree, and that one beyond is a large-leafed dogwood," explained Mary Esther. "This little white flower is a stellaria and the pink one is a true geranium. Our potted ones are not true geraniums, but they are closely related."

The group stumbled down the stony path above the terraces of Fairy Glen and onto the Tehri Road. A train of half a dozen mules passed with chains of brass bells jingling gaily around their necks. Three *dudhwallas** carried round cans of milk on their backs.

The wooded hill rose abruptly on one side and the road fell off steeply on the other as our shoes crunched along on quartzite pebbles.

We soon turned off the main road into a footpath leading along a ridge. We passed a tangle of rose bushes, the white flowers emitting the delicate fragrance of spring. There followed several bushes with yellow berries.

"Yellow raspberries are good to eat," said the leader, and in no time, the bushes were stripped of their sweet, juicy fruit.

The picnic spot at last. The ground fell away on all sides. Looking back, we could see Landour hillside and sections of the path we had just come over. Immediately to the north was Pepper Pot.

"Another time, that would make a longer hike. But you have to be careful up there," warned Mary Esther, "for there are numerous berry bushes of which the Himalayan black bear is especially fond. Just be careful that you do not run into a *bhalu*** over there."

By now everyone was ready to eat. The sky was hazy and the sun warm. What an ideal place to eat and relax. Dimly to the far north, a range of snow mountains stood against the horizon.

"Immediately in front is Nag Tiba, a little over 9,000 feet high. That makes a good two or three-day hike," claimed Mary Esther. "Some day, you may want to climb to the higher ranges. Dotai Tal is a lake at 10,000 feet and is full of brown trout.

"There are numerous hikes one can take. To get near the great ranges is a mind-stretching experience and no one ever returns the same."

There was real enchantment among these Himalayan hills.

I had arrived in Mussoorie in May when the winds blew strong from the south, bringing dust from the plains of India. Suddenly, after four weeks had passed, a great gray blanket of clouds swept in from the southeast, accompanied by bolts of lightning. Then one could actually hear the heavy monsoon rain

* Milkmen.
** Bear.

approaching from the lower valley. The monsoon season in Landour and Mussoorie is something to experience. At some points the rainfall is fifty inches, and in others well over one hundred inches. Occasionally, ten inches would fall in an hour. As the rain rushed down the steep hillside, it took earth, rocks and small trees with it.

And did our roofs leak! After all, ours were only servant houses, built of mud and stone. We had to put any dry things back into our tin trunks, and hope we might sun-dry the rest, should the sun ever reappear. Meanwhile, anything leather, such as shoes, sprouted generous coatings of mildew. Landour, at 7,000 feet, was just the right elevation to receive more than a generous amount of rainwater. It was not very comfortable.

But there were compensations. Hillsides were soon covered with a multitude of monsoon flowers. I don't know how many kinds of jack-in-the-pulpits there are; the one here looked different from the ones I used to see in the U.S. And there were the pale purple lily-like flowers that the children called "peacock flowers." Another, a sort of orchid, they called "Grandfather's whiskers."

The one I like best was called "hyacinth orchid." It was pink with a spiral stem of flowers, and had a fragrant perfume.

But one of the things I didn't like at all, were the land leeches. They were in certain places like cowsheds and on ends of grass along narrow trails. One would crawl up your leg and you wouldn't even know it was there until it dropped off bloated with blood, leaving a spot that itched for days. Leeches were one thing I could do without!

To make up for this discomfort, was the smell of the damp earth washed clean by the rain. The deodar trees added their distinct contribution. After all, I was in Landour to study language, which required long sessions indoors, so I did not mind the monsoons too much.

Our *kuchcha* (poorly constructed) quarters at least made life bearable. The idea came to me that possibly the mission might rent that empty house down the road where I often went to study. One day, I gathered Mr. Freymiller and Tyrell and together we went down to look at the place. It must have had eight or ten rooms with a long veranda overlooking the valley below and a range of mountains. It would be quite adequate for members of our mission, especially those with children, as some of the older ones would be coming to Landour for school the next spring. I had gone down to see the principal of Woodstock School and explained our situation. There was some hesitation on his part, because our children had never been in a proper school, only their own small school We decided we would petition Mr. Whipple, back at our mission, that he consider the possibility favorably. The idea was accepted and the mission folks would be housed in Hazelwood the following year. An anonymous gift of $10,000 made by a friend in American paid for the place, making this possible.

In my new beautiful surroundings, I often thought of Howard. The Bible School authorities back in Wisconsin had given us permission for a long final walk before I left for India. We were told we could not write to each other, but I just kept on hoping that someday Howard would come and share these beautiful hills with me.

One day, a new missionary arrived and she blurted out, "If you are hoping that Howard will come to India and join you, he never will, for he is dying of tuberculosis."

I hadn't known that he was ill, and to get this news was devastating. I prayed to God in my helplessness. If it were God's will, may Howard get well and come to me. We loved each other, though we could not correspond. However, I would leave it all in the hands of God. I knew God was at my side and whatever He planned was right for me. I could only hope and wait.

Chapter VIII

Village Hospital at Siwait

A field of blue flowering flax, which sloped gently southeast from the main bungalow, had been chosen for the new mission hospital building. At the lowest part of the land, the beautiful blue of the flax was pale and the foliage, normally bright green, was a sad gray from the *ooser,** in which very few plants will grow, but it was an ideal spot for a brick yard. That same section still held water from the monsoons, so it wasn't necessary to use expensive well water for making the bricks. Mud was made by the workmen treading and working the clay soil and water with their feet, then casting the mixture into brick molds that were placed in the sun to dry.

Meanwhile, as soil was removed, a large oval ditch resulted, in which the dried bricks were replaced in a honeycomb pattern, interspersed with charcoal and covered with sod, then lighted so the bricks would bake slowly. The fire was kept lit by the draw from a smoke stack. As the bricks were baked sufficiently, the smoke stack would be moved and more bricks and charcoal added, making a great oval going round and round until sufficient bricks were done.

The floor plan for the hospital was a rectangle that included two large wards, one for men and one for women; an operating/labor room; an isolation room and out-patient clinic area; an office/admitting room, and bath and storerooms. A man who claimed to have experience in building was hired to oversee the

* Lime soil.

construction. I soon found that he did not know a rectangle from a parallelogram. Eventually, due to his ignorance of geometric forms, I had to relieve him and direct the digging myself, out under the hot sun, though that was never our original intention.

From time to time, I had to take a day off and go to Allahabad to canvass for funds to proceed with the building and for the beds, bedding, and furnishings that would be needed. I took my "little black book" and started with the commissioner, Sir Maharaj Singh, the highest ranking civil service officer in the city. He was the son of a Hindu ruling price in Patiala who had become a Christian, and thus been disinherited by his father. To compensate him, the British government had given him a civil service post. Lady Maharaj Singh was formerly Gertrude Maya Das, of a well-known Christian family. One sister, Constance, was the principal of Isabella Thoburn College in Lucknow. Another sister, Dr. Maya Das, was often very helpful to us as we attended the patients in our clinic.

The Commissioner's house was a spacious white-washed bungalow, surrounded by a wide lawn bordered with hollyhocks, cosmos, sweet peas, phlox, antirrhinum, bachelor buttons and roses. He and Lady Maharaj Singh greeted me warmly and gave a very generous sum of money. After I wrote his name and the amount of his donation in my "little black book," he tipped me off as to the next government official I should call on, for protocol was very important among the officials. I went down the line and soon had not only the money we needed to complete the building and furnishings, but had made many friends for the hospital as well—friends whom I was able to call on in the years to come.

"Come in and have lunch or a cup of tea whenever you come in to town for shopping," Lady Maharaj Singh had invited after showing me her flower gardens. "You need a change from the village life."

I did just that for many happy visits, always coming away with an armload of sweet peas or gladioli ,or whatever flower was in season.

I also called on the justices of the High Court, which was in Allahabad and not in Delhi, the capital. I called on each justice in his office, after first getting the signature and promise of a donation from the chief justice, who asked me to come to his home at four o'clock.

"I'll have your check ready for you," he assured me.

At four my driver drove me to the chief justice's mansion, where the bearer in his white uniform and turban showed me up the marble steps and into the drawing room. A tea table was set up in front of the fireplace, but I found I was alone. This gave me a chance to observe the excellent decor of the house and furnishings, which included relics of other countries—China, Burma, Ceylon—and the trophies of big game hunts in India, as well as service memorials in frames on the white-washed walls, denoting honors received. There was the ever-present portrait of King George V and Queen Mary.

After a while, the justice came into the drawing room and sat beside me on the sofa. I poured each of us a cup of tea and inquired about her ladyship. He told me she was in England. His objective in inviting me here alone was soon clear as he put his arm around me and began caressing me, which irritated and repelled me. I was angry that he had invited me under the guise of a benefactor when all along he had had other ideas.

Hot and roiled, with my blouse and hair disheveled, I saw a door open from one of the side rooms. Out stepped a gentleman and his lady, dressed in formal evening clothes. They stood for a moment, silhouetted against the arched doorway leading to the garden. She was wearing a long brilliant flame dress and looked regal as she waited for an introduction.

"Miss Owen, I want you to meet two of your compatriots," he said.

"I'm so glad to see you. Please help me out. I must go home," I cried.

They smiled and acknowledged the introduction, but quickly stepped towards the door saying they would be late for their dinner engagements. And no amount of calling or entreaty would make my host loosen his grip on me.

"It's no use. I've already sent your chauffeur off," he declared.

Finally, however, when he realized I was unyielding, he arranged to have his driver take me home.

Following my first year in language school, it was a joy to return to my station at Siwait to use the Hindi I had been learning. I could also follow Urdu conversation now, and my added knowledge brought me closer to the people I had been called to serve.

It was with eagerness I returned to Landour the second summer, for I now had a partial command of the language. And since Mr. Whipple had arranged the purchase of Hazelwood, we did not have to live in servants' quarters any more. Furthermore, his son Norman was accepted at Woodstock School, soon to be followed by a half dozen more pupils from our mission.

Language school went well. We had the usual Saturday outings until the rains began. Then the peacock flowers bloomed again, along with colorful dahlias, golden reinwardtia, and on the forest floor, carpets of blue strobilanthes.

The monsoon rains were heavy and we had not seen the sun for a week, but Hazelwood shed the water pretty well, a great contrast to our experience the year before. Then it was time to return to the plains.

I got a seat in the zenana carriage with five other ladies, two Muslims and three Hindus. It was a thrill to be able to follow the conversation, whether Hindi or Urdu.

One of the Hindi ladies asked me what kind of cream I put on my skin to make it so white! I wasn't up to telling her that it was a matter of chromosomes.

"Where did you come from?"

"Where are you going?"

"How many children do you have?"

That question always seemed to have high priority. When I confessed that I didn't have any children nor a husband, the ladies raised their eyebrows in surprise.

"Don't your parents love you, and can't they find a husband for you?"

It was a little difficult to explain that one.

All of my compartment-mates were quite friendly, and we were all going as far as Lucknow. We unrolled our bedding and settled in for the night.

At Hardoi next morning, the bearer brought toast and tea. Tea wasn't tea without milk and sugar. In this case the sugar had a rather dark hue, while the milk had hardly seen a cow. However, the tea was wet, sweet and warm.

I had to change trains at Lucknow. This time, our compartment had no less than thirty women, children and wailing babies. Our departure was delayed half an hour or more, for a report had come in that beyond Rai Bareilly, the track was under water and in danger of being swept away. In Lucknow itself, the Goomti River was in spate and part of the city flooded.

Eventually, our train pulled slowly out of the station. On either side of the tracks were flooded fields, and continuous rain slowed our progress. We reached our Siwait station an hour late. A servant had come to meet me, but we couldn't take the short-cut to our compound because of the flooded fields. At the gate, Mr. Whipple greeted me under the big old Mohuwa tree. It was good to be home again.

Next morning, a man from the station came running up with the news that the train had been derailed only half a mile down the track. Six or eight sections of the train had meshed together and turned over in the mud, and many had been killed. Would I come and help the injured? I flung together my kit with emergency items, jumped into the car and drove around to the station. From there, I hurried down the track.

Two carriages at the end of the ill-fated train were still on the track, the other five were now kindling wood, splintered and flung across the flooded fields. People were helping the injured from the wreckage. I decided we should take the injured to the Railway Hospital in Allahabad and had them put in the two carriages. We used the third class benches as stretchers. I was in water and mud sometimes up to my knees, as I directed relatives to carry their patients to the first class compartments.

In one of the compartments still on the tracks, a prosperous buniya* sat on a bunk. He expressed no emotion, said not a word, never lifting as much as a finger to help us. This made me angry. I wanted to tell him off for being so callous towards his fellow countrymen, but it was a good thing I held my peace, as we were soon to meet again.

After about an hour, an engine appeared, attached the two sections full of patients, and moved on.

Allahabad is one of the larger cities of United Provinces in North India. The High Court was located here and the court language was Urdu. Numbers of prominent Indian families made their homes here, including the Nehru family, where I had gath-

* Business man.

ered my grape leaves the year before. By now, I had stopped there several times.

The Nehrus were heavily involved in the Free India Movement, and were a target of the British government authorities. Our mission felt we should remain aloof from politics and political leaders, but the Nehrus were so good to me that I felt they were my friends, not political enemies.

In this same city was also the Presbyterian Mission, called the Jumna Mission, home of the well-known agricultural program headed by Sam Higginbottom, as well as the Naini Leprosarium.

On the way down from the hills, I had had plenty of time to think things through. Medical problems were so pressing, yet our mission had no plans to send us American nurses nor any doctors. None of our people would permit themselves to be vaccinated nor inoculated. In India, smallpox was rampant. My conviction grew that I should take more medical training, but the executive staff of our church back in Wisconsin had never approved of my going to a medical school in the U.S.A. to study.

I was happy to be in India with work to do. We were right in the midst of both Mohammedan and Hindu villagers who lived in harmony with one another, but I knew I could do more for these people if I had formal medical training. I investigated the University of London Medical School and took the Senior Cambridge Examinations to satisfy the entrance requirements. Due to the impending war, however, the American consul would not allow me to go to England.

One day I took a delivery case into Allahabad. It was then that Dr. Mabelle Hayes asked, "Why don't you go to Lady Dufferin Hospital here in the city and get your diploma in midwifery?"

That was music to my ears.

"Yes, I would like to, if my mission authorities will give their consent," I replied. With this training I would be able to help more patients back in Siwait, so I resolved to go to Mr. Whipple and plead my case.

It was with considerable hesitation that he finally said I could have six months leave for more training. What a happy day that was! In less than two weeks, I was ensconced in the nurses' quarters for the six-month period of midwifery training. I had no money and received no pay, but Mrs. Benjamin, superintendent of nurses, offered to board me. Here in the hospital, I could observe and learn a lot in other areas besides obstetrics.

Mrs. Benjamin was a dedicated Christian woman. As I got to know her, she told me a bit about her life story. She was from South India and had been married at the age of thirteen. A few months later her husband died, leaving her pregnant. She later gave birth to a son. That season her church was holding evangelistic meetings. She regularly attended these and, on the last day, all those who had received a blessing were asked to bring a gift to the altar. People went forward with vegetables, eggs, rice, chickens. Poor Mrs. Benjamin had brought nothing except her tiny son, so she went forward and put her baby on the altar. The pastor was not a little surprised. He took up the child, gave him a blessing and handed him back to his mother, asking her to raise the child for the Lord.

Mrs. Benjamin then took up nursing as a means of supporting herself and her son, and the boy, Christy, was brought up in the Christian tradition. When he completed high school, the question of college arose. His mother could not afford it, but the agent of the Northwest Railroad,* who had taken a liking to the boy, offered to send him to Edinburgh for four years of university education. Once in a while, at meal times, Mrs. Benjamin would proudly relate an incident or two that Christy had mentioned in his letters.**

With six months training in Allahabad, I was ready to take my examination in Ludhiana, some 400 miles west-northwest of us. It was the location of a well-known English-American hospital, and I was glad to go there and meet Dr. Edith Brown and her colleagues.

The examinations took three days, two of them set aside for written papers and the other, oral. I passed in the top group and saw my diploma, but they would not give it to me because I lacked nine months of the residential requirements. So back I went to Lady Dufferin Hospital for the winter, boarding again with Mrs. Benjamin.

Then a door opened for me. The doctor on night duty asked if

---

* The agent is the top official of the railroad.
** Christy Balaram—see page 109

I would take cases for her. From then on, I got practically all the abnormal delivery cases that came in at night, including craniotomies, versions and forceps deliveries—about five hundred of them. I also got to supervise the midwifery trainees on normal cases. All this gave me excellent experience.

During this period, my roommate was a girl of a well-known Christian family. Occasionally she gave money to a gentle, old Brahmin beggar who came around for donations. Clad in nothing more than a loin cloth, he made a pathetic figure as he carried half of a human skull in which to receive his gifts. One day news came that the old man had died. Because my roommate had been kind to him, he left her one hundred rupees in his will—$35!

When I had a day off, I enjoyed visiting friends at the Presbyterian mission across the Jamuna River. Among these were Dr. Sam Higginbottom and his wife, a delightful couple. Dr. Sam had a strong staff, including Mason Vaugh, Brewster Hayes, and others, and he was on several government commissions, working happily alongside his non-Christian colleagues. He was also one of the leading farm experts in India.*

The medical work was headed by Dr. Douglas Forman, whose parents had worked a long time in India. One of his special charges was the Naini Leprosarium. The families of some of the inmates lived in lean-tos against the wall outside the building, and it was felt that something should be done for those who spent hours just sitting. Mrs. Vaugh initiated a basket weaving project, which netted them a little money to feed their families.

Spring brought strong winds from the south. Dust of the Gangetic plains filled the air, to the point of discoloring even the snow ranges of the higher Himalayas. It was time for Mr. and Mrs. Whipple to get the children out of the heat and to the mission house in Mussoorie – Hazelwood. Mr. Whipple planned to return to his work at Siwait after three days.

To save money, the whole group traveled in crowded third-class coaches—quite an ordeal, with all those smells, the noise, the crying babies, and the temperature well over 100 degrees.

Just a few days before, a Moslem friend of long standing had appeared on Mr. Whipple's veranda. One of his children had just

---

* See *Christ and the Plough* by Sam Higginbottom.

died and the other two were very ill. Would Mr. Whipple come? He went, and he gave what comfort he could, then excused himself as soon as possible and hurried away. But it was too late—the damage was done. He had been exposed to the dreaded smallpox!

Their train compartment was overcrowded with thirty others, and luggage completely filled every corner. When they arrived at the foothills, several of the children traveled up the hill in baskets carried on the backs of coolies and the others walked. Mrs. Whipple had a sedan chair, while Mr. Whipple rode out ahead on horseback.

The first part of the ascent was over a treeless, rocky terrain. And heat! After about an hour, Mr. Whipple developed a splitting headache and felt woozy. He got off his horse and lay down in the shade of a lone tree to wait until the rest of the party caught up. When they did, Mrs. Whipple saw that her husband was really ill, so she had him switch over to the sedan chair.

They finally managed to reach Hazelwood, where Mr. Whipple went right to bed. The next morning, Mrs. Whipple knew that his illness was serious and sent a telegram for me to come up and help nurse him. She readied a bed for him in the servant's quarters, which served as an isolation ward, as it appeared to be smallpox. She and one of the older girls had both had the disease, but none of the younger ones had. The municipal health authorities quarantined the whole family. Mrs. Whipple stayed down in the isolation area to nurse her husband. It was an agonizing few days, for it was soon evident that he was not going to make it.

It was a beautiful, bright Sunday morning when he breathed his last. Friends made a coffin and covered it with white cloth. That evening, six stalwart porters carried the coffin to the Landour cemetery, a little beyond the language school. As I was living apart, I was the only one of the mission allowed to go to the gravesite. An announcement had been made in Kellogg Church that morning, and several missionaries came volunteering to sing, though the word "smallpox" was frightening. (I had vaccinated myself earlier, despite mission policy.)

When the last spadeful of earth was replaced, a silence settled over the cemetery and a soft breeze blew through the *deodars*. Another pilgrim had found the end of the trail—heaven.

Mrs. Whipple took over the responsibility of running the mission, and I returned to my work at Siwait. Then it was spring again! Warm winds from the south promised to turn hot in the near future, and the *amaltas* shook out grape-like clusters of bright golden flowers. The magpie robin bubbled over with song, while the spotted and ring doves filled the dawn with their love calls.

On my birthday, we had a cable from the U.S. to say that Howard Bitzer and Henry Harvey were coming to India. Could it be true? Howard, coming here? You can imagine how a girl just turned twenty-five might feel. What did the Lord have in mind for me? Was Howard *the* man? I could only wait and hope. It would be still some time before the men would arrive.

What a long summer it was!

Mrs. Benjamin's son, Christy Benjamin, was near graduation in Edinburgh when he began spending time on the continent in brothels and taverns, squandering the money given him for his education. He returned to India, and his mother was very disappointed to learn that he had not received his degree. He was remorseful when he talked with me in Siwait, asking my advice on what he should do. I suggested that if he returned to Scotland, he should consider going to our Glasgow Missionary Training School, as he needed to let God direct his future.

While he was with us, he had a visit from his benefactor and sponsor, the railway agent. A large white and gold parlor car pulled up at Siwait railway station, and he and Christy had a good visit for several hours. He never disclosed what transpired there, but the outcome was that Christy went back to Scotland.

There, he met with Howard, who was passing through Scotland on his way to India. Howard did not wait until he arrived in India to begin his ministry, but was instrumental in helping guide a young Indian's decision. Christy later came back to India to help the village people, donning a *chamis* and *dhoti** and working with the farmers in their fields. He joined the Methodist Church and worked at teaching school, eventually rising to bishop.**

*Native shirt and loin cloth which the villagers wore.
** He was known as Bishop Balaram, following the Telugu custom of taking the father's given name as the son's family name.

Howard's long-awaited arrival came in November. Mrs. Whipple announced that she would go to the station to pick up the two men, and so it was that I finally saw Howard for the first time in five years. He had matured a lot; he was now twenty-four.

The mission group welcomed the arrivals, and Howard and I simply smiled at one another. Then they were settled into the long house, which had five rooms and a veranda extending the length of the building. It was set up with men housed at one end and women at the other, though we all ate together and saw each other many times a day.

The next day, Howard and I managed a few moments together. He said our friends had sent some presents with him. He opened up a little Estey organ.

"It was given to us as a wedding gift," he said, "from your cousin Josephine."

We smiled, and he sat down and played a few songs for me on the organ, making my heart flutter. Just to be close like this was pure joy.

I took him down to the hospital to show him the progress on the construction and to introduce him to the workers.

Just then, a villager came to call me to attend to a man who had been bitten by a snake. I got my snake-bite kit and headed to the village. When I got there, a crowd had gathered and someone was piercing the man's ears with a sharpened stick, screaming into one ear to blow the devil out the other. And they poured buckets of water over him (a good way to keep him awake!).

I lanced the area of the bite and used potassium permanganate in the wound, to prevent clotting of the blood, after determining that the snake was probably a cobra, whose venom was a blood-coagulating type. He survived, but we will never know if it was *because* of the treatment or in spite of it.

The season heated up so that we put our beds out under the open sky. A mosquito net was all that was between me and the stars. One night a cyclonic storm came up with lots of lightning, thunder, wind and rain. Howard came running over and helped me get my bed up under the veranda. I could only thank him, without letting him know how I was feeling inside. Those weeks and months, both of us kept rigidly to our requirements that no expressions of affection should pass between us. Besides, my patient load was heavy, and serious cases had to be rushed to Allahabad. There were many other things to think about besides love.

Now it was mid-summer. The rains were quite heavy and the humidity was very high. It was so hot that no vegetables would grow, and our usual limited menu made us yearn, occasionally, for even a glass of pure water with a little ice in it.

About this time, young Henry decided he wanted to learn more of India than just Siwait. One could travel great distances on just a pittance in third class, so he decided to do just that.

The Punjab was frightfully hot that time of year. Very few Europeans chose August as a month to travel, but that didn't discourage Henry. He wanted to push on to the Khyber Pass region beyond Peshwar.

But before he got there, he began to feel the heat. The days were so hot he felt he was burning up. With no immunity to water-borne disease and with the prohibition against modern medicine, he was really taking his life in his hands. He got as far as Rawalpindi, where he collapsed and was taken to the Military Hospital.

Typhoid!

The hospital sent word to Siwait. Howard decided to go up to Rawalpindi to see Henry. When he arrived, he found the patient quite ill and delirious and wired for me to come immediately.

When I got there, I found Henry very weak—too weak to be moved. Meanwhile, Howard had to go back to Siwait. I hated to see him leave, but there was no other choice. We simply said "goodbye," and he left.

I nursed Henry until I was finally able to get him onto a stretcher to travel back to Siwait. It had been a long ordeal—about six weeks, all told, that he lay there.

By late summer, the hospital was completed. How glad I was that we had made the veranda wide, for as many as a hundred patients were waiting there each morning when I arrived. Some had walked a long way and were weary with fatigue and thirst. Outside in the yard we had installed a water tap, which was a popular spot and refreshed many a faint, way-weary patient.

I would see the very ill first and, one by one, get to the rest. Often, when the situation was particularly sad, I would step into my little office to stifle a tear, or perhaps to say a prayer when I felt entirely inadequate for the job I was facing. Over my desk, I had the poem:

> My Prayer
> "I stand by the side of a current
> That's deeper far than the sea,
> And the storm-beaten craft of every draft
> Come in to be healed by me;
> And some have more sin than sickness,
> And some have more grief than pain;
> God help me make whole body and soul,
> Before they go out again."

After a prayer, I could go back to my task refreshed and with renewed vigor.

Not long after the completion of the hospital, a village man crawled up the steps to see me. In his folded arms, he was carrying something wrapped in a dirty cloth, which at first I took to be a baby. When I started to examine him, he fell to the floor, and I discovered he was holding his intestines, which had been ripped out by an angry water buffalo. I had him placed on the examining table, and started intravenous glucose solution.

What a mess! His intestines were full of straw, chaff and dirt which had to be cleaned out. I washed and bathed them in sterile solution, after which I tucked them back into place, then put in another pint of sterile saline solution.

May and Baker, a pharmaceutical company in England, had sent out some M&B 693, which they wished to have us use and report back on. I sprinkled some of this powder in the abdominal cavity and then began to sew him up. The tear was rather irregular and I matched the edges as best I could. Leaving a Penrose drain in to help drain the wound, I drew the rest of the skin together. I propped him in a Fowler's sitting position for better drainage, and he healed with not a degree rise in temperature. In three days, he could sit up by himself, smiling, and soon he was able to be up and about.

When Dr. Everard came for his weekly visit, I showed him my patient, thinking he would probably want to replace and improve some of the sutures.

"No," he said, "your work is perfectly all right; I wouldn't touch it."

That gratified me and the patient went home happy, with his innards intact once more.

"I saw a smallpox case," boasted Howard when I cautioned him about the disease being rampant just now.

"You have? Where?" I asked with concern.

"On a train, yesterday. A woman got into our compartment with a baby who had it."

"Then I must vaccinate you at once," I said and hurried off to get my vaccination tray.

When I returned, Henry and Howard were talking together. They began to treat it as a big joke, refusing to let me vaccinate them.

"What kind of a wife will you make, always worrying about your husband?" Howard added.

This brush-off distressed me. I turned on my heels and left without saying another word.*

A few days later, Henry came to tell me Howard had a fever and was not well. I went over to see him, and as I ran my fingers over his forehead and wrists, I could feel little nodules under his skin. I knew he had smallpox.

"We must get Howard out of the compound or we shall all be quarantined," I stated. "I shall take him to the Civil Hospital in Allahabad at once."

We made him comfortable in the station wagon and drove to the hospital. In a separate, distant building were two empty isolation rooms. I made Howard comfortable in one of them, while I took the other.

---

* The mission's attitude toward vaccination is not surprising when one looks back into its history. A quote from *The Burning Bush* of April 7, 1905 reads: "It is revolting to us to let an old sick cow with a dirty poisonous pus exuding from her udders defend us from the ravages of the disease of Hell."

On the front page of this issue was portrayed a sketch of the three Hebrew children standing immovable before a golden calf inscribed "VACCINATION," choosing the fiery furnace rather than bow down.

Also see pages four and five of the issue.

Nine terrible days followed. The doctor would come once a day and stand at a distance to give me orders. None of our mission people ever showed up. It was smallpox, to be avoided by all means. The case was so severe that the pox covered every area of his body. The pain increased daily, and I could scarcely find space between the eruptions to insert a hypodermic needle in order to give relief.

I couldn't go out to get food or needed supplies; these were brought to us. We talked and prayed together, and I read portions of the Bible to him.

As I held the Bible in my hands, he looked wistfully at me and said, "I'm sorry we brought that Bible with us. It was my mother's, and now it will have to be burned."

As the disease progressed, he became less and less responsive. One of the last days, when I read a portion from Revelations about the new heaven and earth, a flicker of appreciation passed across his face, but he was too weak to respond.

Then his eyes became affected. Big pustules covered his irises, and I took a feather, dipped in olive oil and drew it across his tortured face. I knew he would be blind, should he recover, and that he would never ask me to be his wife. I resolved, quietly, that I would take the lead and see that we were married anyway. I would be his eyes in the future, and learn Braille with him.

On the eighth day, when I was getting very weary, relief came. The mission at Siwait sent Ellen Freymiller (who had had smallpox) to help me. I got some sleep—much needed sleep—that night, while Ellen kept the vigil beside Howard's bed. The next day he remained in a coma and, in the evening of the ninth day, Howard breathed his last. At the moment, a surge of relief swept over me. I praised God that his struggle was over and that, forevermore, Howard would be with our Lord.

There was a lot to do. We had to burn all his clothes and mine. We had to wash ourselves with a Lysol solution, and I had to give myself a new vaccination in case my immunity was not against any new strain of smallpox that Howard might have had. Both our rooms had to be scoured with disinfectant. I was very thankful for Ellen's help.

About ten o'clock the next morning, a horse-drawn hearse arrived. After we had placed the body in the carriage, Miss Paull, the nursing superintendent, came over from the hospital. She clutched a little prayer book and pedalled her bicycle up over the hill to the cemetery. It was a pathetic scene silhouetted against the sky—a horse-drawn hearse followed by a lone nurse on a bicycle with her cap flowing in the breeze. That was all.

However, the Lord gave me joy in my heart and a composure impossible without the Divine Presence. That evening I walked out into the grounds, looking up at the moon, and it seemed the heavens opened and a joy filled me such as I have never known—peace, perfect peace!

I *would* see Howard again! I would carry on my work and only Heaven would tell the end of the story!

During the long summer afternoons after Howard died, when there was no light penetrating our wooden shutters, no electricity for reading, no radio or television, nor anyone to converse with, I had very troubling thoughts of sex. Before Howard died he was always in my thoughts and dreams. I believed that one day he would come, we would marry and have a family. These dreams were sufficient to still the sexual urges for the time. Now the future held no such hope. I would get up in the night and walk over to the grove—walk and pray for hours, until finally I was so tired I knew I could fall asleep.

I wanted a normal sex life, which I could not see in my future. My body cried out for satisfaction. All my training from childhood taught that masturbation of any sort was evil, even causing mental illness if pursued. Remember, this was before one could pick up a book and learn how to dealt with the problem. Back in the twenties, there was little available, even in medical books, and none available to me in India.

I remember how my arms *ached* to hold an infant of my own. I was in the baby ward one night and picked up an infant who had been orphaned. My nipples actually hardened and hurt with longing. I told the nurse I would take the baby home with me and give him his two o'clock feeding, and that she could come and get him after that. She may have thought I was thinking of the baby's needs to be picked up and loved, but I was thinking more of my own.

Carrying his warm bottle and a blanket, I wrapped him up

and held him close to me. When I got to my quarters, he was hungry. I got into bed and put him to my breast. I shall never forget the thrill nor the orgasm that followed as he sucked hard on my erect nipples. Then I gave him his bottle.

The storm raging within me was stilled. This was all I needed. I needed to know that I was a normal female and that I had the body, the breasts, the pelvis of a woman. With this knowledge I could sublimate the experience. I would pray and surrender it as an offering to my Lord, since there wasn't any alternative available. This was a part of the price I had paid in accepting His call. There was no other option that I could see in my future. But I no longer wondered about my feelings or my sexuality. I now knew and accepted the choice I had made.

Chapter IX

Rubies from Burma

I returned to our mission station at Siwait after my ten-day ordeal. For the past five years, the mission had forbidden any thoughts of my marriage, and now with Howard gone and the long vigil I had been through ended, I needed to get away. Someone suggested that Mrs. Whipple and I go to Burma for a while. She also needed to get away, and this would be a good time. The days were warming up, and hot winds were beginning to blow. A trip such as this would take us out of the insufferable heat of northern India. I quickly accepted the suggestion; I loved to travel, and Burma was an area with which I was unfamiliar.

Packing was an easy matter, as we lived very simply, possessing a minimum of worldly goods. Most of our luggage consisted of literature, the gospels, the *Burning Bush* magazine, calendars and children's Bible storybooks which we hoped to sell to get revenue for the mission.

Mrs. Whipple turned over mission affairs to Henry Harvey. He was kind and thoughtful of others, especially the half-dozen children of the mission.

Our train passed through Allahabad and pressed on towards Calcutta, where we booked passage on a British India steamer to Rangoon. The Bay of Bengal was a bit choppy, sending Mrs. Whipple to bed. But I enjoyed the smell of the sea water, the exercise on deck and meeting fellow passengers. All too soon, we were moving up the Irrawady to our dock.

I noted that the Burmese women were very colorfully dressed in their beautiful *longyis* (skirts) with orchids and *kachnar* (Bauhinia) flowers in their hair. We engaged a horse-drawn vehicle and told the driver to take us to the YWCA. We moved into the traffic of Rangoon. After about twenty minutes, we reached the "Y," which had a number of inexpensive guest rooms. This was in the downtown area, which would be handy for us in the selling of our literature.

After we settled in, I suggested to Mrs. Whipple that we go out and get a meal. It was not long before we found a tidy little Chinese restaurant. Inside were cubicles curtained for privacy. We chose one and accepted menu cards from the waitress. After a few minutes, she reappeared holding a bowl with warm towels for washing our hands. I took mine and enjoyed the feel of the steaming cloth. As the girl offered Mrs. Whipple a towel, my companion suddenly jerked back and refused it.

"I know what they are doing," she said in a loud, frightened tone. "They are trying to seduce us!"

She bolted from the table, flew out the door and ran down the street. I was stunned and chagrined. I apologized to the waitress, left the cafe and hurried after Mrs. Whipple. I hadn't realized how frightened she was.

Back in our room, I tried to explain that this was a Chinese custom and there was nothing to fear. But with a mind full of fear and suspicion, it was impossible to convince her.

We spent a few weeks in Rangoon where our sales were moderately good. After subtracting our expenses, we still had a nice balance to send the mission. It was beginning to get hot in Rangoon, so we made plans to go to a semi-hill station to work.

After an evening meal at the "Y," we decided to go for a little walk. Down the street, we saw an ice cream parlor and stopped. Ice cream was rare at the mission in India.

While sitting and enjoying our dessert, we talked over our immediate plans. Maymyo would be a possible place to start.

Sitting at a nearby table was a well-dressed Englishman. He overheard us mention Maymyo and came over to introduce himself, giving us his card.

"You ladies are going to Maymyo?" he asked, and responded to our affirmative reply with the suggestion that we come to his office next morning. "I think I can help you."

His card indicated he was the agent of the Burma Railroads. I said we would be glad to come, but Mrs. Whipple froze. Later, I told her that, in my opinion, the man was very pleasant-looking and meant no harm to us; that we were obviously missionaries and he simply wanted to help.

The next morning, we took a horse carriage to the address on the card, which turned out to be a large building. I handed my card to the guard who stood at the door. The agent soon appeared and welcomed us, but Mrs. Whipple refused to come inside, saying she would sit outside to be sure I came out of his office.

He told me it was the custom to give favors on his last day in office. He would like to give us a three-months' pass on the railroads in Burma! I responded cordially, and we spent a pleasant ten minutes, with a friendly parting and good wishes from the agent.

Outside, I showed Mrs. Whipple what I had—two first class passes for three months on the railroads of Burma! She couldn't believe it!

The next day our train pulled out of Rangoon. Our compartment was a roomette, with a table during the day which turned over into a bed by night. The meals we ordered were served in our room. This was luxurious travel compared to our third-class experiences in India.

For the next three months, we covered most of the cities in Burma. We often went our separate ways. When Mrs. Whipple went to Moulmeinn, I traveled, via Swebo, to Mogok. I had heard of the ruby mines up there and wanted to see them. I arrived in Swebo about nine p.m. and inquired around to find out how I could get to Mogok. I learned that a man with a truckload of empty kerosene tins was heading that way, so I contacted him and asked whether he might have an empty seat. He consented and, in a few minutes, we were off.

But what a road! Part of it travelled through swampland, where logs were laid cross-wise to make it passable for vehicles. We were being soundly shaken, while the noise from those empty kerosene tins was deafening. I thought the trip would never end, but about midnight, it did. I looked around for a place to stay and found a bed in a fourth class "hotel" in the bazaar.

Meanwhile, word went around that an American lady was in town. After a fitful sleep, I was awakened by a knocking on my door. A peon handed me a note. It was from a Baptist missionary—Mr. Hanna, who, I later learned, was a grandson of Adoniram Judson.* He wrote saying he was sorry that a compatriot of his had to stay overnight in the bazaar. Would I please come to his house and occupy their guest room? This I did with alacrity.

Such pleasant surroundings. And to be in the home of a descendent of the very first American missionary to Burma!

One of his many activities was to publish a mission paper. I asked whether he could use sketches as illustrations. Mr. Hanna looked over some of my artwork and was pleased, so I made some sketches for him, glad to be able to repay him for his hospitality.

That afternoon I decided to go for a walk, taking a path that led down to a little stream. There I saw a man squatting in front of three containers and some sections of bamboo, tapered at the end and stuck in the bank. He was operating a well sweep balanced on a pole.

The basket end would be lowered into a small pit and then brought up full of gravel. This he would swish in the stream, washing out the soil. Then he'd take the basket in his hands and begin to separate the contents, placing one or two stones in the first container, a few more in the second, and quite a lot in the larger third one.

I saw a glint of fire and asked if it was a ruby. No, it was a spinel, quite attractive but not worth very much.

"A ruby is like this," the worker said, showing me several stones that looked like tiny brown potatoes. "I put any large ones I find in the first bamboo cup. These are the ones which get my employer excited. He sells them in London and New York.

"In this one, I put the smaller rubies and they are sold in places like Rangoon and Calcutta. And in this larger container go all the rest of them. These, we workmen get as our commission. If I walked on the streets of Rangoon, I could sell these for two or maybe three rupees."

"Could I buy some of the larger rubies?" I asked.

"No, these must all go to my employer. But you can have as many of these small ones as you wish."

---

* Adoniram Judson went to India in 1820, and thence to Burma where he started a mission.

I pulled out my handkerchief and he filled it for three rupees.* I put it back in the pocket of the coat I was wearing and
promptly forgot about it.

The next day, Mr. Hanna took me to see what he said was the
largest crystal ever found; it was in a rocky cave on the side of a
nearby hill. From the path, we could see the countryside and, for
miles around, green rice fields. The primeval forests had been
burned off bit by bit, and each year a new crop of rice was planted. Rice grown on this virgin soil was considered the best flavored
and most choice.

On arrival at the cave, Mr. Hanna stepped back to allow me to
enter first. An enormous cloud of bats immediately took wing and
swarmed over my head in their fright. I screamed, which is what
Mr. Hanna had hoped for. He thought it was a huge joke.

After the bats had cleared out, we focused our flashlights on
a crystal about five and a half feet long by four feet high and
three feet wide. The reflected light broke into prisms of flashing
color, changing with each movement of the torch—blues, orange,
lavender, red—it was beautiful. Wooden beams had been placed
above it, to keep the roof from falling in until such time as it
could be removed intact. Mr. Hanna did not know where it was
going eventually, nor what plans had been made for it. Years later, when I heard that the Japanese had taken Burma, I wondered
what had become of the beautiful block of crystal. I have never
been able to find out.

From Mogok it was on to Hsipaw, and from there to Lashio—
the last station on the railroad. How different were the Shan people from the Burmese! Their homespun jackets were mostly
browns and black, with headgear of similar color and necklaces
and amulets of various stones—the only color some of them wore.
The Lashio weekly market was colorful with fruits and vegetables, and over all, awnings of bright cloth, which provided shade
from the sun and shelter from the rain.

From Lashio, I took a bus to Namtu, which was farther north.
There I was accosted by a local policeman, inquiring what my
business was and if I was a reporter up there to report on the
war.

---

* At that time about $1.

"What war?" I asked. "I haven't ever heard of a war up in these parts."

I explained I was a missionary doing colporteur work for a mission in India. He accepted my explanation, but said he was obliged to turn me over to a responsible local person who would keep a watch on me. And I was not to take pictures nor write any messages! In other words, I was under house arrest.

The person assigned to look after me was an American metallurgist from the Minnesota School of Mines, who put me up in his bungalow and treated me as an honored guest.

The supply of silver in the then-British-held mines in Burma would run out in twenty years and they were trying to take over the Wah country, just across the river, as it was very rich in silver. My host had been recruited to assay the ore and had no military duties. So, he took me down to the bluff overlooking the river (a small tributary of the Salween), where guns had been mounted, aimed at the Wah people who responded with their simple crude guns made of hollowed-out green bamboo with reinforcements of copper bands placed at intervals around them. My host had collected several of these to take back to Minneapolis as souvenirs.

This war was being carried on very secretively. The Italian war in North Africa was capturing the headlines in the newspapers and there wasn't a line about the little Wah war.

After a delightful stay in Namtu, it was time to join Mrs. Whipple in Rangoon for our return to India. I purchased a second-class ticket on the Irrawady Flotilla boat to Rangoon, where we would get the ship to Calcutta.

There were a lot of passengers on board. First class was in the forward section of the boat, while second class was at the stern, with deck passengers (3rd class) in between. The first night was a sleepless one. The crew and others gathered in the dining area on deck just outside my door and played poker all night. They made such a racket throwing their chips that I went to the purser the next day.

"Would it be possible to have a first class cabin from eight P.M. to eight A.M. and use the deck (third class) the rest of the time? Wouldn't that equal my second class ticket?"

"Yes," the official said, "that would be possible."

What a relief that second night!

We stopped at Pegan, the place of 10,000 pagodas. Many smaller ones were falling into decay, in contrast to the three or four large ones that were in daily use. I asked about the sad state of so many of the structures. I was told that to put up a pagoda brought much merit to the builder, but to repair and keep up someone else's pagoda brought no merit whatsoever. This accounted for the condition of most of the shrines.

When we reached Bassein, we transferred to a river launch headed for Rangoon. It was a delight to see the golden Swe Dagon Pagoda rise from the horizon and glisten in the afternoon sun.

I found Mrs. Whipple at the "Y" and we spent the evening recounting our adventures. The next morning, we bought tickets to Calcutta, and late that afternoon boarded our steamer for India. The sky was slightly overcast, so that the lowering sun tinged both sky and water with a brilliant crimson.

This was good for my soul. I had been in a state of shock. My dreams of marrying Howard and working together in India had vanished. Our time in Burma had taken my mind off my grief for a bit, but now as we returned to our mission, pangs of disappointment resurfaced. I would have to throw myself into caring for patients to forget. The flood of color on the Bay of Bengal reassured me of God's presence and that He would lead me always. I thought of the poem which so appropriately spoke the feelings in my heart:

> "I sure
> Have had enough of bitter in my cup,
> To show me never was it His design
> Who placed me here, that I should live in ease
> Or drink at none but pleasure's fountain.
> Henceforth then it matters not, if storm or sunshine
> Be my earthly lot, bitter or sweet my cup.
> I only pray, 'God, fit me for the work.
> God make me holy
> And my spirit nerve for the stern hour of strife.' "

I had chosen to go to India alone, without Howard, and now I would have to go *on* without him. God was my Helper, my Friend, my Consolation.

The wind was fairly strong the next morning. Mrs. Whipple had, again, retired to her cabin and there were numbers of vacant places at the breakfast table. Out on the deck, I met a group of eight American school teachers. They had been traveling together for some weeks and, when in Burma, had wanted to pick up some rubies. They were bemoaning the fact that they had docked in Rangoon on Sunday, when all the shops were closed, and had come away without a single ruby.

I remembered my stones, tied up in a handkerchief in my coat pocket. I had put that coat away, as it was warm in Mandalay, and hadn't worn it since. I went to my cabin, extracted my coat, and pulled out my cache. Back on deck, I spread out the contents, amid "ahs" and "ohs."

I gave each of the ladies several small stones, and they were delighted to have real rubies from Burma. Weeks later, I began hearing from all eight of them. The St. Louis girl said she took her stone to be appraised and learned it was quite valuable. In return, she sent me a camera, which, it turned out, cost $100. Another sent me a ring and a few smaller gifts.

To think, these stones gave so much pleasure to the group. I never told them I had only paid one dollar for the lot!

The mission decided to send Janet McLaren and me to canvass in Ceylon. In Bombay, we were to pick up a car that was shipped from the States, then drive to Ceylon and use the car for our work. We drove to Poona, Mahabaleshwar, Miraj, Bangalore, Mysore, Tinnevelly, and Trivandrum, working each town as we went.

We stayed in the Pandita Ramabai Mission, where girls were being cared for and trained in a beautiful Christian atmosphere. Ootacamand, near Bangalore, was a hill station of great beauty. Giant eucalyptus, bougainvillaea of all colors, and green grassy pastures made it a joy to behold.

As we went down the coast, we stopped at *dak** bungalows. We drove up to one where the conspicuous white *National Geographic Magazine* van was parked. Kurt Wentzel, who was also overnighting there, greeted us. When I asked him what brought

* Inexpensive government quarters.

him to these out-of-the-way places, he said he was trying to get a photograph of elephants—bathing, if possible.

"We passed a herd of six or seven down at the river we just crossed," I said.

He dashed off and got some great shots of the elephants bathing in the river, splashing water on each other. Kurt was so grateful he offered us some color film—film that could not be bought in India at that time.*

We moved on to Kolar, where many Europeans lived and worked in the gold mines 8,000 feet down in the earth. A doctor's authorization was needed to go down the full distance, so we only went down one vertical mile, where we saw paved streets, electric lights, and electric cars running about in the bowels of the earth.**

We were cordially received at Donavor, Amy Carmichael's mission, where we saw children literally being snatched from a life of slavery and prostitution in the temples and being brought up to love and serve the Lord. Donavor is divided into compounds made up of a "mother" and six or eight children of different ages, and the house is a haven of love, where people translate the Gospel into day-to-day living.

We crossed by ferry over to Ceylon (now Sri Lanka) with our car. Colombo was hot and humid, so we headed up the mountains to Nuwara Eliya. The road was winding, with deep forests and dark coves. Janet remarked that if we kept climbing like this, we should arrive at the gates of Heaven in the morning. When we arrived, we found many Europeans who had also fled from the heat. Business was good, and yet there was time for sightseeing and pleasure.

---

* In recalling this event with Mrs. Grosvenor in 1953, at the Woodstock reunion of the class of '32 in Washington, D.C., she said, "Of course I know Volkmar Wentzel. He is still a valuable member of our staff."

She was Anne Revis, a little girl with two braids, going along the *chakkar* to school when I had last seen her in Landour, India, in 1928.

** A sign at the main shaft of the mine read, "If you smell eucalyptus oil, go immediately to the nearest exit. This is the only fire alarm you will have." At a sign of fire a gallon of eucalyptus oil was poured down the main shaft. I could see why we use eucalyptus in chest complaints. It is penetrating.

One very interesting sight was the collection of rock frescoes at Sigiriya, where one is suspended on iron balconies to view paintings that have survived fourteen centuries of time and erosion. The soft colors have been preserved and become more beautiful as time goes on.

The Parahera festival at Kandy was exciting as the huge, highly-festooned elephant was paraded through the streets, bearing the sacred tooth of Buddha. We loved walking through the Peradeniya Gardens, where I asked the gardener how he kept the lawns so smooth and green.

"One hundred years of mowing and rolling," was his reply.

Later, while we were in Colombo, we received a telegram asking us to come to Bezwada (near Madras) to meet with Edwin Harvey from Scotland. We started out in the evening of a bright moonlit night, driving north partly to avoid the heat and also to arrive at the railway station Talimanaar, where we were putting our car on the ferry for India. We waited in the early morning light for the train from Colombo, which was due at five-thirty.

When the stationmaster saw us he asked, "Where did you spend the night?" We told him we had driven all night and had spent the night in our car.

"Don't you know that is dangerous? There are leopards and wild elephants in these forests."

At seven, when the train finally arrived, the remains of an elephant who had charged the train was on the cowcatcher!

On the ferry to Danushkodi the water was very shallow, and so clear we could see the stones at the bottom. We recalled the story of Ram enlisting the help of Hanuman and the monkeys to build a bridge for him to carry his wife, Sita, back to India. I could understand now how it could be.

When we arrived in Bezwada, I was excited because William would be there, and I did not know what it might mean. After Howard had died in Siwait, I was approached by William, but I was not ready for marriage with anyone. My pain was too fresh and I could not shift gears that quickly. But my time in Burma and the time in Ceylon had changed things. I no longer lived with the anticipation of life with Howard, and I did not want to face life alone. I decided that I would marry William if he asked me again.

The first day in Bezwada William asked me to go for a walk

with him after dinner. It was a gorgeous night with a big full moon.

We sat out on the hillside for several hours and he constantly repeated, "Juanita, there is something I must tell you."

He seemed affectionate and warm, but very distressed.

"You don't need to tell me if it pains you," I replied.

"No, I must," he kept saying. We talked of many things, but he kept on coming back to the same theme.

"I must, I must. I really must." But he didn't.

The next day was a repetition of the night before. We went for a long walk and he referred to me, always, as his best friend and told me how much he wanted me, but always ending with, "I've something I must tell you, but I can't."

Of course, I wondered what could be so important. I was leaving for Siwait the next day and hated to be going with a big cloud of mystery hanging over me.

We started off early the next morning. All along the trip, I spoke very little to Janet as we travelled. On our arrival in Siwait, the question that had bothered me was answered. A letter was conveniently dropped in my path to the hospital, with the envelope, addressed to one of the lady missionaries, lying there as plain as day—now the puzzle was clear. His wedding day was already set and his fiancé was heading for Bezwada.

It was not until some years later that William wrote to me. He had received his orders from higher up and they did not include me. If he differed with the order, he would be sent home. That was final and irrevocable.

God still had my life in His hands. I prayed and asked for His help to go on. He became closer than friend or lover could ever be. He was my Helper and Comforter. I would survive.

> "Because He lives I can face tomorrow;
> Because He lives all fear is gone;
> Because I know He holds the future,
> And life is worth the living just because He lives." *

* By William and Gloria Gaither

The long mudwalled bungalow in Siwait where Juanita lived her first six years in India. The doors and windows were solid wood so one had a choice of leaving them open when the hot winds blew or closing them and being in darkness.

At night they slept out in the open to get what little air was stirring. They slept under mosquito nets which, besides keeping out the mosquitoes, protected them from snakes and other night-creeping things.

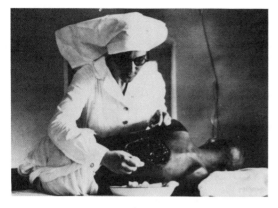

Caring for a patient with a long-standing decubitus and malnutrition.

Below, dressing an infected turtle bite. This was Juanita's first patient before the hospital was built. They were working outside on the ground.

A patient being brought to the hospital at Siwait.

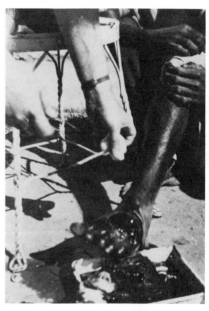

Patients who came from far and were not able to walk would often take the ekka. This was a two-wheeled horse-drawn cart carrying three or four passengers. This was the kind of cart Juanita often took to go to the villages to care for maternity cases.

Juanita in Lombardi costume in South India.

In front of the Eden Hospital, Calcutta Medical College, India.

In Mandalay, Burma.

Nursing students and staff of the Memorial Hospital, Fatehgarh, United Provinces, North India, 1952.

At left: Howard spent his summers on the farm.

Below: Howard on arrival in India.

Bottom: Bitzer Memorial School in Allahabad District in India.

BOOK FOUR

WAR CLOUDS GATHER

1933-1945

Chapter X

An Elephant
for a Patient

In the summer of 1938, Henry, the leader of the mission, took his wife, his mother, and some young students overland by car to England and Scotland, where the students were to continue their training. In their absence, Miss Janet McLaren, a missionary recently arrived from Scotland, was put in charge of the mission accounting. She was very sympathetic with those of us in the mission who had not had a vacation in many years (ten years, in my case) and decided to do something about it. She gave each member of the mission 25 rupees ($8.50) and leave for a ten-day vacation (one week and two weekends), to be staggered so the work would not suffer.

"We are all going for a holiday," she announced. "You can have the use of the old van, which can take some of you. You can each decided *where* you want to go and if you want to go together. It is so hot here; it would be good to get into the cool air of a hill station."

Never having had such a break before, we all agreed that this was a splendid idea.

I joined in with a group driving to Almora, some 250 miles into the mountains north of us. We took our food and bedrolls and slept out under the stars. Off and on during the night we could hear the call of a jackal or the hooting of a night owl.

At 5,000 feet the air was cool and invigorating. The fragrant smell of the pine trees was like a breath from another world, and the warble of the verditer flycatcher and the melody of the gray-winged blackbird were heavenly. After a short time in Almora, we were again ready to brave the heat of the plains.

The blistering winds of the "loo" from the southeast filled the air with dust. Eventually these air currents would draw moisture from the Bay of Bengal and from the Arabian Sea and give rise to the monsoon rains.

What a great relief it was when showers began to fall. Soon, however, we were surrounded by a sea of mud and could no longer walk through the fields to the railroad station. We had to go around the long way on an elevated road. With the temperature well over 100 degrees and the humidity always near 100%, we were in a constant lather of perspiration. We would fondly recall our brief Almora experience.

It was not only humans who were severely affected by the weather—animals were affected, too. A camel, owned by a neighbor in a village close by, went mad. When the owner's seven-year-old daughter attempted to feed it, the beast grabbed her arm and swallowed it up to the shoulder, then swung the child up in the air, her arm in tatters. The father ran with her to our hospital to see what could be done for her. Upon examination, I saw there was no flesh, muscles or nerves left on the arm. I told the father that to save the girl's life, the arm would have to be amputated.

"Oh, no," exclaimed the distraught father. "No man would ever marry a girl with only one arm."

I tried in vain to persuade him, but he gathered up his daughter and departed.

Often my cases were not in the hospital, but out in the surrounding villages. A call came in from a woman in labor in a Mohammedan village about fifteen miles away. I got my delivery kit ready and secured an *ekka walla** to take me to the village and bring me back. The driver was a Mohammedan, and it was the month of Ramzan, when Muslims were not allowed to eat food or drink water from sunup to sundown.

We set out about five o'clock, when it was not so hot, and got to the village before dark. The woman was in good condition, and we had a forceps delivery about an hour later. When we were through, I called for the *ekka walla* in order to return home. He

* Driver of a two-wheeled cart.

was nowhere to be found.

It was now cold and I had missed my supper. I had to wait for him until long after midnight. I spent the night alternately sitting on a brick and standing with a crooked neck, as the roof was too low to stand up straight. When the fellow finally returned and we bounced along that road back to the mission station, I resolved never to engage another Mohammedan driver during the fasting month of Ramzan.

A petty rajah in a neighboring village owned an elephant. One day a servant came running in to report that the elephant was sick and asked if I would come and treat it. I had had no experience with elephants, but I went over to investigate the situation. The rajah was very cordial and took me out to the stall, where the beast was sitting down.

"Kali has constipation and hasn't defecated for a week," the *Mahout** informed me. "Could you give her something to make her well?"

All I could think of was castor oil. Estimating the weight of the animal, I gave him a pint of it, and the *Mahout* managed to get most of it down Kali. To my relief, the animal got better. The rajah was a good friend ever after.

Then there was the call from the Rajah of Annapur, some distance away. His wife was pregnant and ready to deliver. He sent his car for me and we drove to his palace.

When I asked to see his wife, he replied, "Sorry, she is invisible."

After twenty minutes, she became "visible," and I was able to deliver the child.

Not long afterward, word came from the Maharajah of Rewa, an important state in the United Provinces about 150 miles from Siwait. His wife was about to deliver and he wanted me to attend her.

The Maharajah met me and ushered me upstairs to the bedroom to refresh myself. The upper walls and ceiling glittered with hundreds of little mirrors set in a beautiful geometric design and, with colored lights reflected in them, made a galaxy of splendor.

* Elephant driver.

Meanwhile, the Maharajah had to do his *puja** in his worship room.

I looked around a bit to see what might be available for the delivery. I opened a beautiful large teakwood cupboard and was astonished to find it full of cow dung cakes! Next, a servant appeared and asked whether I would like to tour the palace. He had something very special he wanted to show me.

First we went to the Durbar Hall or audience room, whose dome was a replica of the planetarium in Chicago, with constellations and planets rotating in the "sky" above. He then conducted me to the spacious trophy room, which was full of mounted tigers and tiger skins. Beyond them was a smoking room, the walls of which were completed filled with mirrors that gave distorted images. Another room was a great banquet hall. On all sides were large mirror panels bordered with tiny electric lights, which blazed forth in splendid glory when the switch was turned on.

We ascended a winding stairway where we came to a room with a very large bed. The servant literally grabbed my shoulder (something an Indian never does), and in an evident state of excitement, hurried me through the bedroom into the bathroom.

"Look!" he said. "You've no idea of what's coming."

He turned on the faucet and water gushed out.

"See! This water climbs upward!"

That was the wonder of the palace to him. He showed me a high water tank in the yard and pointed out the course of the water. He couldn't get over the fact that the water came up and out of the faucet. It was magic!

The Maharani was delivered after a short, quite normal labor. These delivery cases in the homes of the well to do were time consuming, and my work at the hospital needed me more, but with the shortage of funds, they were a source of income that we greatly needed. (They also gave me a chance to see how the wealthy, high-caste Hindus lived.)

Whenever the mission was low on funds, they would send us out to distant cities to sell literature—books, calendars, etc. In mid-January, 1934—in the cool season when travel was more comfortable—I was working in Jamalpur in Bihar Province. I did

*Prayers.

like to meet people, but often was shy in approaching them for funds.

The hostess where I was staying invited me to dinner the next evening. She said she had a friend who was anxious to meet me. I accepted.

That night as I lay in bed a feeling came over me that I should return to Calcutta and not attend that dinner. I did not know why. Maybe my sister in Calcutta was sick and needed me, or maybe I just did not want to meet the friend. I tried to silence the urge, but it grew even stronger.

The next forenoon, I went to my hostess and asked to be excused from the dinner that evening, for I felt I must go to Calcutta at once. I would take the noon train. She said she was very sorry, but she understood.

It was several hours to Calcutta. I traveled in ladies' third class with several others. Along about two o'clock, I felt the compartment swaying back and forth and the ride became very bumpy. I remarked to the woman next to me that the railroad company should do something about such a rough roadbed.

When we reached Howrah Station, a boy was running about yelling, "Read all about the terrible earthquake in Jamalpur," (and Bihar).

I bought a paper to learn we had just passed through the area of the most severe shocks and greatest loss of life. The train following ours was derailed and never did arrive.

Soon after, I heard from my hostess. She usually fed her baby about two each afternoon and had been in the outside kitchen, warming its milk, when the first tremors occurred. She grabbed her baby and ran out of doors just as the house collapsed behind her. She reported that the room where I had been staying (and where I would have been taking a siesta at that hour) had caved in, killing all who were in those quarters at the time. The catastrophy was widespread, extending as far away as Kathmandu, where 4400 were reported killed.

I found my sister in good health. Why then did I have such a compulsion to leave in haste and go to Calcutta? I believe it was another of those promptings God gives one. Or was it, perhaps, a nudge from my guardian angel? It did seem, following Howard's tortuous death some months before, that I experienced such tokens of God's tender care more frequently than before. I could literally feel His loving arms around me, holding me close.

The hot season came early. The mission was again low on funds, so I was asked to canvass in Patna, capital of Bihar State. Late that afternoon, I decided to stay overnight at a nearby *dak* bungalow. I found the caretaker's quarters and learned that all the rooms in the long, narrow building were empty, so I could have my choice. I selected the one next to his place at the end.

Since it was late afternoon I went to the market to get food for supper. Walking along to the bazaar in still bright daylight, a voice kept hounding me, "Don't sleep out tonight; it isn't safe. . . don't sleep out tonight; it isn't safe."

I wondered if I was just getting timid, which I had never been before. I argued with myself that I felt perfectly safe. However, at the persistence of the message, I yielded.

"Okay, I won't sleep out," I relented.

I went about my shopping without further urging and walked back to the *dak* bungalow.

The caretaker prepared and served me a simple curry and rice supper. I ate it out on the veranda because the room was so stifling, with not a single breath of air stirring. As I was eating, the servant brought my rope bed out of my room onto the veranda and started putting up the mosquito net.

It was then that I again heard the same warning, "Don't sleep out tonight; it isn't safe."

When I asked the caretaker to put my bed back into that hot room, he protested.

"You can't sleep in that oven," he explained.

I almost reneged, but then the message was repeated, "What did I tell you? Don't sleep out tonight; it isn't safe."

When I insisted, the caretaker reluctantly put the bed back in the room, grumbling all the while. I always carried a lock with me in case of need, usually to lock my tin trunk. When it came time to go to bed, I locked the bathroom and back doors with bolts from the inside. When I came to lock the front door, I found the bolt had been removed. What to do? I took the lock from my box and reached my hands through the venetians and managed to put the lock on the outside of the front door. Then I went to sleep in spite of the heat.

About midnight I heard a rumpus. A bunch of men had reached the first room at the far end of the veranda and began to smash in the door. They finally succeeded, only to find the room empty. They came on to the next one, cursing and talking. I could understand part of what they were saying. It was a robber gang bent on getting loot.

Crash went the second door. Nothing again. More cursing as they approached the door next to mine. This was locked, and after an inspection, they found it was empty. Then they came to mine. A full moon was streaming down on the metal lock I had put on it.

The *dacoits** looked at that lock and said, "Nobody here either."

They turned and went away noisily, cursing their luck. I felt grateful to God that He had warned me so strongly and had kept me safe.

My selling work also took me to such cities as Lucknow, Delhi and Cawnpore, as well as to Fatehgarh to the American Presbyterian hospital and friends there, among whom was Dr. Adelaide Woodard of Seattle, a great medical chief. She often handed over cases to other doctors on the staff and trained them in medical procedures.

At one point, she became exasperated after four of her women doctors resigned to be married, one after another. She wrote home to her Mission Board in New York, "Please send me a doctor who is cross-eyed, bow-legged, partially toothless and who looks like wrath and destruction. Then I would not have them going off and getting married!"

The Presbyterians sent out Dr. Bethel Harris, who came from a long line of Presbyterian ministers. She had graduated from Women's Medical School in Philadelphia and had always wanted to be a missionary in India. Dr. Bethel represented none of the characteristics described in that letter, but was just the opposite. The two doctors quickly were in gear together, the young one learning a great deal before she had to go to language school in Landour the following spring. After another winter at the hospi-

*Robbers.

tal, Dr. Harris returned to the hills for her second year of language study.

I attended a dinner party that Dr. Woodard was giving for members of the mission. At each place was a bouquet of small flowers tied up with white silk ribbons. Dr. Woodard picked up hers, opened it and burst into tears.

I sat up in alarm. What was the matter? The rest of us opened our bouquets.

"Announcing the engagement of Dr. Bethel Harris to Robert L. Fleming."

"Another doctor lost to the cause of the Fatehgarh Hospital," moaned Dr. Woodard.

Evening time in India has its own noises, smells and skies. The dogs seem to bark more often and louder, and the smells are of pungent curries cooking on open fires, mingled with the odor of the hookah and the scent of the cooling fields rising after the heat of the day. Women's voices call the children, while the tinkle of bells on the homing cattle add to the reverberations of the temple bells in the distance—some melodious, some dissonant with the clanging of brass on brass. Over and above all the trees and huts with their grass roofs, was the sky—especially in the monsoons—with its red, purple, and gold rising to a deep azure at the zenith.

Walking along the narrow slippery path between the flooded rice fields, which reflected the colorama of the sky, my mind was on my errand more than the beauty of the evening. The men who had come to call for help said the woman had been in labor three days and was near death. My adrenaline was heightened as I walked along, wondering what I would find.

I entered the thatched roofed hut through the small doorway, and in the light of a flickering flame, I saw a woman lying on a pile of straw and writhing with pain. A small blue, bruised arm protruded from her vagina, and I immediately knew I had a transverse lie to deal with.

There was no use even thinking of removing her to the hospital—she would never survive the trip, so she had to be delivered here on the floor. I poured a dram of chloroform into the drop bottle (ether was far too flammable to use near the open flame).

Handing it to a woman nearby, I scrubbed up and donned sterile gloves.

It was a case of amputating the gangrenous arm, after turning and delivering the child by breach, all the while keeping one eye on my conscripted anesthetist and simultaneously keeping mental count of the drops of chloroform and watching the patient's respiration.

Once she was over the long ordeal, she fell into a deep sleep. Advising the family on her care, I explained our hospital facilities and urged that she come there early next time she became pregnant.

Walking back to the hospital, I kept listening for the wailing that always followed a death, and I breathed a sign of relief when I heard none. I said a prayer: "Thank you, God. You were there when I needed you."

That summer Mrs. Freymiller had to stay up in Landour with the children, so she was unable to carry on her Sunday school in Agra where she and Mr. Freymiller were stationed. I was asked to take her place in Agra on Sundays and carry on my work at the hospital in Siwait during the week. This necessitated an overnight train trip (over 250 miles) every Saturday night and a return trip each Sunday night—all of this in a crowded third-class carriage where I was frequently obliged to sit on a kerosene oil tin or on my suitcase in the aisle.

I was often very weary, but in the early dawn as the train would cross the river into Agra, the sight of the Taj Mahal reflected in the sparkling water of the Jamuna with the sunrise glow on her alabaster dome made all the weariness worthwhile.

Chapter XI

Sat Tal Ablaze

Back in Siwait, I found a letter from my mother, who kept in touch regularly. She had enclosed a check for $600 to be used as I saw fit. Up until now, we all lived in mud houses and thatched roofs with no windows. This meant that in hot weather, when we closed the door and solid wood windows against the heat, the room was dark. To lower the temperature somewhat, holes had been made in the walls of the six rooms of the mission (which were in a long row bordered by a wide veranda), and a rope was strung through them. Attached to this rope in each room was a *punka**, a long piece of grass matting attached to a bamboo pole that was placed at right angles to the rope. A man was hired to sit on the porch and pull the rope back and forth, thus moving the *punkas* and fanning all the rooms simultaneously. Sometimes he would lie down and pull the rope with his toes. Alas, too often he fell asleep. Another method was to have water poured over split-bamboo-and-grass mats over the doors. During spring and summer, the days were so hot one regularly took a siesta.

The roofs of our quarters were something else again. They harbored a variety of vermin which produced a series of squeaks and sounds throughout the night. Fortunately, few of them ever fell on our bed, but there was always that possibility.

In our room were the three beds with no room for any furniture, except a desk. We sat on steamer trunks. There were also two canvas steamer chairs which we kept on the back veranda. A

*Improvised fan.

little alcove in the back room was curtained off for hanging our clothing. Everything else was placed on a single shelf. Each of our primitive rope beds was protected by a mosquito net.*

Monkeys are a source of fun and amusement when performing with an organ grinder on our streets or in a municipal zoo, but in the wild, they are something else. There was a troop of monkeys in a grove at Hajiganj, and one of them stayed around the mission house as he frequently got tidbits from the kitchen. But while he was docile with the men, he took advantage of us women. One afternoon as I lay on my bed, he came into the bedroom, hopped up onto the desk and picked up a full ink bottle. I held my breath for a moment, expecting him to throw it at me. Instead, he *turned the cap* and poured the ink out over the desk, looking at me all the while as if to see how I was taking it. Then he ran out wearing what looked like a grin.

I was incensed and told the men of the mission that they would have to get rid of the monkey. He was a big nuisance and was giving us women too much trouble.

"You encourage him in doing these things because he knows you are afraid of him," they said. "Next time you see him, carry a big stick and give him a whack. He won't bother you again."

I decided to try it. When I came out of the dining room one day soon after, he was standing in my path. I raised my big stick. He jumped on me and clamped his teeth into my arm. I hit him hard enough that he released his hold on me, and that was the last time he bothered me. I still have his teeth marks on my arm.

One of the pleasures we had in Siwait was our swimming pool. No, not a pool as one would find in America, just a concrete reservoir tank to hold water for irrigating the fields. But it was cool—actually cold—water from our deep well.

Formerly, water had been brought up in a buffalo skin by a pair of oxen, but Tyrrell installed a kerosene engine that pumped water and, at the same time, ran a generator that supplied electricity for three or four hours a day, beginning at sundown. It was a great treat to jump into the cool water after a hot day (of 110°-125° F) and, after cooling off, having a light to read by and some-

---

* One morning I woke up with a snake coiled on my net and had to lie with the snake there until help came.

times, for a couple of hours, an electric fan!

When the monsoons broke, it was an exciting time. For weeks there would be the buildup of humidity, the thermometer climbing to 115° or more and great cumulus clouds blackening the sky. Each day was full of anticipation, waiting . . . waiting . . .

There would be thunder and heat lightning, but no rain—until it broke eventually. Then the rain would come down in torrents, drenching the fields and roads and filling up ponds that had been dry for months. Fish—mud fish—filled the ponds almost immediately, having been dormant in the dried mud at the bottom of the ponds for so long.

The first drenching rain caught Marjorie Whipple and me unawares. We were down in Hajiganj, and to get back to the mission, we had to wade in several feet of water. Even on the road that had been raised by five or six feet, and sloped on the sides, we were still in water up to my shoulder and Marjorie's neck,, and I had to keep one hand under her chin to help her stay afloat. All around us were floating squash and rotting pumpkins washed in from the surrounding fields. Needless to say, we showered thoroughly and took doses of preventive medicine when we got home.

As was my habit before retiring, I walked over to the hospital for a last check on the patients. In the maternity ward, one of my patients, Bundi, was awake and crying. She had delivered a seven-pound baby girl the day before and was having a very normal recovery.

"Bundi, why are you crying? Are you having pain?" I asked.

"No, I have no pain, but please promise me something. If I should die, will you take care of my baby?"

"Bundi, why do say that?" I asked. "You are not going to die. You are doing fine."

I tried to reassure her, but knowing that patients are often right and that I might be missing something, I checked her over carefully—pulse, heart, lungs, all seemed fine. I looked under her pillow and clothing for any drug or instrument hidden there, for I knew that Bundi was a second wife, and her husband's other wife had a son.

"How can I take a girl baby back to my village? I will be laughed at by the other women and abused by my husband. That kind of life would be unliveable."

Taking her hand in mine, I told her of God's love for her and how He would be her helper. I committed her to His care and left her for the night.

At two in the morning the night nurse called me. Bundi had died in the night. No sign of drugs or instrument was found, but we knew that the Indian "will-to-die" power is very potent. We had no facilities for post-mortems, and the Hindu caste family would not have allowed it in any case.

Villagers who needed me would come up to the bungalow and call out for help, awakening the whole house with their loud and insistent voices and disturbing everybody. Thus, it was suggested that I should live closer to the hospital so others in the mission would not be distracted and wakened in the night.

I knew I could better the situation if I could build my own little house. Then came Mother's letter with the means to do it. The hospital building was completed and there were leftover materials I could use. I sat down and drew a plan. For once, I had the mission people siding with me. They were more than happy when I suggested putting up my own place a little nearer the hospital.

It was a simple, square house with brick walls and a reinforced roof covered by 1-1/2 inches of concrete. Four times larger than the room the three of us were now sharing, this structure would have a living room, a bedroom, a smaller dressing room, bath and kitchen. And the large windows in both bedroom and living room were *glass!* I designed a fireplace to heat the two front rooms; it worked perfectly.

One day I walked into Ram's store in Allahabad, where I was greeted with a warm welcome. After making my purchases, the owner would take no money from me

"How come?" I asked, very surprised.

"Do you remember the day of the wrecked train near your station?" he asked.

Of course I remembered it.

"I was the man sitting in the coach watching you pull patients out of the muddy fields," he informed me. He was always generous to me after that.

I was called to help a woman who had been in labor several days. We left our car outside the village, as the paths through the village were too narrow. Walking into the village, I heard groaning which seemed to emanate from a hut where the *pasi** boy who herded the pigs lived. The hut was scarcely larger than a huge wicker basket turned upside down. I bent over to look in and then remembered I was going to an obstetric case and dare not contaminate myself before the delivery. I would see the boy afterwards.

After the delivery, I wasted no time getting back to the *pasi* boy's hut. As we neared, I heard no more groaning. I bent down and had to crawl on my hands and knees to enter. There he lay, quiet and motionless, in a pool of vomitus, his lifeless body now cold. I was too late.

Saddened, I backed out of the hut wondering how many others in the village had succumbed to the cholera epidemic. All the way home I was humming the song I had learned in Sunday school:

> "Into a tent where a gypsy boy lay
> Dying alone at the close of the day,
> News of salvation they carry said he,
> But nobody ever has told it to me."

I was returning from one of my trips to Calcutta—taking the night train back to Siwait—and the air was nippy. The weather had been hot when I had left Siwait. I realized I would catch cold if I rode all night in weather like this, so I got off the train at Asansol and went up to the bazaar to purchase a blanket.

The shops were filled with all sorts of blankets—lovely Italian rugs, Lal Imli blankets, and rough horse blankets. I went into one shop where the *baniya* greeted me, asking what type of blanket I was looking for. He had imported wool blankets for 35 rupees, Lal Imli wool ones for 20, and some scratchy horse blankets for 4.

I explained I wanted one just for the overnight trip and I was short of funds, so I would take just a cheap one.

"But which one do you really like?" he asked.

---

* Swineherd caste.

"Well, if you're asking my preference, it would be this one," I said, pointing to a beautiful Italian rug in blue plaid, "but I'm not buying that one; I don't have the money. As I told you, I'm traveling, and it's just for one night."

He took down the blanket I had pointed out and began wrapping it in newspaper. Again I remonstrated with him, but he insisted.

"Why are you doing this," I asked.

"I have it in my heart that way," he responded in English.

Then he told me he was educated in a Christian school, and seeing I was a missionary, wanted to repay his debt to the missionaries.

Times had changed somewhat in the mission, and although we still received no stipend or money, we sometimes got respite from the heat in the form of a vacation.

Henry and Creo were planning a vacation with their new baby in Sat Tal and invited John Whipple and me to go along. They had rented No. 10—Fisherman's Cottage—right on one of the lakes (Sat Tal means Seven Lakes), a lovely spot nestled in the deep woods, with chipmunks scampering up and down the trees and red-billed magpies flitting from the branches with their long tails fluttering.

Dr. E. Stanley Jones—Brother Stanley to all the members of the group—had purchased the grounds in the mountains near Naini Tal. He held annual seminars there for Bible study and for the deepening of the Christian life. Meetings each morning were open for discussion, and one day talk centered on the early church policy of communal living, which Brother Stanley was pursuing in a limited measure.

As I was interested in a lot for a cottage, he and I went down the hillside after lunch. At a point between Ram and Sita Lakes, one could see the sun rise over one lake in the morning and set over the other in the evening. We sat down on the ground and talked about the discussion of the morning. He was interested that we were living in our mission very much as he had envisioned the early church. We talked all afternoon on the pros and cons of the system, until we noticed the sun was beginning to set over Ram Lake.

He stood up suddenly, looked at his watch and exclaimed, "and today was my day of silence!"

One evening while we were at Fisherman's Cottage, a forest fire broke out and was coming up over the side of the mountain, carrying billows of smoke and ash. Brother Stanley, always mindful of the safety of his guests, came to the cabin, bringing his daughter Eunice, and gave us instructions.

"We have placed a boat here for you," he said. "If the fire gets close, take blankets, some drinking water, flashlight, and the baby's needs and get into the boat and row to the center of the lake."

Eunice stayed with us. We got things ready and then sat on our porch, our eyes smarting from the smoke, watching the advancing flames come up over the hill. Animals and rodents fled down past our house, yapping and howling in their fright.

Henry and John came frequently throughout the night to check on us, as did Eunice's fiance, Jim Mathews,* and Brother Stanley, and then they would return to fighting the fire. It was an all-night vigil, but by the early light of dawn the fire was contained and we went to bed for some much-needed rest.

Storm clouds of war had been hanging over us ever since Neville Chamberlain had gone to Czechoslovakia in the fall of 1938 and returned with the pronouncement, "No war in our time." We had been watching events closely, and I frequently listened to my radio in the evening. Times were tense. The provisional government of the United Provinces had resigned and events were closing in on us.

I came in from the hospital one evening in suspense, only to find the radio dead. My servant had inserted the speaker plug into the electric mains, thereby burning out the unit. I was dismayed. It was the only radio in the mission. And there was no one within miles who knew anything about fixing a radio. I would have to do it myself if it got fixed at all.

So, I spread a sheet over my bed, locked the door, and proceeded to take it apart, laying it, piece by piece, on the sheet and marking with a number each part on a diagram. I soon found the

* Now Bishop Mathews.

burned part (I don't know its name), took it out and gave it to Lauki, my servant, with instructions to take it to town to a radio shop and get a part like it. He had just over an hour before the shops would close, and he had to cycle twelve miles.

He was fortunate to obtain a part like the burned one, but it was about an inch too long to fit. I got a small metal saw and cut it down to size, put it in place, and wonder of wonders, it worked! At nine that night, we learned from the BBC news that we were at war.

Chapter XII

The Nehru Family

My early contact with the Nehru family in Allahabad—
when I had asked the gardener for grape leaves and Moti Lal
Nehru had come down the steps and asked me to stay for
tea—was most fortunate. When I first started collecting funds for
the hospital and drew up my subscription list, Lady Maharaj
Singh suggested that I begin by asking Moti Lal for a donation.
When I approached businessmen in the city, they would examine
my list and, seeing the signatures of Sir Maharaj Singh and Moti
Lal Nehru at the top, quickly subscribed as well. When the hospital building was at last complete, Lady Maharaj Singh donated
bedding for it and lovely, soft bright red Lal Imli blankets —a
cheery accent in the hospital.

Ranjit Pandit was the husband of Vijaya Lakshmi, the second
child of Moti Lal (who was some eleven years younger than Jawaharlal, her elder brother). Ranjit had great concern for the ordinary villager and would undertake errands of mercy for them. On
one occasion he was seen transporting two men and a goat in the
back seat of his car. And occasionally, while flying the Congress
party flag on his car, he would bring in a village woman who
needed medical attention. He appreciated what our mission was
doing for the common people.*

Vijaya Lakshmi was "Nan" to her family and close friends. I
had first seen her a number of years earlier, a beautiful girl lying

---

* Our mission people were apprehensive of a public display of the Congressional
flag, trying to maintain a neutral status. I tried to convince them that Ranjit was
working for the good of the common people.

across the street with several others, blocking all traffic to the cloth market to protest the sale of British goods. They were practicing Mahatma Gandhi's principle of *satyagraha** against British cloth.

At the time I was rushing in my car to Dufferin Hospital with an acute, abnormal labor case, when I was stopped by the human barrier across the road. I was trying to save the life of one of their countrywomen and they would not let me pass.

A number of the bystanders looked in the car and saw the village woman lying there and saw I was telling the truth. After more shouting, several men stood on the running boards on either side of the car and yelled and waved the crowd out of the way. But not until demonstrators had battered the top of the old Ford to shreds. With the remains of it around our necks, we drove on to the hospital.

Ranjit had come from a Kashmiri Brahmin family in Gujarat. He and his wife greatly loved their three daughters, though they were often separated by political activities. His wife was a most ardent nationalist, and he was a crusader for the common people.

At that time, I felt the Lord was leading me more and more into medicine. I thought of becoming a doctor, as the mission had no plan of assigning one to Siwait. I wrote to headquarters in Wisconsin about it, but the reply was expected: they did not wish me to come back to the U.S. to study medicine as such a deviation would disrupt church policy.

Thereafter, I considered the possibility of going to London instead. To do this, I would need a School-leaving Certificate, which I did not have. So I sat for the Senior Cambridge examination, which I passed in first division, with distinction, in Hindi.

About this time the British Government granted provincial autonomy to the United Provinces to see how the government would run under Indian leadership. This lasted for two years. The British government also appointed a seventy-two-member Rural Development Commission. The only non-Indians on it were Dr. Sam Higginbottom and myself. Our meetings were more often held in Lucknow, the provincial headquarters, than in Allahabad.

*Soul-force the chief element in Gandhi's civil disobedience.

We concentrated on village primary education, building schools and creating radio-receiving centers.

One of the major responsibilities which fell to me was my appointment as Inspector of Prisons.* The Naini prison at Allahabad was the largest in the country. I noted that numbers of women with their children sat outside the walls of the men's section. They had flimsy shelters, comprised of dirty clothes propped up on sticks, to keep off the sun. Their floors were gunnysacks spread out on the ground. When it rained, they were surrounded by mud. Some of these families had been there for several months and nothing had been done for them. Even utensils were at a minimum. The women were cooking extra food for their menfolk behind bars. Otherwise, they had nothing else to do.

We suggested setting up a weaving program. Ranjit Pandit was very helpful in getting this project started. We bought materials and vats in which to dye wool, and we instructed women in how to follow patterns. When a rug was finished, the need for marketing it arose. This led to the opening of the Swadeshi shop over in the city, where we sold locally-made rugs, cloth, baskets, and mats. The whole project was quite successful and brought in at least small amounts of money to those wives whose husbands were confined behind prison bars.

The prison had two main sections, one for political prisoners and another for ordinary convicts. Political prisoners in Class A were given only nine *annas*** for food.

The quarters of a Class A were simple. There was a single room with an iron bed, a table and chair, and a tin box for personal belongings. A dim light hung from the ceiling, by which it was almost impossible to read. There was one small, high window, through which one could see only the sky, a toilet (a hole in the ground), and a place for bathing and washing clothes. Ordinary convicts were housed in long wards with some two dozen beds. They had less food and conveniences.

The year 1939 was a critical time in India. War had been declared and India became an unwilling belligerent. The people of

---

* The British government required that one inspector be a woman to check on the female prisoners.
**About 20 cents U.S.

India had not been consulted in the decision to involve them in a war, which resulted in a general non-cooperative movement designed to embarrass the British government. Members of the National Congress Party courted arrest. They planned to be arrested in a certain order, beginning with the top leader, from Jawaharlal Nehru and on down. Dates were set for apprehension, but usually the victims were rounded up the very next morning.

Jawaharlal was already in the Naini jail and Ranjit Pandit expected to follow soon. He asked me to get him some ammoniated quinine, as he had had malaria and the mosquitoes were reputed to be bad in the jail. When I brought it to Anand Bhawan, Ranjit asked me to put it in a basket beside his door, for when they came to arrest him, he would not be permitted to go back into the house to get anything. There was another item he wanted, which I brought next morning, but he had already been apprehended by the police.

Later, I visited Jawaharlal and Ranjit in jail. I noticed each had books and papers in their cells. One was writing letters to his daughter while the other was working on Sanskrit classics. The two men had a common bathroom and had made a miniature golf course in the second outside courtyard. They used marbles as golf balls and had landscaped the course so that it was quite attractive.

Being jailed was no new experience for the Nehrus. They had been in and out of prison many times. Ranjit's first experience was in 1930 and Vijaya's two years later. The Pandits made going to jail a game in front of the children, and the youngsters soon came to regard it as such. The girls had no fear of the arrival of policemen, the house search, and the leading of their parents away to prison. They knew they were going to prison for the honor and freedom of their country, India. To ease the tensions and apprehensions of the three daughters, Mrs. Pandit would bake a cake and have a party. Tara remembers these parties in her book, *Prison & Chocolate Cake.**

The Rural Development Commission continued its work during the war, but met less and less often. Ranjit Pandit had been the moving force in the organization, but he now was in jail. How-

* See Bibliography

ever, I was able to continue to give my BCG vaccinations* with vaccine which the World Health Organization supplied.**

Years before, I had met Miss Hotz, a most remarkable Swiss-English lady who then owned the three leading hotels in India—the Cecil in Delhi, Lauries in Agra and Wildflower Hall in Simla. At the time of our meeting, I had been working in Delhi and was overtired.

I went to the "Y" to get a room, but they were full. Someone suggested I try the Cecil Hotel a short distance away, pointing out that Miss Hotz, the proprietor, was a kind lady who might help me out. I made my way there and contacted her. She was indeed all that the person had said.

"I'm afraid we are full. Every room is taken." She hesitated, then asked, "Would you mind sharing a room with a quiet old lady?"

"That would be fine," I murmured, glad for any place to lay my head. I was shown to the room where a cot had been put in for me. In no time, I was asleep. When I woke up in the morning, to my astonishment, I discovered that the "old lady" was Miss Hotz herself. She was such a generous person. After that, she would not think of my staying anywhere else whenever I came to Delhi.

I learned that Amy Carmichael from South India had been in Delhi, and Miss Hotz again had shared her room. On the table lay a book Miss Carmichael had written, *Gold By Moonlight*. On the fly page, she had written, "To the Rani of *Kuchh Parwa Nahin*,*** which is what Miss Hotz called herself.

These war years brought numbers of new contacts.

When the war started and prominent Indians were jailed, the mission folk said to me, "See! we told you so! The British will win out in the end."

I sensed a growing aloofness among my colleagues, which

* B.C.G.—Bacillus Calmetti-Guerin vaccine for tuberculosis.

** At one of the Rural Development meetings in Lucknow, the governor, Sir Maurice Hallet, awarded me the SANAD, a large certificate which he had signed, "For meritorious service in rural development in the United Provinces."

*** "To the Queen of No Account." Lit: " it does not matter."

was to lead to the deepest crisis of my life.

World War II had a profound effect on India. When war was declared, and the self-government experiment in the United Provinces came to an end, India was thrust into the conflict, and from then on the Non-Cooperation Movement gained momentum in opposing the British government in India. I was not politically minded—Indians, Britons, mission folk, all who helped the people of India were my friends.

Early war years first brought American Flying Tigers to Alla-habad. The need for a V-Room became clearly evident. We ladies of several missions in and around Allahabad got together and organized such a place. We took turns supplying coffee, dough-nuts, pie, etc., so the strain on the pilots of flying over the hump might be lessened by visiting the V-Room for fellowship and an evening snack. One of the men liked to play the piano, and num-bers of others would stand around and sing. We got to know some of the men personally, two of whom I especially remem-ber—Frank Jones and Maynard Hallman.

Neither Frank nor his pal was a Christian. On a beautiful moonlit night, while flying on his bombing mission from India to Burma, Frank looked up into the sky and a beautiful array of clouds.

"God, if there is a God, give me some sign to prove it," he demanded.

Not long afterward, he felt an urge to fly left, off his course. He argued that this was against the rules, but the urge persisted. He knew he was expected to keep rigidly to plan, still the con-stant nudging caused him to reconsider. Eventually he did turn left for some distance. In the second valley, he noticed a white cloth fluttering near the ground. A flyer was down there, so on his return to base, he reported what he had seen.

Little did he realize that the man down there was his best friend, Maynard Hallman, who also was praying. Maynard knew there was little chance of being found in that trackless jungle, but he called on God, whom he had ignored up until then, say-ing, "Oh, God, if there is a God, let someone find me."

When he unexpectedly heard the hum of a plane, someone coming to help, he felt convinced there was a God interested in his welfare.

After his rescue, Frank and he compared notes. Both became convinced that God had been with them all the time, and then and there, they resolved to become practising Christians. I met both men in Rochester, New York, some years later. One was a successful Dodge dealer and the other a Chevrolet dealer. Both were well off and both continued to give more than a tithe to missionary work.

On one of my times to take doughnuts and pie to the V-Room in Allahabad, I noticed a soldier wearing an American Chaplain's badge. I stepped up to him and introduced myself.

Captain Hood said, "Well, I have been wanting to meet the missionaries, because I want to have some of my men see what you do in your work."

"My work is in a hospital, and I am the nurse in charge," I replied. "I would like to have you come to Siwait and see the mission. We are only about twelve miles out of town."

"How many should I expect," I queried.

"I would bring a truckload—about twenty men," he answered.

So I went over to the bazaar and bought potatoes for a salad. I saw several more Americans that day who said they were also coming, so I went back to the bazaar and bought more potatoes.

August was a hot, humid month. All the other mission personnel had left for the hills, and I was the only foreigner who remained. What could I do tomorrow to entertain Captain Hood and his men? Well, I could feed them. I had my servant cook up lots of beans and I made mayonnaise for the potato salad. We had plenty of juicy limes on our trees for pies, and we boiled tamarind pods for a cool drink. No refrigerator, no ice, of course.

It was then I remembered the rajah's elephant—the one I had dosed with castor oil. The raja had been so grateful that he had said, "Anytime you would like the use of the elephant, just let me know."

This was the time! Yes, he would have his *mahout** bring the elephant over for the evening.

When Captain Hood arrived, there was not one truckload of men, but two. But since I had expected as much, I had food enough for all of them. I had my cook make lemon pies to finish

---

* Elephant driver.

out the rest of the meal.

My house was too small for so many, so we sat around in my garden and talked and sang. Then the elephant arrived, much to the surprise and pleasure of the group. None of them had ridden an elephant before, and they took turns and snapped pictures of their buddies as the *mahout* directed his animal around the compound.

At the end, Captain Hood asked whether there was anything they could do for me. I replied that I had heard about Irving Berlin's song, "God Bless America," but had never heard it sung. The men formed a pyramid several tiers high and burst forth in song.

There in the center of India, 12,000 miles from home, we sat under a full moon and they sang in the moonlight. Tears streamed down my face as I listened to these men singing of their homeland and mine. It had been sixteen years since I had left America, and my pent-up emotions just let loose. I so appreciated what my guests had done for me.

Other men back at the base heard about the good time the first group had had at Siwait, and about the elephant, and they wanted to come out, too. A few other gatherings took place, and the rajah kindly cooperated. There was always fun and picture-taking. The second time, along came a large bag of goodies. After they had left, I found some dollar bills hidden under the book lying on my table. Such memorable occasions!

With the arrival of September, my mission colleagues returned from the hills. They learned of parties for G.I.'s and highly disapproved, since they felt one's energies should be directed toward the suffering and needs of Indian villagers, not toward American soldiers. I was informed that I would no longer be permitted to live in the house that I had built near the hospital, but had to move into a room in the big bungalow under surveillance, and share the bathroom with another lady. I guess they figured this would make it impossible to have any more parties.

I had always wanted my living quarters to be comfortable and tastily decorated. It was the difference between personal and institutional living. Mother had given me the $600 I had used to build the house, and I had used odds and ends left over from

other construction. It had not cost the mission anything. I had
built it purposely some distance from the big bungalow so villagers calling for the nurse at night would not disturb others. But
now I had to move back.

I said, "Yes, I will," but with anguish in my heart.

Whenever I could, I still returned to Allahabad to help in the
V-Room, taking the afternoon train when I had completed my
medical work, and returning by the midnight train. It was a period of continual national disturbances. In an effort to further
embarrass the British government, Indian nationalists were
attacking police stations, ransacking post offices, cutting electric
and telephone wires, and derailing trains. Communications were
being disrupted frequently.

One night I went to the station at midnight, but there was no
train. It had been derailed. How would I get home?

"We will drive you back," chimed several men.

So I hopped into the truck for the twelve-mile drive.

"When we neared the compound gate," I warned, "don't make
a sound, for the ladies will be sleeping outside and we shouldn't
wake them."

As it was, when I approached the veranda, I saw one of the
maiden ladies standing near her door, and I knew she was dis-
pleased. For a moment, I had a most uncomfortable feeling. But
next day, in the hospital, I had a heavy schedule and thought no
more about my late arrival.

I was really tired by nine o'clock when I went to bed, and I
had scarcely gotten to sleep when I was suddenly awakened.

"We are having a meeting in the parlour and they want you
there," I was informed.

"At this hour?" I remonstrated.

"Yes, they are all waiting."

I put on my prettiest blue robe with matching slippers and
went over. As I opened the door, I saw a circle of solemn-faced
people sitting around the room. They came to the point at once.

"You were out late last night with a soldier," accused the
spokesman, "and you came home after midnight. This cannot be
tolerated in our mission. You are a very bad influence. What will
the village people think?"

"But I had no other way to get back; the train had been

derailed," I protested. "And I wasn't out alone with a man, there were ten men in the truck who came back with me," I added.

The group refused to accept my statement.

The chairman gave his verdict: "From now on you will remain in Siwait. No more trips anywhere, and no more parties. You may go to the hospital and to your own room, but everywhere else is out of bounds. You will be permitted to remain here until we can secure passage for you back to the U.S.A. None of us here will speak with you."

The meeting adjourned. Stunned, I returned to my room and prayed to God for guidance. For the next few days, I tried to carry on my work, which became more and more unbearable. At night, I would walk out into the moonlight and talk to God, who I knew was sustaining me. If I had not been spiritually alive, I would not have been able to take the days of loneliness which followed.

I resolved to break rules and go to see my Presbyterian friends in Allahabad—to someone I could talk to. They were most understanding.

Dr. Mabelle Hayes said, "Why don't you join us? We need another nurse right now in Fatehgarh and you would be a god-send. We are going to Mussoorie to our annual meeting, where a transfer can be arranged. Why don't you come with us?"

Our mission maintained policies which completely controlled all our lives. After Howard passed away, a friend of his came to Siwait and made overtures of friendship and even talked to me of marriage, but he promptly received word from headquarters that any idea of marrying me would mean his immediate recall to the States.

Not only did the severe discipline against marriage hold, but families, too, were disciplined. We were supposed to love everyone equally, and it was not considered Christian to love one's own children more than those of others. So, Bernice and Tyrrell were separated. Bernice was sent to Calcutta (in the east) and Tyrrell to Quetta (in the far west), and their two children, Ernest and Kenneth (ages 4 and 2) were given to a woman of the mission to care for.

I begged to have them, as I was naturally attached to my nephews, but I was not allowed. Nor was I allowed to question or interfere with their training. At times when I was present in the dining room, their caretaker would take one of them outside on the veranda and whip him because he refused to eat his vegetables. (Ernest, being older, learned to store spinach in his cheeks until the meal was finished, and then go outside and spit it out. Or a ball of spinach might be found under his pillow at night.) Such was life in a community where love was supposed to be paramount!

There was one thing I *had* to do before leaving. I had sponsored Miriam through her midwifery training and now, though she had finished her time and had her diploma, I felt I could not leave her unmarried and alone in the world. I went in to talk to Mrs. Higginbottom in Naini (near Allahabad). She knew the young men in the Agricultural Institute and could help me find a husband for Miriam. She said yes, she knew a fine young man who wanted to get married, and a couple of days later, she sent for me to bring Miriam to meet the boy. She gave them a seat in the swing on her veranda while she and I went inside to chat. In about half an hour, she got up and looked at her watch.

She said, "I think they have had enough time, don't you?"

We went out to the veranda where the young couple sat in the porch swing.

"We have a problem," the boy said. "We don't know if we can afford all the folks we want to invite to the wedding." It came to about sixty people.

"I think we can manage that," I said, since I was acting as her mother.

We smiled and went home to plan and arrange the wedding, which came off beautifully. It had taken only six days! And I've heard recently that it has been a good marriage.

In the next few days I wound up my business, packed my belongings, and headed for the hills to Hazelwood, where Bernice was living with all the children. Correspondence with Delhi and Bombay confirmed that no ships were leaving for awhile.

Chapter XIII

The Long Voyage Home

There was quite a group of Presbyterian missionaries on the train from Allahabad—medics, agriculturalists, educational personnel, etc. How wonderful just to be able to *talk* to someone after all those days of silence! The clickety-clack of the train's wheels brought joy to my soul as it took me farther and farther away from the Siwait mission.

Bullocks plowing in the fields, water buffaloes submerged in stagnant pools, groves of heavy-leafed mango trees, little whirls of dust on the open field, stands of sugarcane, smoke hanging above villages at dusk, women drawing water in their gleaming brass vessels, a small circle of men squatting around a fire in the dark—unchanging rural India.

The big station of Lucknow had innumerable vendors calling their wares as they paced up and down the platform, red-uniformed porters moving by briskly with unbelievable piles of luggage on their heads. Well-dressed ladies and men emptied out of the higher class bogies, while others waited to find their reserved places. Brown myna birds scurried along the platform, and crows hovered about picking up banana peelings and bits of food. After half an hour and the blast of the whistle, the train moved slowly out of the station.

Early the next morning the foothills of the Himalayas rose beyond cultivated fields and the jungle in the background. The air was already cooler as we pulled into Dehra Dun, the end of the railroad. There was another bustle of porters with luggage, all heading to the exit gate where I surrendered my railway ticket. Then a small crowd of drivers descended on all of us, each urging us to use his taxi for the twenty some miles to Mussoorie. Looking back down the curving way, what a beautiful distant view one had of the Doon and the Siwalik Hills!

The Picture Palace stop was the end of the road. Open-faced shops lined the roadway—fruit stands, general merchandise, cloth, jewelry, photo and post office. Landour bazaar was rich in smells—roasted peanuts, bananas, curries, woodwork and canes, jalebi sweets, piles of tobacco, and body odors from perspiring rickshaw men. Rhesus monkeys chattered from the wall along the road and clambered over tin roofs. Schoolchildren in uniforms carried book bags, while a loaded mule train pushed people aside as it threaded its way along the bazaar road. There were no cars then, as there were some twenty years later when I next passed through Landour Bazaar.

It was good to be back in Landour and to see the shiny rain-drenched needles of the Himalayan cedars. Landour was a Presbyterian stronghold. The mission took over Woodstock School in 1877 from the "London Society for the Promotion of Female Education in the East." It was established chiefly as a girls' school, but now was coeducational and international. Woodstock was noted for its music school, with fifteen or more pianos on the premises.

The mission meetings here were a great contrast to the ones I had been used to. It was at this meeting I was accepted into the Presbyterian Mission and assigned as trainer for the nurses at the hospital at Fatehgarh, U.P., until transportation back to the States was open. There were several doctors and nurses on staff, whereas I had been the only medical person in Siwait.

I shared a bungalow with a lady doctor and another nurse. Several families had small children, one of whom gave us a couple of real scares.

As I was returning to my house from the hospital one day, I saw a pair of little legs sticking out of an irrigation drainage hole. On the other end of the legs was Danny Taylor, who had fallen into the water and had to be quickly resuscitated.

Another time, Danny was licking a spoon which his mother had used to beat some chocolate fudge. As he skipped along, he slipped and fell, automatically performing a tonsillectomy. I took the bleeding boy home, where we flushed him out with cold water. He was fine. I never heard if the tonsillectomy job was complete or not.

In 1943, the war clouds were growing darker and closer. The Japanese had not only taken Singapore and Penang, but had also made landings on the eastern shores of India which, thank the Lord, were repelled. The American Embassy in Delhi was urging all Americans not performing essential war duties, especially women and children, to proceed to Bombay to leave for the U.S.A. I felt I should go, as my agreement with the Presbyterian Board was only "until transportation to the U.S. was available." I knew my three brothers were already in the armed services and Mother was not well.

Most of the news was bad—Britain seemed to be making a last stand. It was in this confused world that we looked for a way to return to the United States. As a nurse, I thought I might be able to accompany some disabled service men. A number of other missionaries were also looking for passage. Finally, word came from the American Embassy that a ship would be sailing from Bombay soon.

I sent my baggage on to Bombay and wired for reservations. The ship was filled to capacity and extra berths had been added.

The *Dominion Monarch* was not a class A ship, but was much better than nothing at all. On it was an assortment of passengers. There were numbers of British and American troops, quartered in third class, and there were three doctors aboard, returning for health reasons. We civilians were placed in second class, and I was given a cabin with the Duchess of Guthrie, a Christian Scientist traveling back to her mother church in Boston. Since it was wartime, we had to keep portholes closed and show no lights. Therefore, she elected to move out in the companionway and sleep there, clad only in a sheer nightgown.

At mealtime or a little before, she would hurry to the dining room and quickly make up sandwiches of the bread and cheese and coldcuts already on the table. She would tuck her goodies in her Boston bag and then hand out her booty to the soldiers who eagerly received it. The soldiers found that food from second class was much better than theirs, so at one meal of tripe and onions, they trooped into the dining room, filled their plates and, at a given signal, turned them upside down on the clean tablecloth and refused to eat. The resulting conference brought a definite improvement to the quality of the food.

We were in convoy, zigzagging our way to Durban, in East South Africa. Suddenly there was a crash! We had rammed the *Duchess of Richmond*, and the convoy came to a halt for several perilous hours. Fortunately, no submarines showed up. We proceeded on our way and reached port safely.

That morning we were back out at sea—headed for Australia —when suddenly the ship turned about and we headed in the direction we had just come from. Our ship was needed to transport prisoners of war from the North African campaign. We were to be in Durban for the duration, we were told.

I had no money, so I went to the Zulu hospital to get a job. They had a place for me and I began my orientation the next day. Meanwhile, we civilians had to leave the ship. Our luggage was all piled on the dock protected by only a thin tarpaulin. We had to find accommodations somewhere. Hotels were crammed full, so I called some old friends, who made room for me and four of my missionary colleagues.

We were in Durban for two weeks. I had started my work at the Zulu hospital when word came there was another ship. Gathering our belongings, we hurried down to the docks. It was a little Spanish ship going as far as Capetown. It had been in drydock for years and was not very seaworthy, so it hugged the shore. To add to our discomfort, the ship was heavily infested with cockroaches—not the little household variety, but the huge ones. We were so glad the ship could not make it any farther than Capetown.

As we were nearing port, I went up on deck and saw the first officer coming in my direction, carrying a little black box.

"Is that, by any chance, a telephone?" I asked him.

It was. I had friends of our mission in the city and asked whether I could let them know we were coming into port. As a result, they were there to greet me by the time we got off the boat.

I went home with them for the evening, and the next day, one of my colleagues remarked, "Why, Juanita, you have friends in every port!"

Well, not quite.

We were then ordered back to the docks. The Castle Line had a ship setting out across the southern Atlantic, and we boarded the *Cape Castle*, a great improvement to that little Spanish vessel. An hour out, the captain announced that there would be a meeting of all captains of ships in the lounge, one of the most unusual announcements I had ever heard, and one I probably would never hear again.

It was the middle of summer and oh, so *cold*. The sea was very rough, and as I lay in my bunk, I resolved not to get into lifeboats if the order came, but just to stay in bed and go down with the ship.

We reached the Falkland Islands on Sunday morning. The sun was bright—such a'calm scene after what we had been through. People were making their way to church, and it was an inspiration just to see them moving along. Then westward we sailed through the Straits of Magellan. The sun came up about 10 a.m. and set soon after two.

The aurora australis was electrifying. The sky was filled with brilliant color; I have never seen anything like it since. After dinner that night, I went back on deck to see whether there were any colors left. In every direction the water was aflame with a bluish glow, as though methylated spirits had been poured over the surface and set afire.

I ran downstairs to alert my friends. They had seen phosphorus on water before.

"But nothing like this, come and see."

So, up they came on deck and were awed at the massive beauty. The water coming out of the faucets was blue fire.* One of the men wondered what it would look like coming out of the shower. There it was sparkling with beauty.

"And wouldn't one look like a ghost under the shower?" He didn't show us.

We spent an uneventful journey up the coast of Chile. Street rioting in Valparaiso prevented us from landing, so we continued northward.

Beyond the Panama Canal there were still submarines about, and we constantly had to be on the alert. All passengers had

---

* The result of the large quantity of guano deposited by the gulls on the shore.

taken two hours watch duty on the bridge for the past two months. As we proceeded up the Atlantic coast, passengers became more and more restless, nearing journey's end at last. When the New York skyline loomed out of the mist, I just stood there and tears rolled down my cheeks. Ninety-three days since we had left Bombay, and sixteen years since I left home for India.

It was June 26, 1943, and my sister Toni was waiting for me. She had become a very successful businesswoman, dealing in clothing of her own original design. Toni had a beautiful new suit of the latest fashion laid out on the bed for me.

Then Toni had a phone call from our brother Bob. He was in San Bernadino and wanted me to come see him before he shipped out for the South Pacific. I bought my tickets, but could only get a roomette as far as St. Louis.

"Everything is full," the railway clerk told me.

"If you should have a cancellation, would you please let me know?" I asked.

The lady behind overheard me and stepped up. "I have a roomette from St. Louis westward, if you would like to share it with me."

We found that we were both from India, she from the south—Puna—and I from the north. Mrs. Jordan was most gracious, and it was wonderful to travel with her.

Brother Bob met me at the San Bernadino station. What a transformation! He had been only eight when I left for India in 1926, and here he was, an officer in the army! How smart he looked in his uniform. We had a wonderful time together before he had to leave for Batan. Later, he was injured at Layte and sent to New Guinea for a long recuperative hospitalization.

From Southern California, I returned to Decatur, Illinois to be with my mother. We had talked over the telephone, but I had not seen her yet. She was the warm, affectionate one in the family, but now even my father seemed to have forgiven me for going off to India. While home, I went over to Millikin University to see about my credits. Fortunately, the college president knew our Waukesha institution and gave me full credit for the subjects taken. I was registered, and when they evaluated the credits I had, they classified me as a junior. This was because I had passed high in first division in my Senior Cambridge examination. Two semesters at Millikin were followed by the University of Chicago for summer school. By January 1945, I had my bachelor's degree.

Realizing I needed more knowledge, I looked around to see where I might study for a master's degree. There were only two places that interested me—Yale and Western Reserve. I chose Western Reserve in Cleveland, which became a good experience.

During this time, I found opportunity to give talks at various churches and institutions around Ohio. There, at Western Reserve, we had a group of nurses and doctors interested in missionary service. Dr. Harvey Fraiser and his wife would have become missionaries, but he had a severe allergy. Therefore, the mission board members felt he was a poor risk, but he was still embued with a fervent missionary spirit. This had been evident all through his medical practice, in Obstetrics and Gynecology.

I have had occasion to visit him since, at his softly-lighted office in Spokane. In one wall is a niche with a long collage of a beautiful robe and sandaled feet. A spotlight on it emphasizes the beauty of the cloth and its warm texture. In front of the painting is a carved bench and a kneeling rug. When a disturbed patient comes in, Dr. Fraiser asks her if she would like to step over to the prayer bench and kneel and place her hand on the hem of the garment. Then prayer is offered, and the patient usually rises with a new light on her face and a peace in her soul.

It was while I was at Western Reserve that I got to know Kate (not her real name). She confided in me that she had gotten away from home at last to go to college and begin a career for herself. Her mother had died when she was in her early teens and since then she had had to be mother to her younger brother and wife and companion to her father, who was very lonely.

Kate evidently told her father about me, for I began to get notes and gifts from him "in gratitude for what you have done for Katie." Some of the gifts were expensive: two dozen red roses, a copy of Ayn Rand's book *Fountainhead,* and a dozen pair of nylon hose which, during the war, were almost impossible to get through regular channels.

Then one weekend Kate asked me to go home with her to meet her father. By this time, I was intrigued and anxious to meet the man. When we arrived, I found her home was a large three-bedroom house. I was well received, and then Kate announced that she had a date that night and asked if I would mind if she went out. Her father would take me to dinner and entertain me.

At dinner he began to talk about my life as a missionary and how I was missing out on all of the good things in life. He asked if I had read the copy of *Fountainhead*, quoting a few passages to me. I owed it to myself to get into the stream of life and find my own self-fulfillment, and to learn what life was all about, he argued.

When we arrived back at his home, he immediately suggested we get into our robes and slippers and have a good talk in comfort. I went to my room and had slipped off my clothes when the door opened and in he came.

From his evening conversation, I had gathered that he was interested in me, but I had expected some talks leading up to, perhaps, a proposal of marriage. I was disappointed. I had hoped that this would lead to a relationship I could enjoy after so many years of abstinence, not just an affair.

He told me that he always had his satisfaction when he wanted it, and Kate had supplied the partner. Now she wanted to free herself of him and date others, and he was desperate. She had sacrificed ten years of her life to his needs. I was not willing to do this.

We went back to Cleveland the next day. Kate did not ask me what happened, nor did I tell her. She was free, and could now look around and find herself a husband. I went on my way, resolving that if I had to get my sexual satisfaction that way I could do without. My philosophy was very different from Ayn Rand's.

Banares, the Holy City, is a favorite place to bathe in the sacred Ganges. Wealthy Hindus have built palaces on the banks of the river. They leave a passageway for pilgrims to pass through to bathe.

On holy days crowds flock to this sacred spot. Once every twelve years it is a very propitious time to bathe, called the Khumb Mela, and at the six-year interval is the Adhi-Khumb, also propitious, bringing millions from all over India.

The dhobi (washerman) brings his clothes to the banks of the Ganges to wash and then spreads them out on the ground to dry. He stands in the water and beats the clothes on a stone slab.

The Indian mail hut Embassy in Bhimphedi.

Below: The clerk checks my passport while squatting on the ground.

Boy carrying a live young buffalo in a basket, his legs folded up.

At right: Our bus had seen better days.

The tomb for Radha Swami which his devoted followers are building. This truly magnificent edifice may one day rival the Taj Mahal in beauty. It was begun some time before 1926 (when Juanita first saw it), and these two pictures taken in 1983 show the progress made in 57 years.

It is estimated that the building will take another fifty to one hundred years to complete. There are no modern tools in use in the building process, and the workmen labor in silence. There are signs posted saying, "Please do not talk to the workmen as they are meditating while they work." The picture at the right shows detail of the arch in the picture to the left.

Below: The Taj Mahal at Agra, India.

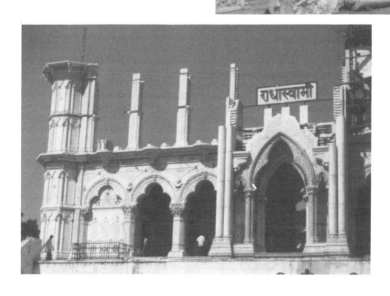

Left: Congratulating Jawahar Lal on becoming Prime Minister (1947).

Below left: With my sister Bernice on a visit to Jaipur.

Below right: Pundit Nehru's visit to Farukhabad.

Left: Bob receiving the second edition of his *Birds of Nepal* from G.U Mehta of Vakil Press, Bombay.   Right: Visiting with Vijaya Lakshmi Pandit and her daughter Chandralekha in their home in Dehra Dun.

BOOK FIVE

*INDIAN
INDEPENDENCE*

1947-1953

Chapter XIV

Freedom At Last

These were worrisome years for my mother. All three of her sons were in the armed forces, and one had been wounded. It was then that she decided to move to California to be near several members of her family. She had been there just three weeks when the war ended.

"Now my boys can come home," she thought. But on that very day, the day peace was declared, she died. It was indeed a bittersweet homecoming for us all.

My work for the master of nursing degree continued to be a challenge. When the weather in Cleveland was warm, it was good. But when winter came, I was ill-prepared for it. I did not have the warm clothing I needed, for my resources were meager. One night that winter, my phone rang. A Mrs. Dingle asked me to come to dinner the next evening. I was surprised at the invitation and said I would be there.

The snow was two feet deep, and I toyed with the idea of staying home to keep warm. At the last minute I decided to go. The Dingles had a palatial home and several cars, and I had hoped they might send one of these for me. But I left my apartment and had to face the elements on my own. It seemed a long walk to the bus that would take me to the Dingle home.

While at dinner, Mr. Dingle asked me, "What do you need for your hospital in India?"

"Among others things, we badly need some sort of vehicle which we can get over bad roads," I suggested.

"Then let's go down to the agency tomorrow and order the type of car you need," Mr. Dingle urged.

So it was that we picked out a Jeep station wagon for our Fatehgarh hospital. But it wasn't until summer vacation that I could take possession.

Sammy, one of the missionaries from Fatehgarh, was in the U.S. and was planning to return soon. I asked her to take the Jeep on the ship with her, as I had to stop on the way out to evaluate nurse's training programs in the Philippines, China and Thailand. She consented.

It was a brand new vehicle, but if we could put 6,000 miles on it, it would become a used car and the duty in India would be much less. So we drove and drove, visiting numbers of national parks on our way west. The road along the steep grade above the Snake River was muddy and Sammy was driving. We slid a bit this way and that.

"You know, I have never driven in mountains before; this is fun," she exclaimed, as I looked down over the edge of the road with a several hundred foot drop.

"Let me take the wheel, Sammy," I pleaded, but nothing doing.

How we managed to get down to the level road I don't know. It was a nightmare.

Sammy had gone on ahead to her ship and I volunteered to get the jeep onto the dock before five o'clock, when the ship was due to sail. After an adventure down a one-way street and a resulting discussion with a police officer, I rolled onto the dock just in time.

After finishing my studies at Western Reserve, I had a few weeks to myself before I needed to pack for India. I had heard much about the good work that the Frontier Nursing Service* was doing, and this was an opportune time to visit their facilities in Kentucky; I might glean some knowledge I could use in India.

I was met at Hazard by a vivacious nurse called Cherry, who became my guide and mentor and who showed me how the nurses served the vast mountain area, both by delivering babies in their homes and by bringing difficult cases to the little hospital in

---

* The Frontier Nursing was founded by Mary Breckenridge in England to send missionary midwives to the "primitive peoples of the Kentucky Mountains."

Hazard. I was then outfitted with the navy blue uniform and tie and knee-high boots, which she called Wellingtons, and we rode horseback the next morning to an isolated village to check on a woman who had a case of albuminaria with hydramnios.

What a wonderful country, with its deep woods and rushing rocky streams, where our mounts enjoyed drinking the cool water as we passed through. Announced by several dogs, we found the patient waiting for us, propped up in a wicker chair with a patchwork quilt thrown around her. Cherry checked her vital signs over carefully and examined her urine.

"I think we'll have to bring you in to Hazard. We need to have you close so the doctor can treat you, dear. I'll go back and we'll make the arrangements."

The patient seemed relieved that she would be under good care.

As we left, Cherry said, "It's not the close villages that are our problem. Tomorrow, Kitty and I will take you by plane into a village deep in the mountains. Leave your suit and boots outside your door tonight, so they will be ready for you in the morning."

How we slept after our day in the fresh mountain air!

I awakened early to the bright throaty call of a redbird. My boots and suit of yesterday were neatly cleaned and pressed at my door. I opened the curtains to see a beautiful cardinal just outside my window. Soon Cherry came, accompanied by a friend whom she introduced as Kitty.*

"She will be with us for the day with her trusty Cessna."

She took us to the little air runway in a very old Scout Master, the British version of our Jeep, and soon we were tucked in the Cessna and winging our way over one green-firred mountain range after another, with an occasional rooftop and hut peering out from between the greenery and dark shadows of the pine forest. We came to a place that seemed to have no opening in the mountains—just a vast amphitheater of forest—and we began to make a turn. Down, down we went in circles, until the floor of the huge sugar bowl came up to meet us. A meadow, from which Kitty shooed the cows as she approached, provided us a soft

---

* Kitty was a major during the war, piloting transport planes from England to France.

grassy landing. From here we would walk to a rustic unpainted log house not more than a furlong away.

This was a happy visit. A beautiful baby girl had been born one month before in this house and this was the first check-up of mother and ˋchild. It was weighed, checked and hugged, and Cherry pronounced, "Mother and baby doing fine."

I felt right at home with the Frontier Nursing Service and would have enjoyed staying longer, but I had to move on. Through the Student Volunteer Movement, I was asked to visit and talk to medical and nursing schools of the Eastern seaboard, which involved schools at Wilmington, Delaware; Boston; Washington, D.C.; and Johns Hopkins in Baltimore. I was nervous and apprehensive, but I enjoyed meeting students interested in missionary service.

As I entered the main door at Johns Hopkins, I saw straight ahead a large sign which read:

LECTURES TONIGHT:
6:30 p.m. Dr. Blalock & Toussig   NEW HEART TECHNIQUES
7:30 p.m. Juanita Owen   MEDICAL CAREERS IN MISSION

I froze when I saw the lecture hall with its high-rising seats and the little podium down in the center of the pit. I listened through the Blalock-Toussig presentation, which was quite new at the time.

When my turn came, I walked down the aisle and stood waiting for the room to clear, but with the exception of just a few, nobody moved, so I began. I gave a quick resume of the different types of medical work available in various countries and the crying need in the Third World for both doctors and nurses.

I returned to New York with my report and found another request.

"Now that the war is over, we hear reports of nursing schools wanting to open up all over the Orient," Dr. Dodd said. "We need to know their plans and how we can help. We'd like you to stop over en route to India and look into this. The war has awakened these countries to the need for nurses and also had broken down some of the prejudices against girls going into nursing."

He spoke of China, Thailand, the Philippines. Japan was out, as no passports were being issued for Japan by the State Department.

In the Board Rooms in New York, a Mrs. Kerr said, "I have a sister-in-law in Tokyo, as assistant secretary to MacArthur, I'll drop her a line and tell her you're passing through."

A week or so later I was on a ship bound for India. As we neared the lovely islands of Japan, I pulled out my passport and there it was, plain as a neon sign: "NOT GOOD FOR TRAVEL IN JAPAN. DO NOT ASK TO GO ASHORE, IT WILL NOT BE PERMITTED."

As our ship passed through the blue-white haze over the harbor water and pulled up at the pier in Yokohama, I stood at the rail, admiring the beauty of the morning light on the distant hills. I was saddened that almost the only buildings standing were tall smokestacks surrounded by rubble walls. In between them small vegetable gardens had been planted, and here and there a straw-hatted man seemed to be pulling weeds.

A limousine bearing the American flag and the standard of General MacArthur drove up and stopped at our gangplank. A lady in western dress got out and waved up at our ship. She spoke to the guard at the bottom of the gangway, then resumed her spot right below me, but very, very far down. I moved a few paces forward and she moved up, then I went a few paces astern and she moved down. Finally, a Mr. Owen, who had been a missionary in Japan before the war, stepped out on the deck.

"They're paging you on the loudspeakers, Juanita," he informed me.

I answered the page hoping it might mean that I would be able to go ashore, as I badly wanted to do so. Sure enough, it was Mrs. Kerr who was paging and I went down to meet her.

"I've been waiting some time," she said. "I'll take you for a drive around, and since I have four passes, you can bring three others if you like."

I thought of Mr. Owen and included him and two friends, and off we went to Tokyo, flying MacArthur's flag. Devastation was everywhere, except for the Imperial Palace surrounded by its moat and the few unscathed buildings that MacArthur had ordered saved for use as his offices after the surrender. The gardens of Tokyo were still beautiful in spite of the rubble around.

The people were solemn and pensive and walked along the streets with their little bundles under their arms.

Our next port of call was Shanghai, and two ladies from the Women's Medical Hospital met me and entertained me royally. There was tension in the air, though, and not knowing the language or customs of China, I confined my survey to the school of nursing—its vital statistics, curriculum, and post-war aims.

Next was Manila, where I boarded a plane to Dumaquete. There, Mary Marquis had been appointed dean and was in the throes of planning a School of Nursing for Silliman University. Mary had been a classmate of mine at Western Reserve, so I knew her well. She had had basic nursing, but no courses in education, nor curriculum planning. She was reaching out for help as she wired the Board (Presbyterian) asking that I might stay a while and help her.

The reply was favorable.

For several days, we took books, papers, contract forms and a lunch down to the beach house and, in our swimsuits, put together the four-year curriculum for the School of Nursing, and wrote up contracts with the science, humanities, and other faculties of the university. We submitted these to Dr. Carson, the president of the college, for perusal and discussion with the other deans.

But it was not all work. When the sun began to set each evening, we would walk along the beach and gather shells and swim in the surf, letting the spray cool and refresh us. Dumaquete was a very pleasant assignment, indeed. But I needed to be on my way again.

My next stop was the School of Nursing at Ling Nang University at Canton (now Guangzhou). When I visited the school, I felt tension in the air and, not knowing Chinese, I could not validate the feelings I had. The anti-American antagonism was almost palpable, and only a very short time after I left, the borders were closed.

On my BOAC flight to Bangkok, I found takeoff in one of the flying boats an exciting experience. The harbor at Hong Kong was full of sampans and junks, and before takeoff, the pilot had to clear the area. So, round and round we circled in the harbor, until he had cleared space enough, and then with a mighty splash and billows of water, we were airborne. The plane had three sections—one was for seats, the second was a lounge, and above the seats were the berths. The service was excellent, with white-gloved stewards, silver service, and an excellent cuisine.

On arriving in Thailand, I took the train to Chiangmai and arrived at McCormick Hospital, finding myself among old friends from the war years. Dr. and Mrs. Cort had had to evacuate Chiangmai and walk over the Burma Road into Assam and India, just ahead of the invading Japanese. They had only the barest of belongings with them when they finally arrived in Fatehgarh. They had worked with us, helping in the Memorial Hospital until the end of the war.

While they were in Fatehgarh, I had assisted Dr. Cort in surgery. It was difficult for him as he had cataracts in both eyes. I had to dye all our sterile linen a dark green, so the reflected light of the white linen would not close his irises. This allowed him to see around the cataracts. I always had to catch small bleeders for him and tie and sew up the places that were hard for him to see.

In Chiangmai, we relived the war events, and I was happy to learn that the Thai Christians had buried and hidden the Corts' silverware and valuables and had handed them all back, intact, upon the couple's return at the end of the war.

During my stay, Dr. Cort did me the honor of taking me down on the train to Bangkok, where he showed me the sights of the city and introduced me to the royal family.*

My time was running short. I wanted to reach Delhi before the Independence Day celebrations, which had been stepped up to August 15. Bidding Dr. Cort goodbye, I took a plane for Calcutta, arriving at 3:30 p.m.—just the hour Mahatma Gandhi was due to arrive in the city.

The road in from Dum Dum airport was lined with ruffians armed with knives, and here and there bodies were lying in the gutter, some covered with blood.

Calcutta has been known for centuries as the city of Kali, the

---

* He had had the young prince in his class as a medical student and, on his return to Thailand, Dr. Cort ordered the body of the ex-king to be exhumed and examined, as he felt somewhere there had been foul play.

Hindu goddess of destruction and violence. Kipling called it the "City of the Dreadful Night," alluding to the massacre at the "Black Hole of Calcutta."

The monument to it had been torn down, but the legacy of Kali still activated atrocities of unbelievable magnitude, as the city was then filled with 400,000 beggars, lepers, homeless people and gangs of hoodlums armed with knives, claws, and pointed steel prongs that could scalp a person with one blow and put out eyes equally swiftly.

"What has happened?" I asked my driver, his full beard telling me he was a Moslem.

"Don't you read the papers?" he asked.

I confessed ignorance, as I had just arrived from Thailand.

"We are going to kill all the Hindus and take this part of the country for ourselves. It's been ours for hundreds of years and nobody can take it from us," he swore.

We came to Dharamtala Street and he stopped his car.

"This is as far as I go—this far and no farther! Across the street, you can get a taxi with a Hindu driver; that is, if you can get across. You can see there is fighting going on. You'll be lucky if you're not killed."

"But I have this luggage. I can't carry it all alone," I demurred.

"Take what you can and I'll watch the rest until you come back across for it."

I started to cross the street and two young boys, not as interested in the killings as in the thought of earning a few rupees, came to my rescue. I managed to get a taxi to take me through the bedlam down Dharamtala Street to Sealdah Station, in the midst of the shouting and brick-bats and glass bottles flying in every direction. I could only hope that Gandhi's arrival would make the people see reason and cease their killing.

At Sealdah Station, the train was crowded and very noisy. I sought out a second class compartment marked "Ladies Only" and, once inside, locked windows and doors and turned out the lights, hoping no one would know I was there. Though from what I could learn, there was no animosity against the English this time, or Americans, but Hindus against Mohammedans and Mohammedans against Hindus, a thing I had not known in my earlier experience in India.

Sleep was scanty, and I was tired and frightened from the day's turmoil. And tomorrow everybody who could possibly make it would be headed for Delhi for the big celebrations. The trains were already jammed with people hanging onto the outside steps and almost as many on the roofs of the coaches as inside. The train finally pulled out and the noise of the shouting and fighting was drowned out in the clickety-clack of the wheels.

The morning dawned pink and orange and augered a good day. Delhi seemed peaceful and there was an air of expectancy everywhere. On the parkway to Viceregal Lodge, stands were being erected and workers were stretching bunting and garlands on every lamppost and signboard. My taxi turned at the Kashmir gate into Old Delhi and to the Cecil Hotel, where Miss Hotz greeted me warmly, as usual.

"I didn't know if you would make it," she said. "They moved the date up, as I wrote you, and I thought that might spoil your plans. Well, get along to your room; the *chaprasi** will take your luggage. Then come in for a spot of tea. You must be famished."

Shortly after sundown, Miss Hotz and I donned evening dresses and mounted our carriage for New Delhi. The air was heavy with the scent of jasmine, and wafts of breeze from the trees carried the fragrance of the queen-of-the-night blossoms. We passed the old Red Fort in a blaze of light, as each turret and minaret and dome was garlanded with electric bulbs, and yellow, green, saffron and white bunting festooned the walls and gateway.

We passed through Kashmir gate into Old Delhi bazaar, where the marketplace had little oil lamps and candles everywhere, like a galaxy of stars twinkling in every nook and ledge. The municipality had given out thousands of candles, so each hut could participate in the festive occasion. Bicycles, carts and donkeys were decorated. Garlanded elephants heading for New Delhi were draped in rich gold and scarlet tapestry, with golden chains and bells tinkling as they ambled along. In Connought Place, the shops vied with one another in their decorations and presented a panorama of glittering festivity.

* Orderly.

Entering the main thoroughfare, Kingsway,* to Viceregal Lodge, it was noticeable that the statue of Queen Victoria was missing. Total emptiness filled the cupola that had housed the Marble Queen since 1858, and now displayed streamers of the tricolor flag of the new India.

Viceregal Lodge was never so resplendent as this night. The decorations were elegant, with flowers, flowers everywhere amid a happy mixture of Indian and English motifs. Of the thirty-seven salons and three hundred forty rooms in the Viceregal mansion, four of them were ballrooms, two on each floor, each eighty feet in length. These were festooned with gold-spangled ornaments around lights that were lowered for dancing, and music in each of the ballrooms was varied to suit the tastes of the young and not-so-young Indian and European couples. The tunics of the musicians were trimmed with ribbons and tassels under the flood of light. The music was mostly European and melodious songs of yesterday—songs of Ireland, Italy, raucous jazz, schottisches, waltzes, foxtrots, Spanish rumbas or tangos. Whatever the mood was, it could be found in one of the ballrooms.

There were also bands out in the gardens, far enough removed from each other so they did not clash. European ladies in long satin and brocade evening dresses and Indian ladies in silk saris of all shades of blue, rose, daffodil, mauve, magenta, pink and gold and sliver dotted the garden. These were set off by the dark or white tuxedos of their escorts. Many wore brilliant red and gold turbans or simple white Gandhi caps.

We wandered through the lighted flower areas, admiring the iris, lilies, antirrhinum, phlox, petunias and canterbury bells, and the great circle of roses blooming in spite of the August heat. We were told that over one thousand gardeners were employed, and they were very much in evidence in their spanking new blue-gray uniforms. An announcement had been made that souvenirs were for the taking—ash trays, silver spoons, stationery—and many guests were taking advantage. Marked as they were with the Viceroy's insignia, the items would never be needed again.

As we neared the midnight hour, the principals began to take their places in the rotunda—Rajagopalacharia, the new presi-

---

* After Independence, the name was changed to Raj Path.

dent; Pandit Jawaharlal Nehru as prime minister; and Lord and Lady Mountbatten. Lady Mountbatten wore the cornflower-blue silk sash of the order of the Crown of India. His Excellency wore on his right breast the gold aiguillettes of the world's most exclusive company, the Order of the Garter, the Order of the Star of India, the Order of the Indian Empire and the Grand Cross of the Victorian Order. The ceremony was brief and, as the rotunda was far too small for the thousands of guests, we listened over the loudspeakers in the garden, cool and uncluttered at this hour. At the stroke of midnight, a new India was born.

Back at the hotel, we caught a little sleep before the noisy gray crows and the early roosters in the alley behind the hotel awoke us. I had timed my arrival in India to precede the arrival in Bombay of the ship that was bringing my heavy luggage and the new jeep station wagon that had been donated by the Dingles to the Fatehgarh Hospital for an ambulance. I planned to go from Delhi directly to Bombay, take clearance of the ambulance and drive it back to Fatehgarh in the U.P.*

I left New Delhi by the late afternoon mail train, riding alone in a ladies' second-class compartment. Not long after the train started, I was startled by the sound of shots very close by. The train stopped abruptly out in an arid no-man's-land with not a house or village in sight.

I looked out the window and people were jumping off the train, running away and hiding behind small shrubs, if they could make it, but many fell in their tracks as the gunfire struck the fleeing figures. Peering out through the shuttered windows, I saw bodies thrown out of the third-class compartments like bags of grain and became afraid that any minute they would crash my compartment doors.

Then I heard a man's voice, an American voice, say, "Lady, are you all right?"

I ventured to open the shutter and said I was still alive, but terribly frightened.

"I think you'd better come in here. We'll look after you. This beats Chicago gangsters at their worst."

---

* In English, U.P. stood for United Provinces. In changing to Hindi, the initials do not need to change. The U.P. now stands for Uttar Pradesh.

He helped me cross over the steps outside my compartment onto the first-class steps.

"What is going on?" I asked.

"It's evidently a band of Mohammedan hoodlums, gondas, judging from the Hindus they've killed. How come you are traveling alone at a time like this?"

I explained my errand and he introduced himself as a reporter from the *Chicago Tribune*. I told him I was from the Chicago area and knew Robert Trumbull of the *Tribune*.* We talked a while, and eventually the train started up, leaving white bundles, human bundles, there in that open, desolate area for the vultures and jackals.

When we arrived in Bombay, the morning sky was aflame with all the colors of the rainbow, accentuated by dark clouds coming in from the north. The monsoon sky in India is indeed one to paint. But then, if you did it justice, you would be accused of exaggeration. It is even doubly grand when reflected in the ocean.

I had the Jeep serviced for the long trip to the U.P., adding a couple of five-gallon cans of gasoline for good measure. People in the mission office in Bombay felt I should have a man with me, as service stations en route were nonexistent. A man named Arlan McClurkin was going to Allahabad and kindly offered to drive with me to Cawnpore, which was the turnoff road to Fatehgarh.

Imagine a trip of over 700 miles with no service stations and no rest rooms! Arlan and I decided we had to have a definite understanding. If either one wanted to answer the call of nature, we would stop and observe the rule, men to the front of the car, ladies to the rear. At night, we stopped at government rest houses, which provided rooms and beds and shower facilities—but no bedding and no food, so we carried our own. Often the shower was just a large #10 can for dipping water from a huge earthenware *chatty*** onto the cement floor. But, however performed, a shower was very refreshing after the dust of the road had pene-

---

* Robert Trumbull was a member of the Press Corps who ate at the Round Table at the Cecil Hotel in Delhi.

trated every pore of one's skin, not to mention nostrils, eyes and ears.

Fatehgarh was now home, at least for the next five years, and I found much to be done: nursing classes to teach, anesthetics to be administered, housekeepers (sweepers) to supervise, gardens to attend and always the morning prayers and people to help with their problems. We had a lovely lady doctor who was kindness itself. She was always ready to soothe a fevered brow or stroke a restless infant as she walked through the hospital or crowded clinic, offering to each person a smile that was pure love coming from her inmost soul. You just knew it

But she fled from obstetrics! She would call me to see a patient who was in for delivery and then disappear, saying, "I'll be praying for you." Never mind if it was a podalic version case, forceps delivery or hydrocephalic—she was nowhere to be found.

One day she told the relatives of a patient who was in with delayed labor that the baby would come in "about two hours." It was a transverse lie. I got the woman ready for the doctor, but she was not to be found, so I went ahead. By the time I got things ready, did a version, and delivered the baby by breech, it took just about two hours. They went off singing the doctor's praises.

"She was wonderful. She told us just when the baby would arrive."

And a huge *dali** of sweetmeats, fruit, and nuts were sent to the doctor who "correctly predicted just when the baby would arrive." Of course, she shared the fruit and sweets with the staff and many of the patients, and everybody was happy.

We had gotten into our regular routines in the hospital and things were going well with the new students in the nursing school, when a telegraph message came from the Indian Christian Council in Delhi. Serious fighting had broken out in the city and environs between Hindus and Muslims, with many casualties. Would we send help?

Dr. Carl Taylor, Dr. Lois Visscher and Kay Slager, R.N. volunteered to go. I would take six nurses in the station wagon, together with as much medicine as could be spared, as well as bandages, splints, and disinfectants.

* Tray.

The Dingles would have been happy to know of the station wagon's first errand of mercy. We could not have done without it. On arrival in Delhi, we were immediately assigned to Humayun's Tomb where 150,000 Moslem refugees had been huddled together for days, under indescribably filthy conditions, with no sanitation, no water, and no shelter from either the torrid August sun or the torrential monsoon rains.* We had six babies born that first day, with no water to wash them or our hands once our small supply gave out. There was no place to put the newborns except under the mother's knees, making a tent with her sari. We tried to find a little shade for them near the old wall, but when the rains came and washed away the mud that held the rocks together, they came tumbling down. We then attempted to get the refugees to help us dig a long narrow trench for burying placentas and to use as a latrine, but even able-bodied men sat with their heads in their hands, totally inert from shock.

Water was our primary concern. We had to have water, so I got into the station wagon and headed for Viceregal Lodge. Lady Mountbatten was quick to react to my request. She phoned the military base, and by the time I got back to Humayun's Tomb, the water wagon was there, literally mobbed by refugees with their *lotas*.** After that, the water wagon came regularly and saved the lives of many dehydrated from days of sun and wind. Meanwhile, the nurses carried on, dressing wounds, delivering babies and comforting the sorrowful. Trucks also were sent with tents and some camp cots, which took care of only the most desperate. The rest slept on the ground, in mud most of the time.

In a few days we had used all our medicines and supplies, so I went back to Viceregal Lodge. Lady Mountbatten was standing outside her office, talking to a tall blonde woman in a large Kelly green felt hat and carrying a large felt bag to match. Obviously an American—a Texan, as I soon found out. I stood at a little distance, but stepped up at a nod from Lady Mountbatten.

I said, "Excuse me, ladies, I hate to interrupt, but this is a matter of great urgency. We have run out of medicines and supplies at the camp. All the shops that have not been looted have

* See *Freedom at Midnight,* page 383.
** Brass water pots.

been boarded up and we have no place to turn."

"Let me first introduce Mrs. Salisbury," said Lady Mountbatten. "She is just leaving for the airport to return to the States. I think we can help you. Why not take my plane and get supplies from Bombay?"

"Wonderful," I replied, then a second later asked, "But what will I do for money? Nobody in Bombay knows me and I have no credit there."

Reaching into her big green bag, Mrs. Salisbury pulled out a wad of American dollars and put it in my hand.

"I think this will help," she said.

Lady Mountbatten had already alerted her *chaprasi** to call the airport to have her plane readied, and, thanking both ladies, I hurried off—for a quick change at the "Y" and then to the airport.

The plane was a sixteen-seater, with an all-blue interior decor and a lot of room at the rear. The crew wore white uniforms, and there were white antimacassars on the seats and even white coverings on the floor.

As soon as we were airborne, I took out the wad of money and began to count it. I was amazed—there were thousands of dollars. That would buy a lot of supplies! We especially needed morphine and anesthetics, and all the other medications, of course. In particular we needed a five-gallon drum of vaseline, which was useful for mixing medications, for sunburned babies and children, and for many other uses. The can was greasy and not too clean outside, and the staff spread the floor of the plane with newspapers before setting it down.

It was great to be able to bring in so much help. Day by day we continued serving the needs of the refugees, who now were lessening. Busses with military escorts would come and take away loads of those who elected to go to Pakistan, choosing exportation over the life of fear and danger they were facing in India.

The nurses gradually returned to their work at the Fatehgarh Hospital, but Dr. Visscher, Kay Slager and I were asked to go to Amritsar, which was the last outpost of refugees before crossing the bridge into Pakistan. There, many husbands waited, having

* Messenger

lost their wives and children to abductors. All along the Grand Trunk road, streams of refugees passed each other. Moslems fleeing for their lives to Pakistan were on one side of the road, and on the other side, Hindus who had been caught in Pakistan at the time of partition were carrying their few possessions and hurrying to India, trying to escape being caught on the wrong side of the border. Except for near the bridge, the boundary was still hazy and ill-defined. Clashes between the two columns of refugees were frequent, and the ditch beside the road gave evidence of the toll of lives lost—arms, feet, other human parts only half buried.* It is estimated that ten million refugees passed down that road in the greatest exodus of all time. Tens of thousands of young girls were abducted from that roadside crowd and taken into their abductor's villages. Many a Hindu girl was forced to break her caste rules by eating meat and then repeating the Mohammedan prayer, thus becoming a Moslem.

This was the case with the wife of a man who met with us in Amritsar. He said she had been taken to a village in Pakistan, beyond Lahore. He knew the name of the village and begged us to intercede for her return. Covering him with a rug, we put him on the back floor of our touring car. With a sepoy at each door, one on either side of me, guns at the ready, and with papers authorizing our errand, we crossed over into Pakistan. Both sides had accepted our group and had made us honorary magistrates for the interim.

When we got to the village in question, we asked the headman to bring out all the women who had been abducted. He lined about twenty on the village wall and we asked our refugee man to pick out his wife.

Even from a distance, he had no trouble saying, "That's her, the third from the right," and he began to weep.

"Bring her down so I can talk with her," I told the village headman.

She faced her husband without a sign of recognition.

"I don't know him; he's not my husband," she affirmed unblinkingly, while her husband broke down in tears.

I noticed a tattoo in Hindi on her left arm and, pushing back

---

* See *Freedom at Midnight*, page 469.

her sari, read aloud the words, "Ram Ram Sita Ram."

"You're a Hindu girl," I said. "You'll both have to come inside this room and explain this to me in private."

Inside the room with the door closed, they rushed to embrace each other and the wife asked, "How are the children?"

"I have Ganga Din, but I thought you had Shushila," he said.

"No, I haven't seen her," she answered.

They both wept for the daughter they would probably never see again. After we signed a few papers in the presence of the headman, we took her back to Amritsar with us.

This is just one case that comes to mind. There were hundreds more. We went back and forth between India and Pakistan, working as hard and fast as we could, knowing that our time was short. If the women got pregnant by their abductors and we took them back, they would be killed. After four months, we had to discontinue our efforts, for by that time, most of them would be pregnant and we would only be reaping more death and sorrow. It was a sad end to our endeavors.

So, it was back again to my regular work at Fatehgarh—teaching anatomy, obstetric nursing, midwifery, and supervising the wards, conducting deliveries, and giving anesthesia when there was a need. We always tried to extend the services of the hospital into the community, and conducted Red Cross classes and first aid in the schools. The World Health Organization gave me enough B.C.G. vaccine to inoculate all the schools of the area, as well as our hospital staff. This took extra time, but we felt it was well worth it if all these children could be protected from tuberculosis. We also vaccinated for smallpox, and it is gratifying that the disease is almost unknown today in that part of India.

But I was called away again. A telegram from Delhi said that Dr. Hoskings had contracted bulbar polio up in Almora and asked me to go and help him. I wired back that I would need an iron lung and other equipment.

They arranged for me to meet the plane at Bareilly and fly to the foothills at Haldwani, where a car would take me to Ramgarh. From there, we would have to walk the remaining twelve miles to the outpost, where Dr. and Mrs. Hoskings and their two boys were. I knew from past experience that most equipment available in India, be it government or mission property, was old and often unreliable, so I took a few tools and black electric tape (to repair bellows and wiring), and plenty of sponge rubber. Also, since most American equipment was 110 D.C. and India was 220 A.C., I took an AC-DC converter and a 220-110 stepdown transformer. A lot of equipment to handle and keep track of !

By the time we reached Ramgarh, it was dark and the village people had gone to bed. We called and called and the only ones we could arouse were the dogs, who set up terrific commotion, making it hard for anyone to hear us when we finally did arouse them.

Finally, the driver and I explained our errand. It was important that we get porters to carry our equipment up to Muktesar right away. We could not wait until morning or the man would die. We begged, cajoled, and promised them outrageous *bakshish,* * if they would help us.

People began to come out of huts and they all reminded us, "Sahib, don't you know this is tiger country, man-eating tigers at that?"

Yes, I was well aware of the stories of Jim Corbett—"Man-eaters of Kumaon," "Chowgarh Tigress," etc. Don't think for a minute I didn't think of them.

"But there are enough of us," I countered, "we can ward them off. We'll have one man go ahead and beat a tin can, and I'll bring up the rear on a horse, if you can find me one. [I had seen one tied nearby in a paddock.] You'll get enough money tonight so you can feast for several days."

Soon, our party was formed—the noisemaker was in front, the porters with the baggage in the middle, and I brought up the rear, and each empty hand carried a hurricane lantern. I had a motive in being last. I wanted to make sure no one dropped out on the way, for one piece of equipment missing and all could be in vain. The forest was eerie at night. A speck of quartz or a cigarette wrapper would reflect our lights and look for all the world like tiger eyes. Occasionally, the call of an owl or the sight of a nightjar's eyes on the path would startle me and make me shudder, and I felt goose pimples rise.

It was past midnight when we arrived at the bungalow. There

---

* Payment, sometimes a bribe.

Dr. Hoskings lay surrounded by a group of his students and faculty who, with the Institute doctor, were giving artificial respiration in ten-minute relays, and had been doing so for over twenty-four hours. At his head stood his wife, looking pale and weary with her long vigil.

I set to work opening up the packages and the transformer and converter (both of which *were* necessary, as it turned out). When it came to the respirator itself, I found the bellows were sadly in need of repair. They would never hold air, so I patched until they *did* hold air. Next I cut a collar from the foam rubber to fit the patient's neck and the opening in the machine. We got him in and, wonder of wonders, it worked!

The next thing was to teach him to breathe and swallow with the machine. He made a supreme effort and it was functioning. Now the tired men who had worked so valiantly could go off, one by one, to get some well deserved rest. It was two o'clock in the morning.

I sat by his head, soothing him and trying to persuade him to trust the machine and let himself go off to sleep. At length Mrs. Hoskings went to her room for some rest.

The following morning he was quiet and breathing with the machine, but in the afternoon he got restless. He wanted me to write some notes for him about some eggs he had incubated for his research on lung mites in cattle.* I did, and then he quieted down. I went to my room to take a nap, while Mrs. Hoskings sat with him. It had been thirty-six hours since I had slept and I was soon dead to the world.

About 5 p.m. I was roused by a commotion, with crying and wailing. I went at once. They had taken Dr. Hoskings out of the lung and he was gone.

"What have you done?" I shouted.

The Indian doctor spoke up first. "It was Mrs. Hoskings' orders. She said her husband didn't want to live the rest of his

---

* Dr. Hoskings was an entomologist from the University of Michigan working at the Muktesar Veterinary Research Institute on developing a vaccine to fight lung flukes in cattle. He said the eggs he'd inoculated should be hatching on a certain date and he wanted me to ask his colleagues to read his notes and follow up on his research.

life in the machine. He wanted to die, so we took it off."

It was a sad sight the next morning as our funeral procession went down the mountainside—the coffin and porters, two young boys on horseback, two women in dandies and a group of followers on foot. My heart was heavy, and prayer, once again, my only support.

In February, Julia Bock Harwood, a friend from Decatur, Illinois, wrote that she was coming to India and would like me to escort her around. She was a typical lecturer and wanted not only to see the Taj Mahal at Agra, and the sights of Delhi, but, she added, "Can't you arrange an interview with Prime Minister Jawaharlal Nehru while we're in Delhi?"

I was not in the habit of inflicting interviews on my friends, but for the home folks, I would try. They would be expecting me to oblige her.

So it was arranged, though I was terribly embarrassed when she demanded several poses of him at his #1 York Street home. He was far too busy with affairs of state for this, having only assumed office the previous August. I apologized for the intrusion, but he did give us an extra few minutes to go up the grand circular staircase to "view his etchings" — a collection of his favorite cartoons of himself. The one I enjoyed most was that of Churchill leaning out the second floor window at No. 10 Downing Street and chatting with Nehru as he clung to a rope outside the window, doing the famous Indian rope trick. It was captioned, "Talks at a high level."

We worked our way northward toward Darjeeling, stopping for the night at Ghoom to make the climb up Tiger Hill to see Mt. Everest. We arose at four o'clock to a heavy mist and dark clouds and had climbed for over an hour when we met tourists coming down the mountain.

"It's no use going on up," they said. "It's beginning to rain and there is no chance of seeing Mt. Everest today."

Julia and I looked at each other and decided to go on. A drove of monkeys in the trees were chattering as they sought shelter from the rain.

After climbing another hour we were nearing the top. The rain stopped and the dark clouds began to rise like a curtain in a theater. Here, before our eyes, was the pink glow of sunrise on the top of Mt. Everest and, over the mountain, the tail of a gorgeous comet. Below were all the colors of a rainbow, as the sun shone on the mists of the valley. It was awe-inspiring and we filmed it with both movie and still cameras.

When I got back to Fatehgarh, I told my colleagues of the comet.

"What comet?" they asked.

I couldn't find anyone who had seen it, much less one who could tell me its name. It was some years later that I read in Harrer's *Seven Years in Tibet* that he had seen the comet from Tibet and called it, "The Great Comet of 1948." One of the loveliest sights I have ever seen. It paid to climb the mountain that day.

Summer was approaching. It was already so hot that butter turned liquid and milk soured before it could be used. Water kept fairly cool in the *chatties**, but we were without refrigeration. The garden was turning brown and no amount of water would keep the flowers and shrubs from drying up, it seemed. It was time to think of where to spend our vacation.

Kashmir beckoned—that lovely valley where the water is as blue as the sky above it and as reflective as a mirror. Some of us reserved a houseboat there and headed north, from Rawalpindi to Jamuna and, after 200 miles of road winding up and up through pine forests and scented balsam, we came to our journey's end, Dal Gate. Groups of Kashmiri boatmen all clustered around, noisily begging us to hire their boats. Names and signs on the *shikaras*** put us into hysterics: "Mae West," "Buckingham Palace," "Yellow Peony," "Here I Am, But Where Are You?" and some more clever ones, but all with the additional sign, "Fully fitted with happy spring seats." We tumbled into the "happy spring seats," which were upholstered with springs and fancy embroidered mattress covers and curtained around with the same embroidered material for privacy.

Our houseboat was luxurious. Persian carpets covered the floors, the bedrooms were lined in a row down one side, each

* Earthenware jars.
** Small skiffs.

having a small room for bath and carry-out toilets. Out the window of our boat, a kingfisher perched on a stump among water lilies waiting for his breakfast. The air was cool and refreshing. On the shoreward side of the boat was an apple orchard in full bloom and a bulbul (nightingale) was singing his very heart out. I, too, wanted to sing, "Pale hands I loved beside the Shalimar, where are you now?"

Salesmen of every description came flocking around our boat and, sitting cross-legged on the floor, would spread their wares around them—candy, fruit, vegetables, beautifully embroidered cloth articles, woodwork of carved walnut tables, stands, bookends, and brass and silver creations fit for a king. We decided to wait until we had seen the shops before buying.

"Suffering Moses' " shop had articles of the best workmanship, and we drooled over his wares. He told us his name was given to him by Lord Redding when he was Viceroy of India. The Viceroy had written to him about an order and had misheard his name— Safar Hosein Moses—so he wrote the letter to "Suffering Moses." This caught on so well that other shops sought intriguing titles such as "Joyful Jacob," and "Cheerful Charlie." So many claimed to be the best that Sobana called his shop "Sobana the Worst."

Several of us went shopping on the *bund** to look at the lovely carved walnut furniture. We were in Sobana the Worst's shop when a crowd gathered and Jawaharlal Nehru entered. I had told my friends about my visits to Nehru's home in Allahabad and how I knew him. But today, he ignored me, much to my chagrin.

"Well, so that's the way it is!" I thought. "He does not want to recognize his friends. Well, so much for him!"

A few moments later, he came over and sidled up to me. "Juanita, do you have any aspirin in your purse?" he asked. "I've got one helluva headache."

I reached into my bag and produced the aspirin and requested a glass of water from Sobana. I felt better.

Since Fatehgarh was a cantonment, there was not much in

---

* The river bank.

the way of amusement or social life, but when the commander of the regiment, General Cariappa, came to town, a dance and party was held on the lawn of the district cantonment house. And since women were in scarce supply, all of us at the hospital received invitations. Dr. Cort thought we should go to give the regiment a little diversion from the drabness of their lives. The lawn in front of the officers' mess sloped down to the river and was a carpet of green with flowering shrubs edging the borders. A full moon added to the scene.

They had hired a band whose repertoire contained very little music one could dance to. They played "Isle of Capri" tolerably well, and play it they did, not once or twice, but dozens of times. Instead of being wearied by it, everybody found it amusing and had a good time in spite of it.

The colonel of our Fatehgarh regiment and his wife had completed their tour of duty in India and would be leaving the next day for England. They were at our house for dinner that evening when she complained that they had lived for two years on the banks of the Ganges. She had hoped her husband would shoot a crocodile and she had visions of going back to England with a crocodile handbag and shoes, but it looked like that was not to be.

The next morning their very excited chaprasi came over to our house with a note. "I've got my crocodile bag!" she wrote.

They had been having breakfast on the veranda overlooking the river when they spotted a croc sunning on the bank. The colonel jumped up to get his gun which had already been broken down and packed in his duffle bag. It took a few moments to reassemble his gun. The gardeners and servants had spotted the croc and were shouting and gesticulating frantically. He got in a shot just as the croc slipped into the river.

Walking along the river bank where it had lain, they spotted blood. "It's mortal blood, Sahib." said one of the boys and he wanted to go in after it. Taking a rope he jumped in and tied it onto a leg and together the boys pulled it ashore. It was quite dead and the colonel's lady had her bag!

Soon after my arrival in Fatehgarh, a barrister from Allahabad brought in his four-year-old daughter, a polio case. Her doctor had put her in a full body cast and had told the parents she would never walk again. The father was not convinced.

I had handled polio cases before. In fact, back in Cleveland, I had had as many as twenty-four patients at one time, with four or five in iron lungs. This experience was now standing me in good stead. I told the father that I would try to help his little girl, if he was willing to leave her in the hospital for two or three months. He agreed and left his wife and daughter and returned to his law practice in Allahabad.

I knew the child's muscles had no chance to recover their strength if we left the cast on, so I removed it. I started hot compresses and massage, and after two weeks, I could see an improvement. She was a sweet child and very cooperative. We would make her treatments into a game.

I would say, "Now, we are going to flex your gastrocnemius muscle." And she would repeat it, for she loved the word.

When her father came for a visit later, she said, "Look, Daddy, I can flex my gastrocnemius muscle," much to his astonishment.

We made two parallel bars for her to support herself and with the aid of these, she would try to take a step or two. Our Indian colleagues looked askance at such procedure. "You are going to ruin her muscles," they predicted.

On the contrary, she began to get the use of her lower extremities. She would inch her way forward on the bars by throwing her body first one way then the other.

"Oh, but brides do not walk that way; they walk straight forward. Try," I encouraged.

The progress increased daily, so rapidly that after a three-month period in the hospital, she was discharged, fully recuperated. I can see her yet, running across the station platform, into the arms of a very happy father.

About this time, the Presbyterian Board assigned Dr. Carl Taylor to Fatehgarh Hospital. He had graduated from Harvard Medical School and came well recommended by the Board. Not long after his arrival, there was talk of his joining Dr. Robert Fleming on a three-month bird-collecting expedition in Nepal for the Field Museum in Chicago. But the Mission authorities felt they could let Dr. Taylor go only if a qualified doctor could be found to substitute for him while he was away. Shortly, word came from Dr. Bethel Fleming in Mussoorie that she would be willing to return to her old hospital and fill in for him for the necessary time. Such an agreement was acceptable and Dr. Taylor left at the end of October to join the Nepal expedition.

It was good to have Dr. Bethel Fleming at Fatehgarh again. Some of her former colleagues were still there, and numbers of the Indian staff loved her. Dr. Bethel was a practitioner who would listen and take suggestions. In the past, doctors with whom I'd worked would put nurses in their place. Not so with Dr. Bethel. Although experienced in surgery, gynecology, obstetrics and pediatrics for more than fifteen years, she was alert and picked up anything which would improve her practice. She lived in the bungalow with Mary Taylor, Dr. Carl's wife. Her son and daughter played in the compound with the Fredericks' children and others.

Communications to and from Nepal were difficult, and several urgent letters to the expedition elicited no reply, increasing concern for the welfare of the group. Anything might be happening to them in such an unknown area. Nepal was still a closed country to foreigners. Although members of Rana families could come out and spend time in their second homes in India, that was not for the ordinary Nepali.

At last a letter did arrive, saying that the expedition was going well. In places where Europeans had never been seen before, people turned out en masse to have a look at these strangers. Dr. Taylor reported crowds of patients along the way until he wondered whether the two trunks of medicines were going to hold out.

Suddenly in the middle of January, after two months of no communication, Carl returned two weeks early and fifteen pounds thinner. He had escorted another member of the expedition, Harold Bergsma, who had come down with typhoid. Following several days of high temperature, the case had looked very serious. When the fever came down and he was strong enough, they put him on a litter carried by four Nepalis. Travelling up and down steep hills, it was difficult to keep the patient on the bed. They walked fifty miles, from Pokhara to Tansen, in six days. Dr. Bergsma his father, had come to Tansen to meet Harold and take him home.

"That is how I got back here two weeks early," Carl explained.

We were full of questions about the other two members, who had remained to fill out the three full months of the expedition. Both Bob Fleming and Robert Bergsaker were in good shape.

"As for myself," revealed Carl, "there was one day I thought I was living my last.

"I was about 14 or 15 thousand feet up on Dhaulagiri, where we had climbed with two Nepali hunters to collect birds at a high altitude. We especially wanted specimens of the giant snow cock. I left Fleming and the two hunters warming themselves around a fire in a light snowstorm, for I thought our quarry might be on the other side of a nearby ridge and wanted to have a look. At that spot, there was a steep drop of about 3,000 feet.

"Picking my way, I suddenly slid on a sheet of ice covered with snow. As I gained momentum and neared the precipice, all sorts of things flashed through my mind. I recalled having read that should you find yourself in such a position, take your gun and press the butt as hard as you can in front of you. I doubled forward and tried it. It worked; my movement toward the edge slowed. I stopped only a few feet from a fatal plunge, and slowly inched my way off the ice onto the rocky soil. I was so shaken I just had to lie there a bit before starting back to our camp some 2500 feet lower down. It shook me up so badly that I did not tell the others about it until four days later at our base camp in Jomsom," concluded Carl.

We were greatly relieved to know that the remaining two men were hunting in the lowland *tarai**. Permission to remain in Nepal ended on the thirty-first of January, at which time Mr. Bergsaker would return to his station in India and Dr. Fleming would head for Mussoorie. So it was that Dr. Bethel and children also got their train tickets to Dehra Dun, traveling by bus the rest of the way to their home in the mountains.

The Presbyterian authorities still could see little relation between mission work and an ornithological expedition, but this certainly helped open the doors of Nepal to foreigners, and particularly to the Flemings*. This, followed by my visit to Kathmandu

---

* See The Fabulous Flemings in the Bibliography.

three years later, helped pave the way for us to become a part of the new emergence of Nepal.

My primary job at Fatehgarh was teaching nurses. This was all done in Hindi, but when there was a scientific term which had no equivalent, I would use the English term, plus gestures, to illustrate what I was trying to get across. Most of the nurses in training came from surrounding areas, though a few were from as far away as Lucknow. And we had the two girls I had sent from Kathmandu.

When Uma and Ruki arrived at Fatehgarh, U.P., they only spoke Nepali. It did not take them long to learn Hindi, as these languages had the same Devanagari script. English was entirely new to them, but they made progress in this language, too. At times, the girls were quite homesick, especially at Dusserah time. Like Christmas in the West, it was a long holiday when all who could manage returned home to be with the family. People wore new clothes and they would go to the homes of relatives and sample the goodies made in their home kitchens. It was the highlight of the year and I could understand why the Nepali girls felt despondent at this time.

A job I inherited was that of taking care of the gardens and grounds of the hospital. It was a blessing, since I always like to be out and get my hands in the good earth. There were numbers of flowering trees; the *amaltas* was so beautiful with its large clusters of golden flowers, and the brilliant red blooms of the *gul mohar* contrasted with its cool green leaves in the hot spring months. As the fragrance of guava and mango trees permeated the air, pink-flowered quisqualis vines clambered up brick walls and the orange trumpet flowers were a mecca for the sunbirds.

On either side of our driveway were hedges of poinsettias ten feet high. Sturdy cannas filled several plots, while petunias and nasturtiums added color to the gardens. Occasionally, rhesus monkeys would drop down from nearby trees and quickly swallow a tasty nasturtium "tossed salad."

At dusk, large fruit bats visited the guava orchard for a feast on the ripening fruit. The watchman had tied up a gallon tin with stones in it, and would agitate the rope energetically, shocking the "flying foxes" and clearing them out of the trees.

We often had flowers that we would pick and take to the patients.

The missionaries' quarters were well built, the Taylor home especially artistically furnished. As little Danny Taylor and his mother were walking to church one Sunday, he asked, "Is this God's house?"

"Yes, it is," his mother assured him.

After a thoughtful moment, he said, "Ours is better than His."

From then on, Mary saw to it that the chapel looked more attractive, actually taking some things from their own home so that the contrast which little Danny saw wouldn't be so great.

We welcomed Dr. Carl Fredericks and his family to Fatehgarh. Carl would point out that his family was international. He was born in Hamburg, Germany, his wife in Korea, their first child in the U.S. Now here they were in India, where they had to begin on a new language. Nepal held a fascination for the new doctor, and it was no surprise that he elected to spend the winter holiday of 1951 in western Nepal with his wife and children.

Later his signature was on a letter to the government of Nepal, along with several others, offering to do more permanent medical work there, rather than for just a few winter months. This was the letter I saw on Mr. Gurung's desk in the summer of 1952 in Kathmandu.

At that time, I had advised His Majesty's Government to extend an invitation to highly qualified medical personnel in India who were with the mission boards, for they would have the welfare of the people at heart and would not be involved in money-making for themselves. A year later, King Tribhuvan Bir Bikram Shah and his government accepted the suggestion and permitted several Christian missionaries to start medical work in Nepal. Bethel Fleming was one of them, as was Carl Fredericks. The door was finally open.

All along the border were missionaries who had been studying Nepali and praying for an opening. God was working out His plan and, at last, it had come.

The days melted into weeks and the weeks into months, until it was time for me to return home and enter Columbia University. I was booked on a ship of an Italian line, and since there were six weeks before Columbia began its new term, I elected to linger in

Italy. I rented an apartment in a boarding house, averse to arriving in New York too early and having to pay enormous rental rates. Instead I spent much of the time resting on the beach, which was just what I needed for I was in good condition when I went on to Copenhagen, Denmark.

It was the night of the United States elections and I wanted to go right to my room and listen to the returns on television, but all television sets were already taken.

A pompous American gentleman at the purser's desk spoke up. "Looks like we are out of luck. Why don't we go down and find a bar and watch there?"

Not knowing him, I declined. "If you get any news, do let me know. I am in room 210."

It was nearly morning when the phone rang and my friend said Eisenhower had won! Then he told me he was General Young, second in command under Eisenhower at SHAPE headquarters in Paris.

"Let's go out and have breakfast to celebrate," he suggested.

After breakfast we went out for the day, touring Jutland and the coast of Denmark and Odense, where Danny Kaye had filmed *Hans Christian Andersen.*

Kennedy House on Claremont was a home for missionaries in New York, and that was where I stayed. I had only been there a few weeks when the telephone operator at the reception desk called up and said there was a couple to see me.

"Send them up," I answered.

In a few moments, there was a knock on my door. I was the most surprised person in all New York City when I opened it and saw Sir John Hunt and Lady Hunt standing at my door! They were visiting in the building and heard I was living there. Only a few months earlier, he had led the successful British expedition to Mount Everest when they put Edmund Hillary and Tenzing Norgay on the top—the first ever to make it.

We talked of old times, Sir John recalling the picnic sendoff on the year before, the reconnaissance climb of Mt. Everest in preparation for the recent full assault. It was terrific to see him again, so soon after his party's successful expedition.

Near the end of my first semester at the University, I had a call from the president of the United Nations, Mrs. Vijaya Lakshmi Pandit. She said that when her husband, Ranjit, died, he left a sum of money so that each of their three daughters would have a coming-out party on their 21st birthday. Chand's was next week and Mrs. Pandit had arranged for a party in the Jensen suite at the Waldorf Astoria.

"As you know, an Indian widow cannot go to a function like this unattended. Would you go with me?" requested Mrs. Pandit.

Of course, I would. I remembered an examination scheduled for the following morning at the university, but maybe the party would be over in good time.

Mrs. Pandit came for me at seven that evening and we drove to the hotel. When we entered the room, a crowd of guests had already assembled, including her three daughters. Chand wore a beautiful silver sari and the other two also had on striking saris. Mrs. Pandit moved on into the room, accepting greetings and chatting with numbers of people. I found friends at one side of the room and stopped a bit to talk. Among them was Osa Johnson*. I had never imagined her as the petite lady I now saw.

Then, I went over to greet Chand; she was radiant, as were her sisters.

About nine o'clock, I was looking for Mrs. Pandit to excuse myself, because of my examination the next morning, when the large doors swung open, revealing a huge dining room with an endless number of tables laid for eight people each. I was directed to a table with Dr. Lin Yutang and his wife, John and Francis Gunther, and John Day. What scintillating conversation! People who were only names to me before were very much alive, here and now! The elaborate dinner took two hours to serve, with waiters hurriedly filling final drink orders just before midnight, as blue laws prevented serving such after twelve o'clock.

It was then that I asked leave of Mrs. Pandit. It was not necessary for me to accompany her home, now that her daughters were with her.

Near the end of the final term at the university, I received a letter from the Presbyterian Board about returning to India. I made an appointment to see Dr. Leroy Dodds, who was in charge

* See *I Married Adventure*.

of the India work. I asked him what pension I could expect to have from the Presbyterian Board for my years of service with them. There was no suggestion that a concession might be made for the sixteen years I had been with my first mission, and there was no social security in those days. I would have the magnificent sum of $29 per month, he told me.

I said I did not want to be a burden on my family in later years and that I could not carry on under these circumstances. I would have to resign from the Presbyterian mission.

Back in my apartment, I remembered that Dr. DeVault, head of the medical department of the State Department, who had seen me at work in India, had said that if I ever needed a job, to call him. I put in a call to Washington, D.C. and soon had Dr. DeVault on the line. I explained that I needed to improve my financial status so that my family need not have to look after me in later years. He asked me to hold the line while he called the United States Public Health Service on Staten Island.

Then followed a four-way conversation ending with Dr. DeVault's words, "You are hired! I'll send you the security forms right away."

I sat down and wrote my resignation to Dr. Dodds. It was sad, but necessary, to end my twenty-seven year connection with mission boards.

The American Consular
Building at Guayaquil,
Ecuador.

Sr. Miguel Andrade Marin
and Clarence Falvey
study the blueprints of the
new American Embassy
office building.

The Embassy
office building,
Quito, Ecuador,
South America.

At left the little plane belonging to the Coast and Geodetic Survey which took Juanita to the outlying towns of Liberia where American personnel were working.

Liberian villagers enjoying themselves. When the men under the straw start dancing, they will leap up two or three times their normal height wearing grotesque masks.

The Diplomatic Corp marching in President Tubman's Inaugeral parade in spite of the summer heat and the sun. Instructions were "top hats, dark suits, and gre ascots." Monrovia, Liberia.

A laterite anthill in Ghana. These were bulldozed the day before Queen Elizabeth's visit but are rebuilt in a few days by the ants.

Upper right: A village in Ghana.

Above: Villagers taking their produce to market.

At left: A sweetmaker's shop in the outskirts of Accra, Ghana.

This dug out canoe is made from a single log. Young Liberian boys learn early to handle them in the ocean.

Preparing for a Liberian holiday when the man under the grass skirt rises up into a giant. Actually, he is holding a masked head on a very long pole.

Fanti fisher boats are very colorful, with primitive Liberian art designs.

BOOK SIX

WITH THE STATE DEPARTMENT

1954-1960

Chapter XV

Nurse Assigned to Liberia

My transition was abrupt and challenging.

"Where would you like to go?" asked Dr. DeVault. "We're just setting up a program of embassy nurses and you are number five on our list of choices. You can go almost anywhere."

"I would prefer a hardship post," I answered.

"How about Afghanistan? You've been in that part of the world for a number of years."

"That would be fine. I shall be ready to go as soon as needed."

"Well, that would be at once, as soon as you have filled out the necessary papers and they've been checked. We shall be glad to have a nurse in Kabul; medical personnel are much needed there," added Dr. DeVault.

Back in my apartment, I unearthed my suitcases and began to pack. In the next few days, I purchased warm clothing, including a pair of fur-lined boots. That part of the world is cold in winter, with no central heating, and there is always a problem with keeping one's feet warm.

When my preparations were nearly done, I had another urgent call from Dr. DeVault. An emergency had occurred in Liberia and would I go to Afghanistan via Monrovia? A doctor was about to be appointed to Liberia and they needed someone to set up a medical center for him. This meant that my wardrobe had to be supplemented by some light clothing, so there was further shopping and preparation necessary before I found myself on a plane for Liberia. I was pleased with this change in plans for it would give me an opportunity to learn something of Africa.

Orientation with the State Department meant going to Washington, meeting my immediate boss and other members of the medical team. For the introduction to State Department policies and methods of procedure, we were taken into a room—all thirty of us—to meet Secretary of State John Foster Dulles. He sat at the head of a long table with the new appointees grouped around. After his pep talk, he asked if we had any questions.

"I have, Mr. Secretary," I said. "Yesterday when the newspaper announced that Gary Powers' U-2 was shot down over Russia, the president said he knew nothing whatsoever about the incident. Then today, the fact came out that he was on a mission of espionage which was planned for and well known to the government. Why is it necessary to lie? Isn't there some other way of answering? Surely, we are smarter than that."

"Well, Miss Owen," he said, "if lying bothers you, the State Department is no place for you."

I was troubled by his answer, but decided that in my medical work, I would not be obliged to answer such questions. I would do my job and keep my own counsel.

Monrovia has been called the "Tin Capital of the World." Flattened kerosene tins, used in layers on the roofs of the houses like shingles, shone in the sunlight as we flew over. We landed in Roberts Field in the Firestone rubber plantation. An embassy car was there to meet me and all formalities were taken care of.

The roadway through the rubber plantation was shaded by row upon row of tall slim rubber trees. All had a spiral cut near the base and what looked like little clay cups at the bottom. Black boys, wearing only short cut-off trousers, moved in and out of the trees with bamboo poles over their shoulders and buckets on each end, gathering rubber from the little cups. Their brown shiny backs and slow rhythmic movements seemed paced by the temperature rather than by the arduous labor involved.

As we left the plantation, we immediately hit a dusty, rutted road, with its traffic of jalopies and carts sending up clouds of reddish laterite dust, so we closed our windows, preferring the heat to the the dust.

And the vegetation changed from neat rows of rubber trees to tall palms, with undergrowth of shrubbery and young palms springing up around the mother ones. Here and there, we passed a house with lush hibiscus, jacaranda and oleander bushes surrounding it. Between, or in the rear, were shanties made of oil cans or shipping cases. Then, as we neared Monrovia, the houses increased and so did the dust.

Men and women were colorfully dressed, usually with a brilliant cloth around the head, a fanti print wrap-around skirt, and often bare above the waist, with bare feet or light sandals. The women carried their babies on their backs in a bundle tied around the waist, and usually they had a basket of groceries on their heads with another baby "in the oven," sometimes one, two, or three more in tow, all barefoot and wearing just "a smile and a string of beads."

I discovered there was only one paved street, and that ran past the president's mansion.

The American Embassy building was on Mamba Point, below which was a group of prefabricated houses, all alike. Mine was farthest down the hill, right above the ocean. There was a nice veranda facing south, where one could see the sun rise out of the ocean in the morning and sink back into the western waters in the evening. Besides the living/dining room and the bedroom, there was the kitchen, managed by my servant, Saturday. A couple of hammocks were slung outside on the screened porch; it seemed everybody used hammocks here. I would soon have plants around the house to make it more homey.

My place was situated about seventy-five feet above the sea, on a rocky promontory. When it stormed, salt spray would hit against the windows. We were only about 6° north of the equator, but there on the ocean the weather was delightful. Each morning there would be the breeze from the land with the scent of frangipani and jasmine. In the evening, the breeze was from the ocean, with its salty tang and cool refreshment. There were just enough clouds to reflect the setting sun, sending streaks of color across both the sky and the great expanse of the Atlantic Ocean.

From my home, it was only a five-minute climb up to the Embassy. Ambassador and Mrs. Jones were very cordial. A peon took me to the room I was to prepare for the doctor's office and clinic. It was a well-appointed room with a spacious desk of mahogany and attractive drapes at the windows. The equipment I had ordered in Washington had come, and I saw to the uncrating of the furniture, sterilizer, and examining table. We opened the instruments and put everything in its place.

The American TCA people at Camp Johnson, three miles away, also wanted a nurse and had me set up a similar room for them. Two public health doctors had their offices there. I divided my time between both places.

I wanted to know what health facilities were available in Liberia, so I undertook a survey and looked up various medical centers. I visited the Bomi Hills Hospital and the Firestone Hospital on the rubber plantation. This was a good place to send patients who needed hospitalization. Another location was Cuttington College, some distance out of Monrovia, which cared for women and children, and still another was the Methodist Hospital in Ganta, in the north area of Liberia. These places could look after certain medical needs, but when an officer of the embassy required surgery, I could send them to Walter Reed Hospital in Washington, or Bethesda Hospital in Maryland.

The American government had numbers of agricultural workers stationed in various parts of the country. Every two weeks, I would fly to outlying stations to give shots or medical aid. We used a little Cessna plane from the Coast and Geodetic Survey. Paul Bradley was the pilot.

On our first trip, we took off for Suakoko. As soon as we were airborne, Paul said he thought I ought to know how to land the plane, if necessary.

"But you're the pilot and I'm the nurse. I know nothing about flying," I remonstrated.

"Well, you see," replied Paul, who was a bit on the tubby side, "I have a heart condition and should I black out, you would have to take over."

"Now you tell me!" I exclaimed.

"Just set the plane down on the treetops and radio for help," he suggested.

I kept thinking of green mambas in the trees and prayed it would not happen.

During the first few days I was there, a couple in a neighboring house invited me to dinner. The other guest was the French ambassador. He was single and I was the only single American woman in the station. During the evening, my host and hostess made numerous suggestions that we should get together. The next week, the French ambassador said he was hosting a rather large party and asked me to act as his hostess. I agreed, using all the French I knew to make conversation and to help people feel at home. He was always cordial and over the next few months, invited me several times to his embassy.

All these years I felt that I was standing on the sidelines, watching the stream of life flow past. There were very few single women in Liberia. When American embassy women got together, they would talk of their children, their former assignments, or of the art objects they were able to pick up. The only other unmarried women were two black girls. One had a black companion, while the second was living with a French doctor.

Tom was boss in the embassy. He was a "Havad" man from New England who had a well-developed superiority complex. I was not at all taken with him, and when he asked me for a date, I wondered how I could avoid it. He was in my office at the time, and just then, passing the open door, were Dick and Harry, two young American men.

I quickly called out, "Tom wants to have an evening on the town. Let's all go."

So the four of us had the "date" together. It was a pleasant evening and in due time, Tom said he would drive the two men home and then he and I would go on to the French Hotel. When we reached the embassy gate, I complained that I felt dead tired and needed sleep before my heavy day tomorrow. I excused myself and we all went our separate ways, much to the disappointment of our host, who seemed to have other ideas.

Every week I kept expecting to hear that the doctor from the U.S. was arriving. A note from Dr. DeVault said that they had gotten several applications, but none of the candidates could pass the security tests. It also asked me to stay on, which I did, but I kept hoping that I might get a chance to use my fur-lined boots in Afghanistan. (I was completely unaware that those boots were being devoured in the basement of the embassy by termites!)

The Liberian scene was quite a contrast to what I had known for the past twenty years. I was now surrounded by a number of unattached males, a fact I had to get used to—very unlike our mission in India.

Another invitation came from the French ambassador for luncheon. To my consternation, he met me in a silk bathrobe and undershorts. He invited me in and proposed that we sunbathe on the roof before the meal, and then later enjoy a swim together. To me, this was too obvious. I tried to be gracious in declining his proposals and said that I would have to leave right after lunch. That ended my invitations to the French Embassy.

A great many Negroes whose ancestors had been slaves taken to America had returned to Liberia and become known as Americo-Liberians. Some of them achieved positions of power and wielded that power in unmerciful ways. If a person opposed them, they would just liquidate him, or have a member of the Leopard Society do so.*

One morning the ambassador's wife and I were on our way to church when we saw lying by the gate a woman whose heart had recently been removed. I thought that the Leopard Society had been inactive for some years, but discovered that such killings were going on at this very time, especially in connection with political campaigns, when leaders up for election would eat human hearts to gain power and to triumph in elections. Even the president had had his quota of human hearts stashed away in his refrigerator.**

Seeing this woman by the gate disturbed me very much, and Mrs. Jones called the police.

"Is the woman alive?" they asked.

"No, dead," she replied.

"Then call the sanitation department for removal. We do not attend to that."

A young African graduate, John Coleman, who earned a polit-

---

* The only requisite for membership was the wearing of a leopard skin and lion claws. Their victims bore all the marks of having been killed by a leopard, and no one would be convicted in a court of law. After all, a leopard had committed the crime.

** The same man was elected representative of the Methodist Church at its annual conference in the U.S. and greatly honored.

ical science major in the U.S.A., arrived back in Liberia with his American wife and small child. He felt that the country would be greatly improved if the two-party system of government could be initiated. I met this couple early and they were very warm and friendly.

John felt the procedure to achieve his goal was to form a second party to contest the True Whig Party in the next election. He gathered like-believers around him and planned to turn out literature to educate the people. To this end, he set up a printing press. Government authorities were appalled at such a move and at once set out on a course of exterminating the opposition.

The first newspaper was just coming off the press when men in military uniform raided the plant. There was no more printing, for the press was demolished and the building set on fire. There were continual threats, so the Colemans decided to leave Monrovia for their farm, thirty miles out of the city, where members of their family lived.

A notice was sent out to bring in John, or his father, dead or alive. Consequently, John had to hide in the sugarcane fields beyond his rubber plantation. While in hiding, family members brought him food and water. This went on for several days before the police got wind of where he was and went out to get him. There was gunfire at his home, and the armed forces set fire to the house, which in no time was a mass of flames. The wife and son escaped burned but alive from the inferno, but the grandmother died in the flames.

Walking back over the thirty miles of trails to Monrovia, the mother sought asylum in the American Embassy, for she was an American citizen. It was there she learned that her husband had been shot in the head, then his body riddled with bullets. His father, David Coleman, who was also hiding in the sugarcane, was discovered and shot. The next day the bodies, clothed in tattered rags, were strung up in the main square downtown where people were urged to take pot shots at them. I had to pass the square later that day. The sight was so gruesome, I had to turn my head and look the other way. That was the end of the Independent True Whig Party.

John's wife was eight months pregnant; her hands and feet, already burned, were cut and bleeding from the sugar cane, and she was exhausted from lack of sleep. I put her on my examining table, where I dressed her burns and cuts and gave her antibiotics, all the while talking to her about what had happened. She was worried about burying her husband and his father. A friend, Eloise, ordered two coffins from Firestone and arranged a burial. For this "subversive compliance" with the Independent True Whig Party, Eloise was implicated, and her husband, the minister of highways, was threatened with losing his job. She was forced to crawl on her hands and knees in front of the president to reinstate herself—which she did only out of her love for her husband.

Across the street where the embassy stood, we witnessed a most distressing sight. A Mr. Horace, also a sympathizer in the new party, was being hauled out of his home tied by his feet to the rear end of a jeep. He was dragged along the rough cobblestones, screaming, until his voice was silenced and his body was drenched in the dust of the road. His influence was ended.

National elections were held shortly after. There was a landslide vote for President Tubman and his party. He had now been in office eleven years and was likely to continue for some time. He had minimized the difference in government between Americo-Liberians and tribesmen, making it possible for tribesmen to hold seats in the House and Senate. Now, also, women who held property were able to vote. And education, health and economic development were given attention. The inauguration was in the offing.

The American Embassy building had been very poorly planned. There was not place to store anything. It was built on stilts above great rocks. A plan was formulated which would remove the rocks and make more space for storage rooms. This had to be done by dynamiting—a ticklish assignment, for blasting had to be done in the daytime when the building was occupied. A steel blanket was stretched over the whole area between the stilts, to prevent accidents during the blast. The operation lasted for two weeks during the sweltering days of September. It was led by a khaki-clad American engineer named Clarence Falvey.

One day, as I was walking home for a morning break, I invited him to my bungalow for a cup of coffee. It was a very hot day and my veranda was cool, open on three sides to the Atlantic Ocean. For the next few days, both of us looked forward to the coffee break. Clarence was fairly slim and very neat in appearance. He had said he was from Southern California and had been with this company on a number of foreign assignments. He was well-spoken and had been given heavy engineering responsibilities.

The inauguration came off as expected, with representatives of many countries present. Eisenhower had sent an American deputation including General Twitchel, Mr. and Mrs. Giss and others. All the men walked in the procession down the main street of town, wearing dark suits and top hats and sweltering in the heat. Posters and placards were carried, depicting all the revolutionist people falling into the flames of hellfire. Others carried banners of "Down With the Revolutionaries," or "Heaven Bless Tubman, Our Savior."

After the hot day of marching, the evening consisted of dinner and dancing in the executive pavilion. President and Mrs. Tubman led the grand march down the center aisle and, according to rank and station, other couples joined in. This lasted for most of an hour, to be followed by dances, and ending with another grand march at midnight. No one was permitted to leave until "Their Majesties" had said goodnight.

For several days the *Liberian Age* was filled with stories of Moses, a young man who had studied in Tuskegee and returned to his country with the desire of helping Liberia economically. He started a chicken farm across the St. Paul river and one day as he was bringing produce to market, the boat capsized and he was lost in the river.

His family and relatives called the diviners who said Moses was being held by the river spirits who would not let him go unless a large sum of money was paid them. When the payment produced no Moses, the family sued for breach of promise and failure to fulfill a contract—not a suggestion of fraud or the fact that they couldn't if they wanted to. Moses had long since been devoured by the crocodiles of the river.

Many of the customs of the villagers around focused on the unsophisticated young people in the city. At puberty, girls were taken to the hinterland, where secret camps had been made in the forests, and solemn rites were performed, to prepare them for marriage. One of these was the performance of a clitoridectomy (without any anesthesia), to make the girls more subject to their husbands and less demanding of sexual satisfaction themselves.

On the other hand, while the girls were away at these *sundai* schools, the boys were taken to *poro* schools, where they were initiated into the practices and lore of procreation and ways in which to keep their women submissive and obedient. One way was to hobble them with heavy brass anklets weighing twenty pounds or more. They did not often try to run away.

Back in Liberia, we had a visitor, Rev. Jim Robinson, a black minister from New York who had come through Monrovia with a group of preachers just a week before.

"What happened?" I asked. "I thought you were going all the way to the cape."

"That was our plan, but when we got to Dr. Schweitzer's mission, he asked me to sit outside on the veranda to eat my food. I was not good enough to be seated along with the rest of the ministers [all white] who sat at his table."

I was mortified. "Well, here you won't have that cross to bear."

Mrs. and Mrs. Hinke made him comfortable in their guest room, where he intended to stay until the group returned from their visit to South Africa.*

My workload was rather slack. I would spend the forenoon at Camp Johnson, several miles out of town, and be back in Monrovia for the afternoon. I reserved the first three days of the month to carry out visits to "out stations," where American personnel were working—such as Gbanga, Swakoko, and Ganta. The roads were something else again, as it rained almost every day, making travel difficult. And the bridge to Swakoko had two parellel logs for each wheel. One had to drive exactly between them to make the crossing.

The type of vehicle I was assigned to traverse these roads was a huge Mack truck. They told me in the American Embassy that the vehicle would also do for an ambulance when necessary. I had put in a requisition for a car or station wagon, but the

* John Gunther, *Inside Africa.*

charge d'affaires cancelled it in favor of a truck, which would also be capable of transporting loads for the embassy. Over those bumpy roads, such a vehicle was almost impossible. When it got stuck, it was too heavy to push.

We had a near quarrel over this truck. Soon after, when the charge d'affaires was ill and needed to be moved to the hospital in Bomi Hills, they suggested I use the Ambassador's Lincoln.

"Oh, no," I replied, "we have a special vehicle for transporting patients."

The assignment of living quarters followed the principle that families were each given a house, whereas single persons were assigned to places in "bachelor's quarters," which consisted of a small bedroom, with a shared kitchen, dining room, and living room. I was fortunate at first to have a house with plenty of room, but when a family arrived that needed my residence, I was given the bachelor's quarters above the engine room, to share with a staff lady from the embassy. We got along fairly well, except that rather than walk down a long corridor to the wash-room, she would leave her dirty clothes in our kitchen sink. It was impossible to wash my dishes and clean up until she returned in the evening to finish her washing. Eventually, the embassy assigned me to other quarters.

Not long after this, Ambassador Locker, who had been suffer-ing from high blood pressure, died. His widow had ordered a huge casket—so large it wouldn't go into a normal plane—so the American government sent a transport plane to take the body home.

I was asked by the Department to make a survey of medical facilities in West Africa to find if there was somewhere for Ameri-can personnel to get adequate help when emergencies arose.The Nigerian capital—Lagos—had no adequate facilities.

Ghana was my next stop and I was met by a man from the Embassy whom I knew from Liberia. I expected to be taken direct to my hotel but he suggested we go to the airport for breakfast and see the Queen's plane arrive.

"That's right, Queen Elizabeth comes this morning," I replied. "That will be most interesting."

Driving along from the airport, I noticed how level the raods were which normally are lined with ant hills five or six feet high. "They've bulldozed them but the ants will be back in a few days." A garden party was scheduled for the Queen that afternoon and she would be travelling this road. It must be perfect.

After an uneventful flight we landed at Libreville on the coast from where we were to take a plane to Lambarene in French Equatorial Africa to visit Dr. Schweitzer's hospital.

"Any hurry to get to Lambarene?" the pilot asked. "We'll be stopping here over the weekend. We'll put you up in a hotel on the beach," he added.

"No, no hurry," I replied. The little bus took me to the beautiful hotel right on the beach, where I had first-class accommodations and everything paid for by the airline. It was a restful weekend.

Before departing, I sought out one of the street cafes along the beach for luncheon. The places were all filled except for a table where only one lady was sitting. I asked whether I might share her table and she was happy for me to do so. It turned out that she was an American who had been selected by the Albert Schweitzer Foundation in New York to take his annual birthday gift to him. It was a considerable amount—$1,000 for each of the eighty-three years of his life.

I inquired what it was like in Lambarene.

She said, "Wait and see for yourself. It won't be long now."

The flight was called and it took only an hour to Lambarene. I knew it was not very far and was surprised that we had stopped so short of our destination for the weekend. When we finally arrived, Dr. Schweitzer's secretary and helper, was there to meet me. She had been living in Lambarene for some twenty years.

We slid down the wet clay slope to the water's edge and could look across the river to the famous hospital. Tied to a dock nearby was a beautiful launch, all newly painted and polished. I started toward it, although I was not prepared for such luxury.

"Dr. Schweitzer will not let us use that government launch, although it is free. We must cross in the dugout canoe," she informed me.

So, I put my luggage, what little I had, in the prow. The secretary, being a bit bulky, took a position in the wide middle portion of the canoe, while I sat a little toward the back. It was only a hollowed-out tree, without a seat or cushion, so there we sat on the bottom of the canoe and, as water splashed in, our nether regions became thoroughly wet. I started holding onto the sides of the canoe to keep my balance.

"Don't put your hands in the water," I was warned, "there are crocodiles."

So there I sat with legs stretched out in front of me and my bottom becoming wetter and wetter.

I looked across and could see Dr. Schweitzer himself, standing on the river bank. He had come down to greet me. He removed his hat from a shock of white hair and bowed. Our conversation was all in French. Now, we had the problem of negotiating the slippery, foul road up to the long houses made of bamboo, chicken wire, tin roofs and planks. The incline was so steep, the doctor took hold of my elbow to assist me. I kept facing him at all times, so as not to expose the condition of my rear.

I noted droppings of pigs and chickens on the path. The natives had no bathrooms and so, of course, they had to use the bank of the river. Dr. Schweitzer asked about my family. I was taken down a corridor between long houses and shown my cubicle. The doctor hoped I would be comfortable.

I had lived in primitive conditions before, but was not at all prepared for this. There were no windows. A long roll of six-foot-wide chicken wire extended the length of the long house. It was placed just below the over hanging tin roof. For privacy, one drew a white sheet—now tattletale gray—across the opening. In fact, almost everything in the hospital seemed to be the same gray color. But then, why not, when everything was washed in the muddy water of the river we had just crossed?

Animals, such as chickens and goats, wandered at will. Flies were everywhere. The doctor held that all living things were God's creatures, so why should they not be allowed to live, too?

We were called for the noon meal. Some eighteen people assembled, all white. We sat at a long, narrow table, I in the seat of honor, directly across from Dr. Schweitzer, who was flanked on one side by Miss Houseknecht, his secretary, and on the other by his wife.

There were a number of large bowls on the table. After a

prayer, we helped ourselves to food. I noted that about ninety percent of it was carbohydrates—potatoes, cassava, bread, yams, and breadfruit.

There were bits of other things as well. A servant appeared, bringing a dish with two small broiled fish and placed it in front of Dr. Schweitzer.

"My physician said that I need more protein," he explained, with a slightly embarrassed smile.

"And don't we all?" I answered, but the remark fell on deaf ears.

After the evening meal, which began with prayers, Dr. Schweitzer went to the piano, played a hymn, which the group sang, read a Bible portion and conducted prayers. I was there for five days, long enough to absorb the atmosphere of the place.

The next day, I made rounds with the doctor in his hospital, which was crowded with patients. The long building was divided into rooms, each about fifteen by twenty feet. On either side of the narrow main aisle were bunks for four. Then there was another series of bunks above these. Finally, in a space still higher up and reached by the means of center aisle ladders, was another series of bunks—twenty-four in all.

I noted that the uniforms of the nurses were stained with dirt. Little wonder when livestock wandered freely into the wards! And after stepping in feces and mud, it was distributed on each rung of the same ladder they had to climb and handle to reach the third tier of patients.

A young, personable and enthusiastic Danish doctor came to see me and wanted to talk. It seems he had been chosen for the foreign missionary field at a very early age. Not only his family, but his whole village in Denmark had taken part in helping him secure an education and medical degree so he could come to Lambarene.

"I don't know what to do!" he moaned. "With all these sacred little flies nothing is sterile. I can't practice proper medicine. And I cannot return to my home, since they helped me all these years to get a medical education so I could come here."

"There are many places in mission fields where you could practice," I said. "Why don't you look around and find a group who thinks much like yourself and apply to work with them?"

"Oh, I couldn't," he remonstrated, but he listened thoughtfully and knew that I understood his problem. The turnover in western medical personnel then was rather rapid. Many thought and felt like this promising young man.

Dr. Schweitzer liked pets; he had a pet cat that sat on his desk in the center of his office. A mosquito net-covered bed was at one end, and a narrow passageway led between his room and Mrs. Schweitzer's. In the center of the passage was his famous organ, given him by the Bach Society of Paris. At the other end, the doctor opened a bit of wire netting where there were two young antelopes, and he said that the animals wanted to greet me. If I would put my hand in, they would lick it, which they did.

"And now, would you like to have me play for you?"

"Yes, by all means," I asserted.

His six-foot organ was fronted by a narrow, sloping bench. He sat down and took more than half the space, as he was a big man. He motioned me to the other end of the bench and, grasping me by the thigh, said in French, "Come over closer; I play better with human contact."

He went through a group of Bach numbers. It was a bit difficult to prevent myself from sliding forward and not to be too close to the Great Master.

During the recital, his wife came in from the adjoining room.

"No one ever comes to see me," she confessed.

"Oh, I'll come over at once," I replied. But just then, the lunch bell rang. "I'll come right after lunch," I assured her.

After the meal, I went to her room. It was furnished with one table made out of packing boxes, one straight chair and one old canvas steamer chair. The tattered rug was the usual tattletale gray. On her table was one small #2 tin with a plant in it.

"I like flowers so much, and we have many at home. I recently planted a flower in the yard and put chicken wire around it for protection. Doctor came along and saw it and told me to take the wire away. He said that if animals wanted to eat the plant, I was not to prevent them. And of course, they did.

"I have this tiny plant left, so I keep it inside where someday I hope it will flower."

Mrs. Schweitzer had such pale skin that she looked like a little Dresden doll. She spent a few months of the year at Lambarene and the rest of the time in Europe. I felt sorry for her.

Everyone at the hospital had work to do. Lepers and others came each morning to get their hoes for field work. At noon, they were given two bananas and a handful of rice before they went back to their jobs. In the evening, they returned to hand in their tools and receive their daily pay. One man started to complain about something, but the doctor was very gruff with him and pushed him aside.

Among other animals on the back porch, he had a pelican with a broken wing. Each day, a servant brought two fish from the river to feed it.

"How do you reconcile killing two fish for the pelican when all life is sacred?" I asked.

"Well, this has been a major problem which I have not been able to resolve," the doctor admitted.

And there was a young chimpanzee. One afternoon I went with the nurse to feed the primate. She took him to the front porch and offered him food. He knocked it out of her hand with a playful chuckle. The same thing happened several times before she gave up.

Finally, it was time to take the chimp for a walk. The nurse held one paw and I the other. We had gone about fifty yards when we came to a tall tree. The chimp jerked himself free and fled up into the highest branches. There he sat, daring anyone to challenge him. When we coaxed him with a banana, he finally jumped to the ground with a mighty thump.

Leaving the tall tree area, we came upon an open space where a beautiful new building stood. I was told that this was the French Hospital and, being a medical person, I wanted to see inside. It was very well-equipped, but I noticed it was not teeming with patients, though the treatment was free. There the two institutions were, not more than fifteen minutes of each other, one demonstrating how Schweitzer ran a hospital and the other how modern ones were run.

When I was leaving, Dr. Schweitzer brought one of his books, which he autographed and gave me. It was a copy of *The Mysticism of Paul the Apostle.*

"A lot of people cannot understand this book," the doctor

admitted.*

He waved me off as I slid down the muddy path to the dugout canoe. This time I was careful to sit in a manner that would keep my backside dry.

My flight took me to Lagos. There, sitting alone in a grass shack which served as the air terminal, was a lone American who was shaving. He used a razor powered by batteries, such as I had never seen before. He turned out to be Dr. Frey, head of the World Council of Churches. He was making brief visits to some of the African countries before returning to the U.S. We had a good visit while waiting for our plane.

Only one place remained for me to visit—the Cameroons. There, I met Dr. Green, who showed me around his busy hospital. When asked whether he might take patients from the American government personnel, he pointed out that his staff was overworked and would not wish to have such an arrangement. But he kept a neat, clean hospital and was very busy.

So my work was over, and I returned to Monrovia to draw up my report to the State Department. For serious cases, there was really no place in West Africa, and for other cases, there was none better than the medical set-up at Robert's Field. So, I recommended that those who were very ill be flown to the States for treatment.

Upon our return to Monrovia, we had a visiting fireman from Ghana, Dr. Meyers, whom we wished to honor. I proposed a dinner party in my home, with heads of embassies, doctors and some nurses, and TCA personnel. Everyone thought the plan an excellent one. I asked my servant, Saturday, to take charge of the additional help which would be sent over to assist, and I also needed Clarence to help me with the drinks.

The outstanding feature of the party turned out not to be the doctor, but Clarence. I had never seen him dressed in evening clothes before, and he was really quite striking. And embassy personnel who never looked at him when he was dynamiting the

* When I tried to go through it, it was so ponderous that I joined the others who could not understand it.

rocks under the building, certainly noticed him at the party. Romance at last? Perhaps.

The West African Construction Company completed its work at the Embassy, and several storage rooms resulted. Fortunately, the whole operation was carried out without mishap. After that, the company turned its attention to the well-worn road to the north, over which many troops had traveled during the Rommel campaign in North Africa, and which now was being extended to the border of French Equatorial Africa.

Clarence supervised the construction gang building the bridge. Their huts were a bit beyond Suakoko, so I hadn't seen much of Clarence lately, and I was happy to receive an invitation to celebrate Thanksgiving dinner with his group in their quonset hut. There would be three ladies with their husbands, eight or ten of the American men working on the road, and myself. For the next few weeks, I postponed giving inoculations to any of that group, so I could do it on Wednesday before Thanksgiving. Then I could request the use of the Coast and Geodetic plane to fly me to Suakoko.

Plans for food were made well in advance. The *S.S. African Queen*, regularly brought the food shipments from the U.S. to American personnel in Liberia. The *Queen* arrived punctually, bringing with it Thanksgiving turkeys and all the trimmings. The prospects for an exciting weekend were good. I would fly up on Wednesday, then return with Clarence in his jeep on Sunday, so he could be at work the next day.

They had put up a palm leaf canopy and had decorated our table with the beautiful *gloriosa superba* flowers that grew wild there. Cooking was done in a smoky shack which looked like nothing at all, but what delicious dishes of food the native cooks produced! There were plenty of crows around, and monkeys jumped from branch to branch on the farther trees. And Clarence had his very vicious parrot tied up a little distance away. It was a rather noisy scene.

In these primitive surroundings, we ate our Thanksgiving dinner. It was really a feast. Our gracious hostess made us all feel at home. After the meal, we sat around and talked.

I liked the minister and his wife. I did not know until later that Rev. Paul displayed some intuition as he leaned over to

Clarence and whispered, "If you ever need a minister, I'm available."

Clarence told me that his father had died when he was quite young. His mother was working at the time, so he was sent to live with his Uncle George to help him on his chicken farm in Monrovia, California, and attend high school. When he was graduated from Cal Tech.

Clarence told me more about himself on this picnic than I had ever known before. I believe he knew me better, too. As we drove back to Monrovia (Liberia), I pondered over my past and wondered what the future might hold. We promised to keep in touch.

It was during this time that we had a visit from a member of the U.S. Congress, Frances Bolton. We were already friends, for I had graduated from the Frances Payne Bolton School of Nursing in Cleveland, Ohio, and she had been very helpful to me in our hospital in India. I looked forward to her visit as we had much in common.

Lest her schedule get filled up in advance, I went early to ask the ambassador to allow us a little time together. He did. We were to go to Bomi Hills in separate cars and therein was our visit. On the road, a tree had fallen and, while they were removing it, we sat on a log and talked, but we were soon on our way again in separate cars.

Early the next morning, the bearer from the Embassy called me to come. Mrs. Bolton was sick and needed help. I found her on the floor. The servants and I got her into bed and I ordered some hot tea for her and then nursed her, keeping her quiet and cut off from visitors. The second bed in the room I commandeered for myself, and when she revived, we had another visit.

The following weeks passed rapidly. My term of duty would be up in April. I flew to the several outstations to give the usual shots and medical attention. (I recalled my first flight in Liberia with the pilot with potential heart failure, but I never did have to land the plane.)

Of those several instances, one was particularly embarrassing. Clarence and I were invited to the Port for dinner. We went in the pickup Clarence used for his work with the West African Construction Company. It was late afternoon when we arrived, but still light. We had a pleasant evening with friends, and at about ten o'clock we started home.

At the gate, the guard stopped us and arrested Clarence for not having his lights on when he arrived at the Port. We had arrived long before sunset in broad daylight. The African police took him off to jail. I called my friend, C. C. Dennis, the newspaper editor, and told him what had happened. He came over immediately and we drove quickly to the jail,where he gave the jailers a piece of his mind! Clarence was freed immediately.

There had been only one person from whom I would have accepted a proposal of marriage—Howard. Since his death, I consistently warded off any suggestion of marriage. But now, Clarence was different. I was drawn to him and he was creeping into my thoughts. Though he worked unnoticed in his fatigues along with his crew of local helpers, I felt he was head and shoulders above the other American personnel.

Clarence had been hurt by a divorce some eleven years earlier and was a loner who was not ready to risk being entangled with another marriage. As for myself, I began to feel that I had stood on the sidelines much too long. Instead of completing my tour and returning to the U.S. for another foreign assignment, maybe I should take the plunge.

We decided to have a party. Invitations went out to quite a number of people, including the American, French and British ambassadors. It was a gala occasion. Clarence was tall and handsome in his tuxedo. Several guests asked where I had found such an attractive man, not having noticed him in his work clothes around the Embassy.

Shortly afterward, we decided to get married. My qualms about Clarence had been allayed. We set the date in April. At that time, my assignment would be completed and Clarence would have only one more month of his. I wrote to the Phillips in Denver, asking them to pick out a dress for me—a short white cocktail dress. Using several girls in the shop as guidelines, they determined my size, and when the dress came, it fit very well. It was lace over taffeta with a pink ribbon belt intertwined.

Meanwhile, we had told no one in Liberia of our plans.

We set the date for April 27, 1956. I quietly packed my needed things and put them in the office for Clarence to pick up. I had had invitations printed, but kept them secreted away until the appropriate moment. We wrote to Ross and Peg Wilson at Firestone that we would need the company guest room. Somehow, word got out in Suakoko, for an order was sent to Monrovia for a turkey and all the trimmings.

We were married on Sunday morning, after church service, at the minister Paul Seifer's house. Their mantle was decorated as an altar. A number of church people were present for the wedding dinner, and that night we stopped at the Robert's Field guesthouse. We told them we had just been married, provoking fireworks that lasted well on towards midnight.

The next morning we left early for our forty-five minute drive back to Monrovia, where Clarence let me off at my door. No one was around when I took our announcements to the mailroom. I saved one for the ambassador, asking him not to open it for one hour. I posted a sign on my door saying, "OUT," drove over to Camp Johnson, then to the seashore for the day. I needed time to pull myself together.

The breeze through the palms and soothing birdsong helped to bring repose. Clarence was at work, so it was up to me to book reservations at a beach hotel for a party that night, for the embassy staff and some two hundred guests. On short notice, the proprietor laid out finger food on leaf plates, with a large cake on the center table, and we had our pictures taken with the American ambassador.

Then we felt we were really married.

The best "hotel" in Monrovia was constructed of packing boxes. We had to be careful where we stepped for fear of going through the floor. When we invited guests on one occasion, one of their legs actually did go through. We had to set the chairs over the girders and caution folks not to move them or they might suddenly find themselves on the ground below. We stayed here the rest of the month until Clarence finished his assignment, after which he was assigned to building an oil refinery in Cuba for Esso Standard Oil Company.

In between jobs, we planned a honeymoon to visit places where Clarence had worked in North Africa, including a trip to the Voice of America radio station he had built in Tangiers. There appeared to be acres of antennae. In such work, few men were qualified to erect steel towers. There had been such an expert on the job there, but one day he froze while up on an antenna that was eighty feet high and narrow at the base. In order to get him down, Clarence had to climb up, knock him senseless and carry him down. There was not enough time to send to the U.S. for a replacement, so Clarence had to finish the work himself, truly a hazardous task.

Our itinerary then took us to Robat and Casablanca, and to Tangiers, where he had built a dock. Then we crossed to Gibraltar, hired a car and driver and toured Spain.

At one point the driver asked me, "How come you, an American, married a Spaniard?"

"I didn't," I replied.

"Then you're not married?" he asked.

"We are, but he is an American," I answered.

"But he speaks just like a Spaniard," he remonstrated.

At the French border, we rented another car, traveling through the Riviera and on to Switzerland and Austria. Finally, we arrived in Paris.

At the American Embassy, we ran into the same secretary who washed her clothes in my kitchen sink. She had come to Paris with the French doctor whom she had expected to marry. He had left her at the Embassy, saying he would return shortly, after he announced his engagement to his family. But he never came back. After several disappointing days, she returned to America, where she wrote a book about their romance.*

We scheduled our flight to the States on Air France and had one of the last flights with berths, for new planes had only seats. Since we had sent announcements on to our families, they were expecting us.

*See "Yulan" in the biography.

Chapter XVI

Cuba Just Before Castro

Clarence's next assignment was in Cuba to build a refinery for Esso. We had ordered a new car from Detroit. He had to be in Havana before it arrived, so it fell on me to drive it from Detroit to Key West. Knowing we would be gone a long time, I filled the trunk with household needs, canned goods and non-perishable groceries.

Clarence had been able to rent a very good house in Tarará, a private community on the beach with its own police guards at the gate and located near the Yacht Club. A long row of almond trees lined our street, and palms in our yard made it a tropical paradise. I loved to hear the waves beat on the shore as I sat on our veranda, watching the golden sunsets light up the western sky and the little fishing craft wending their way home with the day's catch.

One boat, the *Pilar*, was anchored right in front of our door and its caretaker, Gregorio, and I became friends. I wanted to learn Spanish and Gregorio liked to teach me. He had been with Ernest Hemingway for years, and many of his stories were of Papa (as he called Ernest) and his exploits. He pointed out the boat alongside, from which Mary fished, as Papa didn't like her tangling up his lines. She was all for red snapper, her favorite fish, whereas Ernest went for the big marlin. Gregorio was the "Old Man of the Sea," which was being filmed there on the beach. (At the time, Spencer Tracy and Katherine Hepburn had rented a house just a short way down our street, which sent the maids into a tizzy, especially when the couple swam in the nude. The girls would peer through the wooden slat fence and always come away giggling.)

I was anxious to get acquainted with Havana and make new friends, so I joined the Women's Club. One of the first programs was a tour of the most elegant homes and the most beautiful gardens. They asked for volunteer drivers and I offered to take three passengers.

When the time came, we drivers lined up to pick up our passengers. I was very happy with mine—Kitty Hill of the American Club in Havana, and Mary Hemingway and her daughter-in-law, Puck Hemingway. We visited several homes, having coffee at one, lunch at another and afternoon tea in the most beautiful garden of all. By the end of the day, we were quite well-acquainted and found we had similar interests. Kitty taught French and Spanish at the Women's Club and Mary was writing,when she was not looking after Ernest and their *finca*.*

One day, Ernest received a telegram from a man who had written a book on flower arranging and who was coming to Havana, hoping to have Hemingway write a preface for it. Ernest did not like the idea and there was no address where one could head off the visitor, so he decided to go fishing and let Mary take care of the guest.

Mary called me and asked me to bring a friend saying, "We've got to have a luncheon for him, he's come so far."

When I got there, she was putting the finishing touches on the flower arrangements. I went into her bathroom and found a bidet full of roses.

"Mary, do you want me to arrange these?" I asked.

"No, they *are* arranged. Every day the gardener fills the bidet with flowers and I enjoy them right there."

When the guest arrived, Mary served us a refreshing drink and took us on a tour of the place. Adjoining the house was a high tower, which Mary had built for Ernest so he would have a quiet place to write.

"He never liked it, so the cats have taken it over, all twenty-seven of them!" Mary explained.

The very large swimming pool looked inviting, so we all had a

---

* Ranch or farm.

swim before we went into lunch. Passing in the front door, Ernest's room was on the left and just inside the door was his writing desk, four feet high.

"Why is it so high?" we asked.

"Ernest always writes standing up and paces back and forth in the room while he's thinking up a word or phrase," she informed us.

On one wall in the main room hung a very large tiger skin.

"I shot him myself," said Mary, "and you'll never find the bullet hole. He was running away from me!"

Soon after we had finished lunch, Ernest returned, greeting the guest as though nothing had happened. I never heard whether the guest got the preface or not, though Jack and Puck were often in our home in the next two years with little Margaux* in her pram.

One weekend we flew over to the Isle of Pines, where Robert Louis Stevenson wrote *Treasure Island*. What an idyllic place! We had been invited by the Finns to their home, "Finn's Finca." Tropical vegetation, including an avenue of Montezuma trees and tree Hibiscus elstus, and brilliant flame bottlebrushes decorated their estate. No cars were permitted on the Island.

The beach was of black sand. Roads had been constructed of white marble, then covered with tar. What a pity! They had added an unusual room to their house which contained the bed, furniture and memorabilia of Henry Wadsworth Longfellow, Mrs. Finn's great grandfather. Since Castro's administration, I have often wondered if the furniture is still there.

Christmas time produced two girls who flew over for their vacation. Gina (Virginia Clare) was Clarence's 14-year-old daughter and was attending high school at a private boarding school in Seattle. The other girl was my niece, Joan Conner, who was in college, while her parents were in Sao Paula, Brazil, too far for her to go for Christmas. It was fun having them in Cuba at our beach home. The Christmas ornaments that year were sea shells that the girls gathered and painted.

---

* Looking on that sweet baby face, who could predict that twenty years later I would see her on the cover of *Time Magazine.*

Times were uncertain in the country, politically. Castro was in the Sierras carrying on guerrilla warfare. His little boy would come to play and he wanted to learn English.

"My daddy is home," he would announce, when his father was trying to keep his movements secret. Castro carried on disruptive tactics day after day. He did everything he could to discredit Batista and the government. Cuba was very unstable and our American Embassy was aiding both sides, not knowing how disastrous the Castro regime would turn out to be.

The oil refinery in Havana Bay was nearing completion. One morning, the workers were greeted with a balloon flying above it with large letters painted across the surface, "VIVA CASTRO." Several rifle shots failed to bring it down, so one of the men had to scramble up there to release and get rid of it.

Our job was finished in Havana so we prepared to leave. The next morning, we took the ferry to Key West. Sailing from Havana harbor, we passed Morro Castle, which was placed in a beautiful setting. We could also see the refinery that Clarence and his men had just completed.

It was a mass of flames.

We watched the refinery burn till we were far out to sea—two years of labor gone up in smoke.

Back home in the good ol' USA, we planned to drive to Hawthorne, California to be with Clarence's mother for a few days. But first, we stopped in Florida to visit with Daisy Douglas,* who had paid me a short visit in India, then to my hometown of Decatur, Illinois, where my sister now lived. Illinois was a radical change from the mild weather of Cuba. When we reached my sister's house, we managed to get out of the car with great difficulty, for we had washed it and all the locks were frozen shut. We couldn't even open the trunk to get out our clothing. It was cold, cold, cold.

We decided to drive southwest with ice and snow along the way. Finally, we reached Arizona. The upper part of Salt River Canyon was deep in snow, but after another hundred miles, sunshine! This was for us. We visited my brother Bill and his family in Phoenix and decided to look around for property in which to

* Daisy Douglas was on the Presbyterian Board of Foreign Missions.

invest. Clarence played a lot of golf in Scottsdale, and while doing so, he discovered an attractive lot, which he purchased. Meanwhile, I had been moving about the city and had found a little house on a lane of palm trees, which appealed to me. This would be our home until we could build our dream house; it would give us a place to come back to when foreign assignments were completed. Meanwhile, we rented it out, then drove on to California.

Clarence's mother was a gracious lady who received her new daughter-in-law with open arms. Numbers of things around the house needed doing and we were glad to lend a hand. We took time to drive up to Seattle to see Clarence's daughter graduate from high school. We had enjoyed Gina's visit to Cuba two years before and were happy to be with her again.

Chapter XVII

The Voice of the
Andes — Ecuador

In September 1958, Clarence took a position in the Office of Foreign Buildings of the Department of State, and he was assigned to supervise the construction of the embassy office building in Quito, Ecuador. The prospect of being assigned to Ecuador was exciting. I had never been in South America; a whole new world lay before me. I expected my Spanish from Cuba would stand me in good stead. Clarence left in October and I was to follow a few weeks later.

Flying through the clouds, we skirted the side of the Andes and had a gorgeous view of Angel Falls, with a "flyer's glory" trailing beneath us as we passed the falls. We began our descent into Quito valley, passing one gorgeous snow-capped peak after another, each with its own shape and characteristics—Cotopaxi, white against the blue sky, and Chimborazo, towering over the valley like a sentinel. I loved these peaks after the flatness of Cuba, for they were reminiscent of the Himalayas. As we taxied to the air terminal, I could make out Clarence waving me in. How good it was to be together again!

He had found us a two-story apartment in a quiet suburb, where bright geraniums surrounded the walls and phlox and antirhinums grew in profusion. He was having it cleaned and painted and we would stay in the Hotel Embajador until it was ready. He also warned me about the altitude of nearly 10,000 feet, pointing out that it was wise to stay quiet the first day in order to get acclimatized.

We would then have to shop around for more furniture, as

what was in the house was rather old and very uncomfortable. And, for a few days, I would be interviewing maids. I would need at least one maid and a gardener with such a big house. Ladies from the embassy were very helpful in this, as well as in telling me where to shop for groceries, what provisions were available at the embassy commissary and who was the right seamstress to make drapes and curtains.

Boys from the countryside brought in terrestrial orchids, which I hung in baskets around the entrance, and we soon had one of the prettiest yards around. A friendly neighbor, watching my endeavors over the wall, introduced herself as Eva Grano (wife of Paul Grano) from Denmark. We grew to be good friends and exchanged plants and seedlings from time to time.

Clarence was busy checking over the blueprints of the new Embassy office building and getting to know the Ecuadorians who would do the actual work. His building engineer was Miguel Andrade Marin, brother of the mayor of Quito, Carlos Andrade. His family took us in as co-workers and friends from the start and we became very close, being invited into their home for all holidays and special occasions. We had not been there long when Clarence received word from the State Department in Washington that he would also be supervising the building of the Consulate office building in Guayaquil on the coast, which meant much traveling back and forth.

It was easy to become part of Ecuadorian society. Our knowledge of Spanish helped a great deal. We had been there only two months when we were invited to the Andrade Marin home, the day before Christmas, to celebrate Bene Noche. At midnight, we moved around the table carrying lighted candles and sampling the great variety of finger foods which had been prepared for the occasion. We could hear the sound of the bells of the city through the open windows.

Miguel's cousin, Jose Gonzalez, was an organist and he would often go up to the church on the hill nearby, open the windows and play for several hours. He got us interested in sending for a little Hammond organ which arrived just about this time. This was Clarence's Christmas present. In a few hours, he was playing, "Silent Night," which he greatly enjoyed.

I began to get acquainted with the missionaries at HCJB

radio station and hospital and there I found kindred spirits. For a dinner party on January 8th, I had invited Marj Saint, Mary Skinner and six or seven others, looking forward to getting acquainted with them. They arrived solemn and quiet, and then Mary quietly informed me that this was the anniversary of their husbands' deaths at the spears of the Auca Indians. We had a blessed evening singing hymns and telling of God's workings in the mission.

This led to an invitation to visit Frank and Marie Drown in Macuma. They had been commissioned to write a book about the Jivaro Indians. "The Headhunters" was the title the publishers suggested. This did not satisfy the Drowns, as head-hunting had been banned some time before, but they solved the problem by so stating in their first few pages and then going on to tell the story of the mission and God's working in the lives of the new Christians in the church. The "church" was a mud-floored building with logs for seats and a conta palm-leafed roof overhead.

Ecuador, as its name suggests, straddles the equator with a backbone down the center of a mountain range running north and south. Many of the mountains rise to 6000 meters, with deep valleys in between and, although on the equator, they are snow covered the year round. This made travel from one part of the country to another quite hazardous, with few areas of large enough size for air landings. There is also a railroad from Guayaquil to Quito, with a road following the rails. But much of the travel within the country is by dugout canoe or bushwacking through the dense jungle.

It was while crossing the river in a dugout canoe that I saw a gorgeous blue Mariposa butterfly. The naked native boys taking me across tried to catch one for me and nearly upset the boat. I told them to forget it, but they didn't. After taking me across, they went back and caught a beautiful eight-inch butterfly for me.

There was one airstrip at Shell Mera where Piper Cubs and Cessnas could land. These were flown by pilots of the Missionary Aviation Fellowship* (called in Spanish *Alas de Soccoro*—Wings of

* Now the Mission Aviation Fellowship.

Help), who serve the surrounding jungle stations by carrying food, supplies, personnel and medical assistance to missionaries in distant places.

I have always had my heart in the cause of mission, and since my husband was busy with his construction supervision, I decided to take advantage of the time on my hands and visit the missionaries. Perhaps I could be of help somewhere.

To get to Shell Mera, we had to fly on an old German Trimotor Junker first south between the two ridges of high mountains to Riobamba, then abruptly northeast to Shell Mera, making a huge "V" between the mountains. Dense forests covered the ground areas, except where rushing rivers cut through the jungle and, too often, masses of clouds obliterated the landscape ahead altogether. We followed the Curaray River and crossed several of its tributaries and then came down on a wide strip of level land—the air base at Shell Mera. In my heart, I said a prayer of thanksgiving for our safe landing.

The buildings of Shell Mera were substantial, but the only wooden houses were those we had seen from the air. All of the native huts were grass-roofed bamboo sheds on 4- to 6-foot stilts with notched logs for stairs. These buildings had been part of a Cat Camp built by Shell Oil Company for oil exploration teams and, when abandoned, had been turned over to the missionaries.

There were several of the latter at the air strip to welcome us, and to pick up their mail and what food and medicines they had ordered. I was taken to the guest room—a clean, austere room made homey and cheerful by sheer cotton curtains blowing in the breeze. And it *was* a breeze, even though a very warm one. Mrs. Keenan took me in for some lunch and then let me rest for the day. I was too excited and anxious to see things to sleep, so I wandered out to the office where the mail was being distributed and one of the ladies was sitting at the radio, receiving and sending messages to outlying areas.

She turned to the pilot, Johnny, and said, "They need you to make a trip to Arajuna. They're asking for some chloroquin."

"That will be our last trip of the day then, since it's important. Would you like to go along, Juanita?" he asked. "We only ask that you pay ten cents a pound for your flight. That helps us pay for the gas."

"I'll be very happy to do so," I replied.

The next morning, Johnny weighed me in at 130 pounds. (I quickly said, "$13, that's cheap!") As we were airborne, Johnny gave me our directions and some of the history of MAF, as we learned to call it.

"We will pass almost over the sand bar where the five missionaries were killed last year. I'll drop down a bit so you can see it better."

Johnny was the pilot who had found the bodies. His other pilot, Nate Saint, was one of the five who were killed and who still had the poisoned arrows in their bodies when found.

We went on to Arajuna where Mary Skinner and dozens of little black bodies swarmed around the plane. We went into her abode, a large thatched hut with only latticed bamboo and mats for doors or partitions. She was English with a high-pitched voice, higher than usual today, because of the excitement of meeting a new friend. She asked me to examine the patient whom she had already diagnosed as having malaria. He was sick and emaciated, and she was urging his relative to give him the medicines and also to feed him. He needed more food, and, of course, an anti-malarial drug.

Mary had a school for Quichua Indian children. She was also preparing to send tapes back to Quito to be used in broadcasts to Indian tribes. We had no sooner returned to Shell Mera than we had word on the wireless from Mary that the Auca Indians across the river were giving bird calls. This was interpreted as meaning that the Aucas were preparing to attack. All of Mary's Quichua colleagues had promptly fled and she was left there alone.

"Could you send me some ammunition? I have a gun here," she requested.

"What bore do you want?" asked Johnny.

"I don't know," came Mary's answer. She apparently knew nothing about guns.

"We had better send you a gun and shells," Johnny advised.

So, out he went, loading the plane with the requested items, and I went with him. When we landed at Arajuna, we found Mary busy tying wire around her house. She had hoped to have it electrified, but the generator wouldn't work. The pilot tried to persuade her to return with us to Shell Mera, but she would not hear of it. He then gave her the gun and ammunition and had her demonstrate how she was going to use them.

Mary was living in a bamboo grass hut which certainly could not withstand attack. That night, she proceeded to make a dummy of herself and put it in the bed and she slept under the bed with her gun. We, in turn, had many sleepless moments and next morning, we rushed over to the radio to find out whether she was still alive.

Her cheery voice sang out, "Oh, I'm all right. Nothing happened the whole night long."

Soon her colleagues returned and school went on as usual.

One of the duties of the embassy wives was to help entertain visitors. Clarence and I were in Guayaquil when Frances Parkinson Keyes arrived there with her secretary-cum-driver-cum-nurse in a large Ambassador car. She was in a wheelchair and she wanted to go up to Quito, some 9,000 feet higher up, over an unmarked, unpaved, twisting mountain road. As Clarence knew and had driven that road a number of times, he offered to drive them.

"No, I trust my secretary to drive me and I'm wary of anyone else," she said.

"Then I'll drive behind you," Clarence said. "Just in case you need an interpreter or mechanic."

Halfway up the mountain, something or other began to leak and, of course, no service stations were available. Clarence made a small plug out of some chewing gum and was able to stop the leak, and they were on their way again. Since the ambassador's residence was closed, she was put in the New Quito Hotel.

The same day, Secretary of the Treasury Douglas Dillon arrived, and to give him more exposure and a chance to meet people, we held a party for him in the Observation Lounge on the top of the Quito Hotel. It was a lovely room built around a large, circular fireplace with picture windows surrounding it, offering a gorgeous panoramic view of the whole valley and the snow-capped mountains beyond.

When the guests had assembled, I went down to Mrs. Keyes' room to help her manipulate her wheelchair in the elevator. I introduced her to Mr. Dillon, and to as many of the guests as I could.

A few days later, she asked, "How come you haven't had a party for me?"

"Well, Mrs. Keyes,* you know the Ambassador is away and usually they like to handle such entertainment themselves," I said.

"Well, why wait for him? I don't want a hotel party. It should be in the embassy residence."

The charge d'affaires thought it over and asked us ladies to open up the embassy and have a party. That meant removing all the chair and sofa covers, polishing the silver and dusting the pictures and furniture as well as planning the hors d'oeuvres. However, it turned out to be a grand party and Mrs. Keyes was satisfied.

Then a day or two later, she said to me, "How come you haven't invited me to your home, Juanita?"

So, we set an evening and I invited the editor of *El Comercio*, Carlos Mantillo, and his wife Doris, and four interesting and well-known Ecuadorians.

"And, Juanita, since you have been in India, you must know how to make mulligatawny soup," she said.

"Yes, I'll see what I can do," I replied.

So we served mulligatawny soup and as we started to take the plates away to serve the main course, she said, "All I want is mulligatawny soup. Just have the maid bring me another bowl."

So, we did, and she was happy. Doris Mantillo had been a guest at Mrs. Keyes, home in New Orleans, so the evening's conversation was lively and interesting.

My role was that of the wife of an embassy man. When colleagues learned that I formerly had served as embassy nurse in Monrovia, I began to get occasional calls for help. I was glad, unofficially, to help out when I could, having noted that almost every wife who arrived pregnant had aborted. The oxygen supply, or lack of it, affected the fetus. When this had happened several times, I wrote a report to Dr. DeVault in Washington, suggesting

---

* She corrected my pronunciation of her name: "It's not keys, it's Keyes. Just remember eyes, then say Keyes."

they not send pregnant women to Quito. The doctor decided to come to Quito and check on the matter. After all, he had lived at 12,000 feet in La Paz and had had no respiratory problems.

I tried to explain my analysis of the problem. Quito is a bowl completely surrounded by mountains. The old forested areas in the valley had long ago been cut down and many eucalyptus trees had been planted on all available land to furnish needed firewood for the population. Newcomers, especially for the first few days, would wake up about 3 a.m. gasping for breath.

When DeVault arrived that first day, I suggested he have a cylinder of oxygen handy. He laughed off the idea as he had never needed any, even at greater altitudes. However, I quietly slipped an oxygen tank and a mask into the closet in his room. About the usual time, 3 a.m., our telephone rang. It was Dr. DeVault, so breathless he could hardly speak and gasping at every word. I told him I had put a tank of oxygen and a mask in the closet in his room. The next morning, he was most grateful for what I had done and understood more fully what I had recommended.

Ecuador is a land of perpetual springtime. It would rain every night about midnight, and then be sunny all day, and one could pick violets every day of the year. Naturally, the garden club was a flourishing organization. There I met numbers of Ecuadorians and American expatriots.

The American Women's Club was well-organized and carried out a full schedule of activities. One of our favorite trips was to the Equator monument where one could stand with one foot in the northern hemisphere and the other in the southern. Or a couple could hold hands across the equator and be hemispheres apart!

Old churches like La Compania and the picturesque streets fascinated me. One would see westernized Spaniards, Otavalans with their large black felt hats, and Quichua Indians carrying bales on their backs. And occasionally Colorado Indians with stiffly varnished hair cuts like beaks to shade their eyes, and colored with red achiote paint and black, red and white stripes and designs all over their sun-tanned bodies.

At Cuenca, on market days, the display of marble carvings,

weavings and genuine Panama hats* made in Ecuador forms a vivid pictorial against the background of the mountains. There, Cotapaxi, the world's highest volcano—higher than Vesuvius, Etna, and Somboli all piled on top of each other—looms majestically against a deep blue sky.

Not far from Quito is the interesting town of Calderone. On All Soul's Day (or is it all Saint's Day?) gaily dressed Quichua Indians gather in the freshly-festooned cemetery to commemorate the departed. For weeks in advance, the villagers make bread dolls and paint them in brilliant colors. If they are remembering a mother, the bread doll may be a mother and child, or if a man or boy who was fond of the horses, the bread doll will be a gaily caparisoned horse with saddle and rider, complete with epaulets and tassels.

And they go to the mountain slopes and pick blueberries. These are made into jam and a large bowlful is placed in the center of the grave. The family gathers around, dipping the bread dolls in the jam and having a merry feast. It is anything but a sad occasion—rather, a joyous time for greeting old friends and relations.

Another important visitor to Quito was Adlai Stevenson. I had been in Cuba when Castro was carrying on guerrilla warfare in the Sierra Maestras and our embassy in Havana was aiding and abetting his activities, even supplying arms. They were keeping two sets of books, to be on the winning side whichever way the conflict went. We knew of Castro's communistic leanings and tried to warn the embassy personnel, but no one would listen.

Here now was my opportunity to reach someone who might be able to alert Washington as to the situation in Cuba. I wrote a short note to Mr. Stevenson, outlining what was happening in that country and left it at his hotel. Late that night, I had a phone call. Mr. Stevenson explained he had been meeting officials all day and had been at dinner that night, thus had just now (after 11 p.m.) received my note. He asked me to have breakfast with him in the morning so we could talk further, and we agreed

---

* These are woven only on damp days to keep the straw from drying out, often woven under water.

to meet in the dining room of his hotel at 8:30 a.m.

We had a table to ourselves and talked. He was very serious at hearing the news, which seemed unknown to him. As we conversed, Senator Smathers came over to our table with some hand-woven Otavalan Indian scarves over his arm, saying, "Adlai, maybe your lady friend here can help me make a choice. These women know materials and colors better than I do."

Stevenson introduced me, and then said, "Excuse us, Senator. Mrs. Falvey and I are talking about very important matters." Evidently he *was* taking seriously what I had felt so concerned about. I hoped he could convey this information to Washington.

There were some strange goings on when we were attached to the embassy in Quito. I began to feel our house had been bugged. The lamps would be slightly misplaced, or the sofa would be out from the wall too far. I had heard about other embassy personnel being bugged, but until now, I had never had the experience. I decided to find out.

When Clarence came home from the office, I had him sit with me on the sofa and then I made up a wild story, quite unique and improbable, to tell him. He scarcely listened as he picked up the paper and was reading while I talked.

The next day, I went to the Embassy commissary and an information officer of the embassy—one whom we thought was a "cloak-and-dagger" man—called me into his office. As he sat down at his desk, I noticed he touched a switch under his desk, and there was a very slight humming sound from the curtained wall behind the desk. He saw I noticed it.

The wall was completely covered by a plain burlap curtain, not covering any windows and certainly not for decorative effect. I started pulling at the curtain, saying as I did so, "You ought to take that burlap down. It detracts from your office and is really quite ugly."

He got very nervous. Then he turned to me and repeated the wild story I had told my husband the night before.

"You surely don't believe that, do you?" I said. "That's impossible. I know those people you're talking about, and they're fine, upstanding Americans. Wherever did you hear such a rumor?"

He turned red, but changed the subject.

From then on, I was careful not to say anything, even in my own house, that I did not want recorded. We'd talk on the golf course; and even there, I'd wonder if there was a tiny mike tucked away in my golf bag!

Guayaquil, known officially as la Cuidad Santiago de Guayaquil, is a port city with a number of docks in the Rio Guyas harbor, several miles from where the river entered the ocean. The Grace Lines have carried on a great deal of trade and travel to that port as have ships from Japan, England, Denmark, and other South American countries. Besides the shipping lines, the river was literally cluttered with barges carrying bananas, cocoa beans, *marañores,* * balsa wood, mangrove bark, rice, barley, coffee and castor beans, as well as ferrying people across the river.

The city itself is a fairly impressive one, with many large office buildings and beautiful avenues and streets of flowering almond, jacaranda, hibiscus, and Rose of Sharon trees shading dwellings of concrete, wood, and stone. There are also some kerosene tin shanties on the back streets. The traffic was hectic, with bicycles, cars, trucks, and jeeps, and pedestrians weaving in and through the wheeled traffic.

A five-story building on the corner lot at Avenida Nueve de Octubre and Garcia Moreno was owned by Emilio Estrada, who had halted construction after it was condemned. He then sold it to the U.S. for a consulate and office building, after engineers had determined it was structurally sound and suitable, and the cracks had been strengthened and repaired. Clarence had to take over the supervision of its reinforcement, completion and refurbishing.

During this process, we got to know the Estrada family very well. Emilio himself a part-time engineer, pilot and archeologist had many interests, one of which was collecting *objets d'art.* One of his discoveries was what was once an ancient refuse heap containing oriental-looking objects that have offered much evidence of distant contact (possibly Chinese) with Ecuador, as far back as 2000 B.C. His museum contains many exquisite artifacts and gold jewelry. He was aided in evaluating and classifying his col-

---

* Cashew nuts.

lection by Clifford Evans, Jr. and Betsy Meggers of the Smithsonian Institute and it was exciting to be in on some of their finds.

The Estradas proved to be a lovely couple and had a beautiful home. We enjoyed trips together and sometimes visited a cousin of theirs, whose home was right on the beach. The cousin had taken sections of vertebrae of a number of whales that had died on the sand nearby and had placed them around his yard for garden seats. They were not bad seats at that!

The ocean was right below their seaside home. One day when we were there, his cousin put on bathing shorts and was gone about twenty minutes. Soon he appeared with fresh oysters. He gave Clarence one which filled his whole dinner plate.

Joe and Gloria Gorelik were another interesting couple at Guayaquil.They were Russian Jews who had come to New York and become American citizens. When they moved to Ecuador, Joe found a woman who wished to sell her Pepsi Cola business, which he bought for $10,000. The business proved to be so profitable that he eventually accumulated several million dollars.

Wanting to do something for the city in return for his good fortune, he built a public library. It was a beautiful building with marble floors and a winding staircase to the second floor. The United States Information Service had set up libraries in many foreign countries and Gorelik tried desperately to get American books for his library. But that was back during the McCarthy days, when everyone with a background like his was automatically suspect. The security department of the Embassy in Quito actually set up a constant watch on him. They installed a telescope on a nearby building and reported his comings and goings, who called, car license numbers, etc.

I wrote to Frances P. Bolton* in Washington and told her the story, yet no books arrived. Then, I contacted Senator Fulbright and explained the matter to him. He was very understanding and the books started coming.

We were dinner guests in the Gorelik home—a beautiful but simple place—and Gloria and I swam in their pool before dinner.

---

* My friend from Cleveland who also visited us in Liberia.

They served an excellent meal which was not especially Jewish. Clarence had to supervise the purchase of materials for the embassy building through Gorelik, so he knew him earlier on a business leave. We were glad to see that some of the misunderstandings about the Goreliks were clearing up, since it was people like these which made our life in Ecuador interesting.

The Consulate building was five stories high. Offices occupied the lower three floors while the upper two were apartments for embassy personnel. They were outfitted completely with American furnishings. A great amount of curtain material arrived, needing to be cut and fitted, and a girl showed up asking for the job of making the curtains. She was rather scantily clothed and had a deep tan. Innocently, she told me that she had recently been to the Galapagos Islands with the American ambassador and his group.

"But, I had heard the trip was for men only!" I exclaimed.

"So it was," she admitted, "but I was special. I had a great time!"

So, this was the gal who got the sewing job!

Clarence's contract was now almost over as both the Embassy in Quito and the Consular building in Guayaquil were completed. For the opening of the Embassy building, the American ambassador gave a lawn party for the diplomatic corps and townspeople.

Just prior to the contract completion, Clarence went to see Dr. Roberts to check on a pink area on his body where he had had an appendix operation some eleven years before. They removed a long string of catgut from Clarence's abdomen. The doctor found it hard to believe it had been there for so long. Whether or not that had something to do with the cancer that later spread to his colon, I don't know.

At the Embassy party, I saw the doctor and asked whether he had had any results of the examination. Yes, he had. Clarence had an advanced case of cancer of the colon, and would have to be sent on the first plane the very next morning to the Naval Hospital in Bethesda, Maryland. What a shock! And what an ending to our two happy years in Ecuador. We immediately left the party and went home to get ready to depart.

Clarence boarded the AGRA plane just before noon the next day, and was soon on his way to the States, with no time to say goodbye to our friends and the local people. I returned to our house and began to pack. The next morning, the movers came and boxed our heavy items. A day later I left for Bethesda, where Clarence's operation was scheduled for the next day. At the Naval Hospital, Clarence was assigned to a room in the Tower and treated like a VIP. I took an apartment not too far away and was with him each day.

I wanted to attend church on Sundays, and a friend in Washington suggested that we go to a little church in a home on Massachusetts Avenue. It was, indeed, quite small. Chairs took the place of pews. Next to me was a lady clothed in black, sitting next to her little boy. Something was said in the sermon which caused her to weep. I, too, was going through a trying period, not knowing whether or not my husband would survive his hospital experience. Perhaps I, myself, was headed toward widowhood. I put my hand over hers and gave it a little squeeze.

After the service, we introduced ourselves. She was Catherine Marshall, the widow of the late Peter Marshall, Chaplain of the Senate.

"Oh, I have read your books and the prayers of your husband," I volunteered.

After that, we met several times on Sundays at the little chapel. She was always solicitous of my husband's health and we grew very close.

When Christmas approached, I was feeling a bit blue. I decided to go to the George Washington Hospital and volunteer my time, from Christmas through the New Year, so that the other workers might get off during the holidays. When I went to apply, who should be in the office but a colleague of mine from back at Western Reserve.

"Oh, we won't need to process you; you can start tomorrow," she said. "Let me show you around."

So, we inspected the wards. When we came to one door, the nurse unlocked it with a key. As we passed along, I thought I heard someone calling my name. I dismissed it, thinking there must be someone else by the same name on the staff, and walked on.

That evening, I had a telephone call from a man I had known in West Africa during the time when the ambassador had died and I had had to send the new charge d'affaires home with cancer. The third man in line, who became the new charge d'affaires, was the one calling.

"Were you at George Washington Hospital today?" he asked. "Did you hear your name called as you went through one of the wards?"

"Yes, I did, but I thought it must have been for someone else with the same name," I replied.

"It was my wife," he said. "May we visit you on Sunday."

"That would be fine," I answered.

Sure enough, Frank, with his wife Virginia and their two children, came on Sunday. She and I had been in the same room when we were hospitalized in Monrovia. Strange to have found folks from Cleveland and from West Africa whom I had known so well.

It was a cold, snowy winter. I had no transportation, and it was most unpleasant travelling by bus back and forth from my apartment to the hospital. I had not seen winter in years, having been in India, Liberia, Cuba and Ecuador—all tropical places. I had to learn all over again how to walk on ice and snow.

The hospital at Lambarene on the river which provides water for the hospital laundry and bathing.

A note from Dr. Schweitzer:

Avec l'antilope Leonie quand elle était encore petite

a Juanita Owen en souvenir de son séjour à Lamba, née en février 1956
Albert Schweitzer

Above: Dr. Schweitzer with his pet antelope, Leonie.

Left: The leper village at Lambarene.

Below: The Timbuktu Mosque with its walls of mud and floors of sand.
At right: A family is traveling by donkey through the town. Their heads and faces are covered to keep out the hot winds and blowing sand.
Lower right: Market cays bring a crowd from distant places.

Don and Juanita arrive in Timbuktu windblown and in need of a glass of cool water.

Don and Juanita with Bishop and Mrs. Amstutz after their marriage in Claremont, California.

Below: Visiting Suffering Moses' shop in Kashmir.

At the equatorial monument at Latitude 0'00° just outside Quito, Ecuador.

Juanita with Arthur C. Clarke and dogs at his home in Colombo, Shri Lanka.

The dress of the villagers of the Mt. Hagen and Gorokha area is very colorful and often awesome—designed to put fear in the hearts of their enemies.

A typical village home on the Sepik River. When the river rises many homes are surrounded by water.

BOOK SEVEN

THE PHOENIX RISES
OUT OF THE ASHES

1960-1978

Chapter XVIII

Phoenix College—
A Challenge

When Clarence left the hospital, we took a quick trip to visit relatives. Then we returned to our little house in Phoenix which we had been able to buy with the bonus the company gave Clarence for his work in Cuba. However, I knew that I would have to work to keep up with expenses. Mutual of Omaha had cancelled all of Clarence's insurance and he was too young to receive social security, though he had paid into the fund for twenty years. I took a position in the Good Samaritan Hospital as instructor in obstetrics and the newborn, a post I held for two years. Meanwhile, I also had to do housework and the cooking, while looking after Clarence during his long recuperation.

When Clarence recovered, he accepted a position in Flagstaff as superintendent of construction. Dormitories at the university were needed and Clarence carried out and supervised this assignment. Meanwhile, it was necessary for me to obtain a certificate in order to teach in Arizona. Thus, when summer came, I temporarily gave up my work at the hospital and went to Flagstaff to take courses required for my teaching certificate. We lived in a dormitory and really had a pleasant time together.

That fall, I went back to Phoenix to the hospital and taught until spring. Clarence had finished his work on the dormitories and was asked to continue work on the building at Lowell Observatory in Flagstaff. We were together again that next summer, and, having qualified, I began to teach nursing and obstetrics in Phoenix College.

Clarence came back from Flagstaff for the winter. Then came

an offer from his old company for him to go to Salonica*, Greece,
and supervise the building of a pier for oil tankers to unload.
When college closed for the summer, I followed Clarence to
Greece, where I set up our apartment, bringing in furniture,
rugs, and all the necessary household supplies. I liked going to
the beach and attending the Women's Club.

During our summer there the government changed and there
was a lot of activity in the street below our windows. The queen
mother had been removed and a democracy set up by a general
election. Papadopolous was elected the first president.

I decided to take Greek lessons from a teacher with Salonica
University. I discovered there were several separate Greek languages. I worked on some conversational Greek, so I could use it
when shopping. Taking a newspaper, I gleaned a few useful
phrases, or so I thought. My teacher went with me to the market,
and when I used a sentence I had found in the newspaper that
morning, she quickly put her hand over my mouth.

"We never use those words," she said. "One does not speak
newspaper Greek in the bazaars!"

At the end of the summer, I had to return to Phoenix College,
for I was working on my tenure. Clarence was still working on a
pier for Esso-Papas which would require twelve more months, so
I could expect his return to America at the end of the following
summer. With Clarence's earnings in Greece, we were able to buy
a plot of land in Phoenix Cudia Estates. From it, one looked out
on Camelback Mountain. We planned for a swimming pool, so I
would occasionally go over to the lot to see where the moon came
up in relation to the mountain. I wanted the swimming pool
placed so that the moon would be reflected in its waters. Having
built a small hospital and my house in India some years before, I
was not totally unfamiliar with building work.

When Clarence returned from Greece, he helped me. This
kept him busy until the following spring, when he had to reenter
the hospital. The treatment given him made him bleed profusely,
so he became weaker and weaker. For the final nine months, he
couldn't leave the house as cancer had affected him, causing

*Also known as Thessalonica

complete paralysis on one side.

I continued to hold my teaching job, for now we had no other source of income. One day I had to leave early to drive across the city for a 7:30 class and didn't get back until late. When I returned from the college, I found he had been lying on the floor all day. It was apparent that we would have to get a nurse. I tried to hire a number of nurses, but when they came to examine the situation, each refused. Finally, in desperation, I called a nurse friend, Catherine Dwyer, in New York. She flew to Phoenix the following morning and was with us for the last month. He slipped away December 20th, 1967.

We had had almost twelve rewarding years together, six of them in foreign countries. We enjoyed our home in Phoenix and had many happy times, in spite of his illness. All this would have been impossible had we not loved each other as we did.

Friends who had avoided me during Clarence's illness began dropping by again, helping to fill a certain emptiness. I had my little poodle as a companion, and he was there to greet me when I returned in the afternoon from college. The urgency and worry I had had about Clarence was now gone and things began to fall into place. During his long illness, there were heavy expenses and no insurance. Now I had large hospital bills to pay, so my teaching job helped me meet my financial obligations.

Soon it was obvious that I could not continue to carry the expenses of our large house, and I began to seek out other alternatives. Perhaps living in Mexico was the answer. After all, I was used to living among peoples of other cultures, and it *would* be less expensive.

That summer, I joined a Phoenix College six-week tour of Mexico, led by our Spanish professor.*

The summer tour of Mexico was fascinating to me, and quite valuable. The climate was enjoyable, especially along the sea coast, where it was cooler than Phoenix in summer. And I got to see how the Mexican people lived.

In villages, they were quite simple, for they were poorer than

---

* In Arizona, we had to earn five college credits every four years to keep up our certification. I already had taken practically all the subjects available, so I chose Spanish to cover the credit requirement.

those in towns and cities, while in places like Mexico City, society was much like that of the middle class in India. The Mexican people in urban areas lived quite comfortably, but usually not as elaborately as in the United States, and what with the cost of living, I could see that my modest income would pay for a couple of servants who would look after the house, garden, and cooking—and I'd still have something left over. Mexico seemed to be a real possibility.

But for now, it was back to Phoenix College for another year.

An instructor with his master's degree, became interested in me. He turned up several times at my house and then asked me to have dinner with him. It was all very informal. Then, he proposed, adding that I would have to get rid of my dog and sell my house. I didn't quite understand about the house (unless he needed money), and there was nothing about love in the whole matter. Actually, he was quite overbearing and had an exalted opinion of himself. Needless to say, I soon disentangled myself.

I had saved enough from that year of teaching to pay all my debts and have some money left over. I decided to take another trip to Mexico, this time driving in my Camaro with my little dog.

One of the more attractive cities I had visited was Guadalajara, where I rented an apartment for two months. Some fifteen thousand Americans lived in the Lake Chappala area. There was a servicemen's club where handicapped U.S. vets and others gathered. Their incomes would not permit them to live north of the border, but in Mexico they could manage. It seemed pathetic that men who had spent years serving their country in the armed forces found it impossible to live in the U.S.A.

But I found the residents preoccupied with trivial gossip. Such a narrow environment stifled me; I couldn't take it. I had brought money with me to buy a bit of property, but decided against it and returned to Phoenix instead.

Back in my teaching role again, a new door opened for me. I asked for a leave to attend an organizational meeting of the Nurse's Association of American Gynecologists and Obstetricians in Seattle. We did have an affiliation with the American Medical Association, but we felt a separate organization would be more effective. The first year, I was a charter member and later elected chairman of District VIII, which included the fourteen western states and extended to British Columbia, Alberta, and Hawaii, as well as to Guam and Okinawa. It was the largest district association of the AGOG in the United States, and as our membership grew, it became a real task to get out 8,000 letters to all of its members.

Then came another responsibility. I was chosen chairman of the Speakers' Forum Committee, which I greatly enjoyed. Our committee chose the monthly speakers and looked after their housing and all necessary arrangements. This brought me into contact with outstanding entertainment people. Pearl Buck, whom I had known in New York, was one of the first.

She told me that she had sent copies of her book *East Wind, West Wind* to twenty-nine publishers and had received rejection slips from all. She then sent the thirtieth copy to East West Association in New York.

It had already been placed on the rejection pile at a meeting of the selection committee when the president, Mr. Walsh, entered the meeting late. Attracted by the title, he asked the meeting to reconsider. The result was not only an acceptance but the beginning of a long writing career, and she married Mr. Walsh!

Another visitor I greatly enjoyed was Arthur C. Clarke, a physicist and scientist who had written many science fiction stories and who shared in the authorship of *2001, A Space Odyssey.*

He related to us how he had taken a couple of boys out snorkeling and swimming off the Ceylon coast, and how they had come upon an ancient sunken ship in which they found bags of silver rupees encrusted with salts and lime and looking for all the world like rocks.

He pulled out some of the coins from his pocket, and I asked if the government of Ceylon (now Sri Lanka) tried to take the booty from him. He said he had written about his discovery, but because of his science fiction stories, the government did not believe he was serious.*

---

* The ship was thought to have sunk in 1702 as the newly minted coins bore the Moslem date of 1113.

Sometimes a speaker would stay in my home; it was a privilege to be their hostess. Erma Bombeck stayed with me a couple of days and later decided to move to Phoenix. Her first book with Bill Keane was conceived on the couch in my living room. She sent me a copy of the book when it was published, and on the flyleaf, she wrote: "The next time I visit you in Phoenix, I won't let you off so easily. I'll send for my husband, the kids, my sister and brother-in-law and Grandma and Grandad. Such enjoyment as you give should be spread around. Erma."

As I sit here writing (in Claremont), I hear a familiar voice and look up at my TV set to see Erma on the Donahue show (September 24, 1987). He was a neighbor of hers in Ohio. I could relate to this; for several years I was her neighbor in Phoenix and we shared a cleaning girl, Shela. We often lamented together on the telephone. I say "lamented" seriously as Shela (not her real name) was always getting pregnant, and we thought she already had enough trouble.

One morning Erma called me and asked, "Did you know Shela was pregnant?"

"No, I didn't," I said.

"Well, she left here Friday evening, went straight to the hospital and had a baby over the weekend. She's back today."

And I was supposed to be an expert on such things!

In 1987 Erma was chosen to introduce the Pope in Sun Devil Stadium with 65,000 people looking on. They tried to cover the word "Devil," which was all over the stadium, but forgot a few. Later during the tour he was introduced in a San Francisco school by another woman—Nancy Reagan. So, women are coming into their own!

Chapter XIX

The Sands of Timbuktu

That fall, I met Don Milligan. He was a book and magazine wholesaler from San Jose who was being treated for emphysema. While at the clinic, I talked with the nurse who worked for Don's doctor. I noticed a whole tray of syringes that were already loaded and lying in neat rows. When I asked the nurse about the dosage, I learned that they were all the same, a "mood elevator." I knew such a thing was useless as far as getting to the root of his problem was concerned. Such treatment made one feel good only for the day, but in twenty-four hours, when the effect had worn off, the patient would be back in the clinic for his next shot. I finally persuaded Don to listen to me, and he began to think that possibly a pool would be helpful. In a short time it did improve his breathing.

For Christmas vacation I had planned to be with my brother Bill and his wife in San Diego. When Don asked me to spend Christmas with him, we came to a compromise. He would go to San Jose for the day with his son and family and I would go to San Diego. The next day, he would fly down and join me.

Don flew to San Diego as planned, and we drove to Phoenix.

Later, he arranged for his son and family to come and visit him in Mesa. He introduced me to his family, and though I enjoyed them very much, I did not want to take on another sick husband. I tried to steer away from him, yet he kept asking me out. A Mesa resident for about two years, he seemed to be a lonely man. He began to talk about marriage, and at length I agreed, but I was determined to complete my year of teaching at Phoenix

College.

We waited until June for the wedding.

Don's health continued to improve. He quit his tranquilizing drug and took to exercising instead. He was a different man.

June came, and with it our wedding. I wanted Bishop Hobart Amstutz in Claremont to perform the ceremony. The bishop had been in a Japanese prison in Singapore in 1943 when his wife and son, Bruce, and daughter, Beverly, had sailed with me around the Cape of Good Hope and Cape Horn to New York. I had gotten to know the Amstutz family very well on our 93-day trip.

On the appointed day, about two dozen close family members living in California were present, and after the reception, we returned home to Phoenix.

For our honeymoon trip, we were booked on an American Express tour of South America. The Bariloche lake district in the Argentine was especially beautiful, and our visit to Quito was most enjoyable. We were in a delightful setting surrounded by mountains, and of course, we had the usual picture taken of Don and me holding hands across the equator.

During lunch time in our hotel, we heard gunshots, and from our second floor window we saw soldiers leading President Valasco out of the palace at gunpoint. I learned that this had happened several times, but on each occasion he had been recalled.

I was fortunate once again to have an opportunity to fly to Mary Skinner's village on the Curare River. Mary related that the headman of her village had developed tuberculosis and had to be taken across the Andes to the H.C.J.B. Hospital in Quito, where he stayed for some time and daily listened to the gospel.

One day when Mary was preparing her cassettes for broadcasting to the Indians, she had a call from the headman. He was afraid he was going to die and asked to be brought back to his village. They got him back over the mountains and carried him to a cot in front of his home in his own village, and as he lay there, a crowd surrounded him.

He raised his voice and said, "I have now become a Christian and want to ask your forgiveness for the wrongs I have done you."

This was a powerful witness. Some of the villagers were already Christians, but their number definitely increased before the headman died. The missionaries' faithful work had borne fruit.

When we returned to Phoenix, Don had a denture that began to bother him. With difficulty I finally persuaded him to go see a doctor. They took a biopsy and it was malignant. The next four years was a series of physical crises.

Still, there *were* enjoyable highlights. One of these was the annual meeting of the Book Wholesalers and Publishers, scheduled at a different location each year, and several lesser gatherings that many publishers attended. They were gala affairs, with lots of talk, food and drink. Atlantic City and Los Angeles were among the cities chosen for these events.

Don was very interested in children with handicaps. A waitress in Mesa had told him of her nine-year-old son who was crippled with multiple sclerosis. She was alone and her meager salary was not enough to pay for his treatment *and* their daily expenses. Don made arrangements for him to be treated at a Crippled Children's Hospital run by the Shriners, and he contributed for years to the facility toward the boy's support. He loved to make children happy, and he was always generous with his money, especially in a good cause.

Those last few years were filled with travel. There was a trip to Alaska, up the Inland Passage to Whitehorse, Fairbanks, and Nome, dogsleds and all, followed by a Carribbean cruise to most of the islands. Another lengthy journey included Australia, New Zealand, Fiji, Tahiti and Java, after which were visits to Iran, Turkey, the Grecian Islands, Egypt and Spain. Still another was a rail trip across Canada, and a drive in New England in time to enjoy the fall colors on the trees.

Don and I both liked to travel, so we planned an around-the-world trip in 1974. Our first stop after leaving Los Angeles was Hawaii, where we visited most of the islands. We enjoyed the orchids of Hilo, the Blow Hole Geyser, and the view of Honolulu and Diamond Head from Pali. We found it very modernized.

Next, we stayed in a grass hut in Tahiti with a glass-bottom floor, which afforded us a spectacular view of the multicolored sea life below us. It was truly an exotic area, but cheap hotels and slot machines abounded, and the people were very upset at the prospect of a nuclear bomb being tested in the South Pacific by the American military forces.

We arrived in Sydney, Australia just after the new Opera House was opened—such a unique design! We also visited Melbourne and the capitol city of Canberra, with its well-laid out streets, gardens and flowers.

In New Zealand we visited Rotorua, the original home of the Mauris. The thermal area was studded with geysers and mud pots, and Mt. Egmont, a still-active volcano, loomed in the distance. We enjoyed the hotel at Milford Sound on the South Island. While there we heard the tolling of bells in a nearby village and learned that several men had been lost the day before in a shipwreck.

Bali is one of the eastern outposts of Hinduism. We arrived on a special holiday when a hundred or more participants had gathered, some from distant villages, to take part in the Hanuman Monkey Dance. On a platform facing the crowd were many men dressed as monkeys, reciting portions of the Ramayana, while at intervals, the whole crowd would lift their arms skyward. How much like segments of our society, where the audience was trying to be just like everyone else. Down at the water's edge, girls exquisitely dressed in multicolored *saris* were floating little lights and flowers out on the water. All these brilliant colors against a volcano erupting in the background made an unforgettable scene.

Fiji reminded me so much of India, since more than half the population had come from that country. The tropical climate and fruits were so familiar. Children went to school and learned two languages, one of them often English. It was stimulating to be able to speak Hindi with the people we met in Fiji, and I was overjoyed when the waiter brought custard apples to our room— one of my favorite Indian fruits!

Ceylon was a garden island far different from what it is today. Don had sold many books authored by Arthur Clarke, and he was invited to visit him in his home. He met us in his garden at Bishop's House in his *sarong* and *kamize** and showed us around his place. I noticed a door stop that looked like a stone, but was really a bag of coins that had rested at the bottom of the sea for

---

* Wraparound skirt and shirt.

two hundred years and the outer canvas bag had long since been encrusted with lime, thus resembling stone. Mr. Clarke would pick up a bag and throw it on the cement floor, breaking it, and two hundred bright, newly-minted silver rupees would roll in every direction, to the amazement of his guests.

We took a trip out to the lighthouse. He had given instructions to be called when any strangers came too close to the sunken ship. He showed us his telescope on the roof of his house and the plaque presented to him by NASA for his support in permitting them to use his drawing of the communciations satellite he had devised in his science fiction writing. A long line of his published books took up most of one bookcase in his office.

Then we went on to Nepal. We had donated some money for a bird book being prepared by the Flemings (Senior and Junior) and wished to know how they were getting along. We checked in at the Annapurna Hotel, where Don stayed in bed most of the time due to the effect on him of the 4200-foot altitude.

Once again, I enjoyed the bazaar streets of Kathmandu, such as Indra Chowk, where the thoroughfare was crowded with cars, rickshaws, cycles and hundreds of people on foot, some of them well-dressed, and others tribal men just in from the hills. The streets were a living kaleidoscope!

We were invited over to Bob Fleming's for tea. Bethel had died two years before, and Bob was living in a three-story brick house in Patan across the river from Kathmandu. On the gate was painted a colorful sunbird. We were taken to his sun porch where two Nepali artists were meticulously coloring in the feathers of birds from the ones they held in their hands. The two Bobs— father and son—had been working for two years on the 950 pictures of the bird book they expected to publish. When we left, we were glad we had sponsored such a project, for there was no adequate field guide for the birds of the central and western Himalayas.

From Nepal we headed for Kabul in Afganistan where I was first assigned by the State Department in 1954.

The Muslim culture of Afghanistan was a great contrast to the Hindu-Buddhist culture of Nepal, although Kabul was also at an altitude which confined Don to his hotel. I had a friend there who called for me in her car, and we went on a tour of the city and a walk through the bazaars, purchasing small items of jewelry with lapis lazuli stones.

The Blue Mosque in Shiraz, Iran, was truly a vision of beauty. Beyond a large square, the blue dome of the great mosque was surrounded by minarets. From there, the muezzins called the faithful to prayer. We stayed at the Shah Abbas Palace Hotel in Tehran which was beautifully appointed with Persian carpets, lace curtains and furniture inlaid with pearl and ivory motifs.

I wanted to visit the School of Nursing set up by Princess Ashraf, the Shah's twin sister. She was very interested in nursing and the building she had constructed for the school was the nicest and most modern I had seen anywhere. The nursing students had Persian carpets on their floors, beautiful furnishings in their lounges, and recreation rooms. A gorgeous outside pool was surrounded with a well-trimmed hedge and adorned with many beautiful flowers. From what I could learn, the teaching and operation of the school was one of the best that I had seen anywhere, including Robert's College School of Nursing in Turkey, which I visited next. The school was headed by Dr. Shepard and the difference was apparent. They were both in Moslem countries.

I spent some time in the bazaar, happy that I could converse with the people in Urdu. We drove out to Persepolis. It was interesting to see the arrangements being made for the heads of state from all over the world coming for the big celebration.

Istanbul was adorned with the beautiful St. Sophis Mosque and the suks* were intriguing. In one shop, I found yards and yards of beautiful lace curtain material eleven feet wide. I bought enough and more, for our home in Phoenix. We paused to do some sightseeing and then we were on to Europe.

I always seemed to arrive in Vienna during a musical festival. Participants represented a variety of countries and the mild climate was conducive to programs in open-air arenas. After a brief stop we left for Paris, and then it was back to New York and Phoenix.

Don stood the trip quite well, though at times I was apprehensive. Now it was so good to be home again to our rose garden,

* Bazaar.

our swim room, and our comfortable bed.

Don's health continued to change for the better. We prayed together, asking God to take charge of our lives. We enjoyed going to church together. It was such a good feeling to have Don with me at worship service. He was always anxious to help other people.

We began to plan another trip abroad. Don was not up to par, but he thought that visits to other places would take his mind off his physical condition. We booked on a flight that landed in Dakar, and then on to Bamako and Timbuktu.

No one warned us to take some snack food with us. The plane from Bamako to Timbuktu was very small and we were permitted no luggage, except a small case which would fit under our seats. The flight was over miles and miles of inundated land—water, water everywhere—and I had thought we were going into the desert! Then the water abruptly ended and the dry, sandy soil appeared, and not a tree or hillock was in sight. Sand, sand everywhere.

After we touched down, we were taken to our hotel in a land rover, and Don and I were given one of only two bedrooms that had a toilet. The rest of the rooms shared a common toilet, with no sexual discrimination! As far as the eye could see, there was nothing but sand and sky.

Don lay down to rest on one of the two cots in our room, while I walked around to the back of our abode to see the culinary department. There was a dining room area, but no kitchen and no tables! The cook would lay a raw chicken on the sand, pick it up without washing it, and drop it into a pot of water over a small cook fire. Clarence had once told me that in Arabia all their food was "seasoned with sand," and I could now see why, though I'm sure they had water in Arabia to wash things in. Here, the water was quite scarce; what little they had was carried from afar and used sparingly.

That evening at dinner the sand was in and on everything! How I wished for a bun or roll such as we had had in Bamako that morning—I was so hungry. Then I noticed that in the soup, the sand settled to the bottom and, by taking the bowl in both hands and making a gentle circular motion, I could siphon off the top and leave the sand at the bottom. But that was it. The bread could set one's teeth on edge, and after peeling the chicken to get rid of the sand, they were so scrawny that one had only a bite or two left. And why shouldn't they be? There wasn't anything for them to eat, except the bones of their cousins of the day before.

Don complained of a fever and I put him to bed by candle-light. I did my best to make him comfortable, but his temperature kept climbing. I gave him a little water and aspirin and hoped it would control the fever, but still it climbed. I lay in my cot won-dering what I would do; my options were few. There was no transportation until 2 p.m. the next day (the plane we had come in had left). There *was* the land rover, but there were no roads, except the one to the airstrip.

Don's temperature did not come down and he began to talk irrationally. He thought he was being held hostage, and I longed for some water to cool his fevered brow. I prayed he would go to sleep and wake up okay the next day. But what if he didn't? There were no telephone or telegraph lines to call for help, and whom would I call? No plane could come before morning anyway, as there were no lights or guidelines at the airstrip, and it was the dark of the moon.

What if he should die there? Where in all that sand could one dig a grave? The sand was nine feet deep, and when the Ameri-can army tried to dig to put in a pipeline during the war, it kept caving in. There was no wood, at least not enough to cremate him. I thought of the ghastly option of putting him out for the vultures, as was the native custom. Most of the night I sat beside his cot, trying to cool his fever and praying that God would bring him through until we could get some help.

It was a welcome sight to see the sun come up the next morn-ing and to realize we had made it. Now, it was only a matter of making it through until the plane came in. At sun-up, Don's tem-perature went down and he sat up and asked for some tea. It was all like a bad nightmare.

I thanked the Lord when we got on the plane that afternoon and he seemed no worse for the night's fever. We decided to go on with the trip, especially as there were doctors in most of the places we would be visiting.

At Accra, Don stayed at the hotel while I went to the Ameri-can Embassy to see the doctor and get some medicine. I was met at the door by the ambassador, Mrs. Shirley Temple Black. She was wearing a native costume—a colorful cotton wrap-around skirt and a bandana around her head. She was doing a good job representing America. I told her I was the first nurse assigned to the Accra Embassy in 1954 and had taken care of the American personnel there, as well as those in the rest of West Africa. It was reassuring to have a doctor there now.

At Kinshasa airport I noticed the biggest transformation since I had last been there, before the changeover. There was a complete lack of the Europeans which had given Leopoldville a typical colony look, with white officers sporting their uniforms and strutting about with *topis** and walking sticks. I was pleased that the kow-towing seemed to be absent, and that the people held their heads high and with dignity. We were there only to change planes and go on to Johannesburg, where we were to get a smaller plane for Swaziland to visit missionary friends. But after our bout with fever in Timbuktu, I doubted the wisdom of getting too far off the beaten track. I phoned my friends and told them we had arrived in Johannesburg, but we would not be coming to Swaziland after all.

Shortly afterward, Don got into the shower and soon called me. I was shocked; he was black and gasping for breath. I helped him out of the shower and onto the bed and then called the concierge at the desk.

"Do you have any oxygen?" I asked.

"Yes. If you'll come right down, I'll have it ready for you."

At 7,000 feet, they were evidently used to these calls.

I left just long enough to pick up the oxygen and hurry back to our room. A doctor was also on his way. As soon as Don got a whiff of the oxygen, he began to turn pink and his breathing eased. We were so grateful! For the next couple of days we stayed in our room and kept the oxygen going. We also changed our travel plans.

Instead of taking the Blue Train to Cape Town, we took a flight to Rio de Janiero, which was as long as we dared to fly, and the captain agreed to pressurize the cabin for no more than 5,000 feet. They also had stewardesses who knew how to care for

* Sun hats.

Don, so he got along fine.

In Rio, we went out to a hotel on the beach and, at sea level, Don relaxed. He gained his strength and was breathing normally, but we rested there for two weeks before we decided we could make it to Miami, where we followed the same pattern of resting, walking along the beach and taking things easy.

I took advantage of this time, and the next day, I went on to Oklawaha to see the Holmeses. Eveline had been with me in Kathmandu back in 1952, and I had seen quite a lot of them in Delhi on various occasions. They told me about a foursome bridge game at the house of Peg Wilson during which my name was mentioned.*

"Not Juanita Owen?" one of them asked.

"Yes, the same Juanita."

"I knew a Juanita when I was in West Africa," one of the players announced.

"And I knew her in India," added a third.

"And I knew her in New York," volunteered the fourth.

None of them had known that the others had known me.

Back at the hotel, Don was feeling better, so we decided to head home to Phoenix the next day. During the next few months, Don was quite active. He was enjoying being back home again.

That was Don's final trip. After a few weeks, he again underwent surgery. The cancer had not only involved the liver, but had extended throughout the abdominal cavity, and in his weakened condition, he lived only two more days. That final Saturday, we had prayer together, and he prayed for all the patients in the hospital. Don talked normally and finally went off to sleep.

Early Sunday morning, we listened to a church service on the radio, and I could see he enjoyed it. A telephone call came in from his son, who said he would be free the following week to come and see his father. I told him that that would be too late, for his father was slipping away.

We prayed together, then he slept and fell into a coma. He

---

*The players were Eveline Holmes, who was with me in Nepal in 1952; Daisy Douglas who was a Mission Board representative; Ethel McIndoe, missionary in S. India; and Peg Wilson, wife of Ross Wilson, head of Firestone Plantation in Harbel, West Africa.

passed away quietly that Sunday morning.

I sat there for a long time, recalling the years we had had together. Those final few joyous months made up for any hardship I might have experienced. It was Don's triumph! I could not weep, for I knew that Don was past all mortal pain and that he was at home with the Lord.

At the memorial service, an Episcopal priest spoke and a close friend read the memorial service. A second service was held at the Shriner's Garden in Seattle, where numbers of family and business friends gathered. Don had been commodore of the Seattle Yacht Club and many friends had appreciated all that he had done. The Shriner service was impressive, as various friends took part, and the ashes were placed in a crypt in the wall of the Shriner's Garden, next to those of his brother.

Dr. Carl Taylor visits the Flemings in Kathmandu. Dr. Taylor and Bethel Fleming along with Dr. Carl Fredericks were the backbone of the medical work and the founding of Shanta Bhawan Hospital.

Bob and his friend, Sir Edmund Hillary with whom he shared his great love for the mountains of Nepal as well as his love for the Nepalese people.

Bob in Nepalese dress is discussing the Bird Book with son Bob and the two Nepalese artists.

At right: Young Bob assumes the role of teacher as his father looks on.

Below: A reticulated python has Bob's interest.

Below: Examining one of the world's largest hornbills known.

Bob chats with two trekkers as he rests by the roadside.

At left: Bob loved music and wrote songs of Woodstock School.
Below: Botany was another hobby. Here he is examining a specimen.

Above: Bob's letters were a joy to his many friends.

Right: Exploring the Karnali River.

Frances P. Bolton (right) on her visit to West Africa. She was the patron saint of my school of nursing, and at the time of this photo was on the Foreign Relations Committee of Congress.

June 1985 at the Cosmos Club in Washington, D.C., where Bob and Senator Fulbright (seated in the background) were being honored. The senator had just related how he had succeeded in getting his "Fulbright Bill" through Congress, and Bob handed the podium to me to reply.

BOOK EIGHT

ON THE WINGS OF A BIRD

OF A BIRD

1979-1987

Chapter XX

Evening Shadows

A friend, Dr. Lucille Dagress, urged me to travel with her around the world, but she wanted to go to India, Nepal and the Orient, where I had been only recently. I demurred. I did not want to visit those same old haunts again, and I was more interested in the Balkans, where I had never been. We compromised. I would go separately to the Balkans and she would join me in Zagreb, from where we would then travel together to Athens, Bombay, Delhi and Kathmandu.

She was very interested in Oriental religions which she had been teaching. To her, Christianity was accountable for two world wars, while Oriental philosophies were gentle. In Delhi, I made it a point to show her various religious shrines.

We first went to a Sikh *gurdwara** where, at worship time, well-dressed men sat on one side of the hall and women on the other. The talk was ecumenical, spiced with passages from the *Holy Granth Sahib.*** The worshippers served themselves sweetened vermicelli from a common ceremonial dish and the atmosphere was cordial.

As devotees left, disciples washed their feet. Other devotees caught the water flowing off the feet and drank it, as do the Hindus who drink water from the holy Ganges River.

The Jama Musjid had a huge platform for worshippers on Fridays, but our visit was not on a holy day, so only a few Muslims were there. The Birla Temple, where several religions worshiped together, was modern and beautiful, and Sarnath was one of the foremost Buddhist shrines, with numbers of devotees coming and

* Temple.
** The Sikh Bible.

going. Priests in their saffron robes were much in evidence, butter lamps flickered at the feet of a large replica of Buddha, and worshippers prostrated themselves in front of it. The atmosphere was calm and peaceful.

Varanasi,* the center of Hinduism, daily draws many pilgrims to worship in the sacred waters of the Ganges. Nude *sadhus*, rubbed with ashes, sat and stared at the sun, while sacred cattle roamed through the streets at will, and columns of smoke rose above cremation pyres along the Ganges River. Hinduism is more a way of life than a religion. For one who was teaching about these religions and had never seen them in action, these experiences were revealing.

Seeing the Taj Mahal is like gazing down over the Grand Canyon for the first time. Words fail as one stands and looks, not to be distracted by a clatter of flying foxes (fruit bats) hanging from the limbs of a nearby tree. And as one makes his way down the long avenue lined with cypress trees, the shrine becomes more intense.

The glistening marble is inlaid with precious stones and Arabic quotations span the archways. The four minarets are tall, slender and graceful. Within the structure, sounds reverberate, and when one sings a chord, it comes back as music from a grand organ.

This is the site of the grave of Mumtaz-i-Mahal, the wife of Shah Jahan, who built the Taj in her memory, then was buried by her side. Visitors glide by in padded slippers. The Taj was just as beautiful this time as when I first saw it fifty years earlier.

Then we were off to fascinating Nepal. Beyond the Gangetic Plain with its many clusters of mud villages, rose the well-remembered Himalayan foothills, crowned to the north by snow-clad ranges. It is always thrilling to fly parallel to the roof of the world. I had written ahead to my two nurse friends, the girls who had come to our hospital for training in 1952. One was now professor of Nursing at Tribhuvan University and the other, the public health director for the Kingdom of Nepal. I hadn't contacted Dr. Fleming, who was on a fern expedition in far eastern Nepal.

It was hard to believe that this now-modern air strip was

* Formerly known as Benares.

once a village cow pasture! Disembarking passengers streamed toward the customs counters, where officials checked visas and we waited for our heavy luggage. There was quite a bit of jostling in that limited area, but finally our bags were carried by porters out to waiting taxis (certainly different from 1952, when only a single rattle-trap Rolls Royce taxi was on hand).

The eight-minute drive to town led along the road bordered by flowering cherry trees, which bloom in the fall. We skirted newly-harvested rice fields to the city and on to the Annapurna Hotel. Here, the nurses Uma and Ruki waited to greet us.

In the heart of Kathmandu, the hotel was surrounded by a beautiful garden. I had invited Uma and Ruki to dinner at the hotel that evening, but when we got to our rooms, there was a note from Dr. Fleming, asking me to have dinner with *him* that evening. I called and told him I had invited the girls to dinner.

"Why don't you join us?" I asked. "You can manage four women."

So, we all had dinner together, reminiscing about old times and catching up on events that had transpired in the intervening years. Uma had planned a dinner in her home the next evening, and our two and a half days there filled up quickly with other plans.

We had many animated chats with the nurses, who brought us up to date on people and happenings, and my doctor companion and I toured the kaleidoscopic bazaar with its cosmopolitan stream of passersby. There were fruit stands, Nepali caps, Tamang wool jackets, Tibetan rugs, and bookstores where little boys begged for money to buy a dictionary and as soon as the benefactor disappeared, promptly would return the book for cash.

The next forenoon, Bob (Dr. Fleming) took me to the American embassy for a little business. We stopped at a nursery and picked out a flowering plant.

"I always buy a plant like this when I am in this part of the city," he confided. We walked through another part of the bazaar and found ourselves on New Road.

"I'm feeling hungry; let's get something to eat," he suggested.

The Crystal Hotel was just across the street, so we found a table in the candle light of "The Other Room." We had chicken sandwiches, but it wasn't the food that mattered. As we talked, we found that we were soulmates. Both of us felt our lives were directed by the Lord, with whom we walked day by day. The joy of that discovery! That was the only occasion when we had a little time alone together.

The evening party in Uma Das's home was quite Nepali. To reach there, we turned out of the crowded Dilli Bazaar, up an incline and into a private compound. What an attractive residence Uma and her family had! Guests included Uma's doctor sister, her mother, and several Nepali doctors whom Bob knew, and the Nepali food and enjoyable conversation were followed by music. The evening passed all too quickly.

The next day we flew to Rangoon. Bob came down to the airport, bringing us each an orchid to wear. Did he think I was a little special? In goodbye Bob simply extended both hands. There was no other mark of affection, only a loving look in his eyes. Kathmandu had meant more than I dreamed it would.

What a different Burma compared to what I had known twenty-five years earlier. Men and women no longer wore the colorful, distinctive costumes. A pity.

The Shwe Dagon Pagoda was much the same, with its impressive cylindrical tower covered with gold leaf. We had to take off our shoes, as usual, and the jute carpet underfoot was rough. We stepped aside to avoid pigeon droppings. Candles flickered in numbers of niches, before Buddhist shrines, with devotees kneeling before several of them in quiet meditation. We were also able to drive around the city and see the sights.

We took a train up-country, where the delightful Mandalay Palace had been bombed and was a burnt-out shambles. I was so glad I had had the good fortune to see it earlier, with all its magnificent lacquer work. Bells still rang in the nearby Arakan Pagoda. Dr. Dagress seemed to enjoy much of what she saw on this, her first visit to Burma, but I was sad over the changes that had occurred these past years and over leaving Bob after my short visit to Nepal.

Upon leaving Burma, I dropped Bob a card. He wrote me, too, regretting the fact that my travels took us farther and farther apart.

Then to Bangkok, with its porcelain-chipped pagodas. At our

hotel, 108 priests were lined up with their bowls to receive special food that brought merit to the givers. We took a boat through some of the canals, which were shallow and smelly. At one point, as we were getting out of the boat, Dr. Dagress slipped and fell half inside and half outside the boat. I had seen a thick gray tube lying in the water under her. It suddenly became very much alive, for it was no tube, but a very large snake, a sea serpent!

The hawkers were selling fish and flowers from their small boats, and my companion bought several pieces of colorful silk. There are delightful things to buy and what an interesting setting in which to shop.

We were soon in Honolulu, where we stayed for a few days. In our hotel, I was attracted by a beautiful white dress, decorated by hand-painted irises, my favorite flower. When I went up to our room, I found a cable from Bob stuck behind the doorknob, and my heart went pitty-pat. Dr. Dagress was curious about it, but I did not tell her what it was. After reading the cable, I went right down and bought that dress. It just *might* be my wedding dress.

When we reached Phoenix, the letters and missives from Bob began to arrive with some regularity. He was evidently as lonesome as I was, for he had been alone the seven years since Bethel had died. He was tender and loving in these letters, and each one reassured me that we were indeed soulmates. Finally, they were less frequent. I had forgotten about his trip to East Nepal from where it was still almost impossible to write. Out in tents in the rain and leeches, one can only think.

I was getting more and more depressed, when Dr. Harvey and Aimee Frazier from Spokane visited me for a few days.

"Let's pray about it," suggested Harvey.

We did and my heart was lifted. It was not ten minutes later that the phone rang. It was a message from Western Union.

"May I announce our engagement?" Bob was asking.

"Why, he hasn't even proposed to me yet!" I thought.

I discovered that announcing one's engagement by correspondence left a lot to be desired. In a letter which followed, Bob asked me to make some wedding plans.

This was January and I considered the month of April, which in Phoenix is delightful. It is pleasant outdoors and flowers are in full bloom. Yes, that would be good time for our wedding, and I wrote Bob about it.

In his reply, he said, "I didn't mean for you to plan for the wedding for I have already done that. We'll be married here in Kathmandu."

That was news to me. I had been to Kathmandu a couple of times recently and was not eager to go again, not even for a wedding. But plans went forward and we set the date for the 7th of April, 1979—in Kathmandu! I packed the new dress which I had bought in Honolulu. It *would* be my wedding dress.

I asked Bob to meet me in Bangkok for a few days to work out the program in more detail. We met as old friends and certainly not as a newly-engaged couple. That afternoon, he suggested we go out and buy our wedding rings. We found a good place only a short distance away. It was good to see Bob's empty hand fitted with the ring. We both walked on the same spiritual plane, and as Bob put it, we were just fitting into God's plan—together we would walk with Him.

The flight into spectacular Kathmandu Valley was without incident. Bob Jr. and his wife, Linda, were there to meet us. How they got all four of us, plus our luggage, into their little Volkswagen, I'll never know. They drove us to their house in Kupandol, then on to the Naryani Hotel, where Bob had engaged a room for me on the fourth floor. As there was no electricity, there were no elevators, and we had to walk up.

Two days later, we were invited to Bob's house for dinner. As we came in, here were Bob Jr. and Linda coming out onto the road. She was carrying a pie.

"Oh, we forgot to tell you that friends had asked us to come over for dinner. However, Nuchhe, the cook, will get you a meal."

As it turned out, there was very little to eat, mainly leftovers.

Towards the evening, an ornithologist friend dropped in and he and Bob began to compare notes and catch up on bird news. I was completely ignored.

When it came time to return to the hotel, Bob tried to get a taxi, and none was available. We walked about a mile, down side streets, to the main road—but no taxis. Bob pointed up the road and said that the hotel was right ahead and that I couldn't miss it. He returned to his bird friend and left me to walk about a mile in the dark. This was too much.

When I reached the hotel, I resolved to take the next plane home. I looked for a telephone, but could not find one, so I went to bed and prayed that God would show me what to do. As a result, the next morning I resolved to talk with the minister who was going to marry us, but I did not know where he lived.

Bob had an appointment at Shanta Bhawan Hospital and took me along. Just as we arrived, another car drove up behind us. Who should it be but the minster! Bob took off in the direction of the reception desk, and I realized this was the opportunity for which I had been praying.

"What brings you here? Are you coming to see a patient?" I inquired.

"No, I have no one in mind," he replied. "I felt an urge to come to the hospital, for someone must be needing me."

"I think I am that person," I said. I unburdened myself; "Bob seemed so cold and unfeeling."

"Oh, Bob is not cold; he has a warm heart and personality," he assured me. "And he is lonesome and needs you."

On the following day, another unhappy incident occurred. It was the celebration of the 25th anniversary of the founding of the United Mission by the Flemings, Millers and others. I had looked forward to the event and we had planned our wedding day with this in mind. When the invitation from the United Missions to Nepal came out, printed in large letters was the admonition, "Do Not Bring Guests." I looked further and saw Bob's name there, but not mine, so I knew I couldn't go. But Bob asked me to be ready by 4 o'clock and I dressed for the occasion. As the time neared, Bob suggested we go and look around the bazaar, for we might find something we liked. It was almost four and I became more and more fidgety. Finally, we drove home, missing the event entirely. I figured Bob had not gone to the celebration because I had not been invited. Later, I was surprised to learn that Bob had forgotten all about it.

The next day, I met Uma, who exclaimed, "Where were you? We all expected to see you there at the UMN celebration."

I made some excuse, not wishing to say that Bob had forgotten. Later, Mrs. Bond, who was one of the principle movers in the UMN said, "Not inviting Juanita was a serious oversight on our part. She should have come anyway." In spite of the "No Guests" directive? I thought.

However, wedding time was a very happy occasion. This time, numbers of my family were present. My brother Robert and his wife Mary, and my brother Ralph and his son Bob, came from far-away America. The ceremony would be in the beautiful garden of Lincoln School, with its three small gazebos on the grounds. The center one, I planned to be our altar. The piano would be near in another one and in the third, we would serve refreshments and the cake. When I announced my plans to the minister who would marry us, he was aghast.

"You won't find me performing a ceremony where insects from the thatch above keep falling on my head," he stated emphatically.

Well, I couldn't blame him; we must do something about it. I hurried to the bazaar and bought yards and yards of light blue cloth, which I stretched and sewed on a little toy sewing machine until my shoulders ached. When the canopy was in place, it completely prevented insects from falling down. The minister was happy and we proceeded to arrange the altar.

I had brought a suit for Bob from the States and had to do some alterations until it fit well. All the sewing I had to do left me weary.

The principal of LIncoln School lent us beautiful azalea plants, which we arranged on the sides of the altar. We took some cushions and rolled them up and placed them on the altar. These proved to be quite wobbly and I found it difficult to keep my balance, but they would have to do. The minister and the pianist came and we went through the rehearsal on a day that was quite windy. I hoped it would be less so the next day.

April 7th—The Big Day! Everything was in order by noon. The wedding party assembled shortly before three. We had three clergymen—the minister of the Protestant Congregation, Rev. Alex Fleming (no relation); Father Moran, my Jesuit priest friend of long-standing; and a Nepali pastor, Robert Kartak. These led the procession, followed by Bob and his son. Bob's sister, Helen, was maid of honor.

I came in on the arm of my brother Bob. As we stood in front of the altar, our soloist from the Philippines sang "My Task," and later, while we were kneeling, she sang "The Lord's Prayer." The usual signing of the book followed. Then we were greeted by our 200 guests, some of whom came to say goodbye, for Bob was leaving Nepal after twenty-five years. Among the guests were about twenty people I had known in 1952, when I first came to Nepal.

At the third gazebo, Bob cut the wedding cake with a Nepali *kukri* knife. Beyond, the hostess of the American Club had set a pleasing table of refreshments. After the ceremony, Ishwar Shumshere Jung Bahadur Rana, whom Bob had met in West Nepal thirty years previously, stepped up to me and placed on me the traditional Nepali golden wedding necklace. Princess Madhuri was there and the two nurses, all of whom I had known in 1952. There were the Carl Fredericks with whom I had worked in India at Fatehgarh, guests from the American Embassy and USAID, and a host of Nepali friends and members of the United Mission to Nepal.

There was much conversation and taking of pictures. On the table were the beautiful Bride of Heaven orchids that Bob had gathered in the Godaveri hills, and which I also carried. Finally, we stepped into a car and were driven to the Soaltee Hotel, where brother Bob took us to dinner. On the walls of the room was a series of bird paintings that our artists had done for the bird book. It was a happy occasion.

Not long afterward, the Protestant Congregation put on an evening program designed around a bird theme, in which six or eight members took part. The narration was hilarious, portraying birds as people-watchers and expressing their observations.

"Imagine having two sets and sometimes three sets of eyes!" (Binoculars, glasses and normal) or "Humans keep their young ones in the nest even after they are full grown." (Bob Jr. and Linda, in the same house with Bob Sr.)

At intervals up on stage appeared human versions of birds of various species. There was the myna bird (a person dressed in an old coat carrying a pick axe), and the hornbill was something else again—what a surprising headgear! Then there was a peacock, in feathers with large ocelates. The narrator went on to say that the Fleming men once collected such a specimen for the Field Museum of Chicago. Once while passing through high grass where a couple of tigers were roaring at each other. The narrator thought they were angry, perhaps because of the human intruders.

"No," my husband called from the audience, "they were in love."

We seldom have had so many laughs in an hour as we did that evening.

Now it was time to pack, but first Linda had a garden sale with people milling in and out of the house. In cleaning out his office, Bob came upon a batch of pickled snakes!

He was about to leave most things behind, but I went into his room and recovered a number of mementos, especially family pictures, which I knew he would appreciate later. There were books, including a beautiful coffee table volume on Nepal given to us by the church members, who also presented us with a Tibetan rug with a strange insect design in the center. And Bob delved into a large, old trunk from which he extracted numerous dried fern specimens for the Herbarium at the University of Michigan.

Finally, we had our parcels ready and went down to the travel agent, who said that customs at the airport would have to go through our things. I took some gunny sacking and cord with which to sew up the parcels. The customs man sat on the ground as he opened everything, after which we had to sew them up again. What a job!

It seemed wise for us to visit some of the United Mission installations, and before we left the country we flew to Pokhara and saw the Boy's School. This institution was created at the request of a government cabinet minister who wanted a school where boys could learn "discipline and character." There were some 250 boys there. When he first saw the terraces full of boulders dropping off toward the river, Bob wondered how one could have a boy's school on that land. He hadn't counted on Bob Buckner, who called in a corps of stone-chippers and proceeded to construct a number of beautiful stone buildings. I thought the campus was very attractive.

From here we flew to Bhairhawa, near the Indian border, where a station Jeep met us and took us to Butwal. The United Mission had built a number of large sheds, as well as private homes, and had electrified the place with power from the river channeled by a mile-long aqueduct bored through a mountain.*

The UMN had enough electricity to illuminate the whole town of Butwal. Recently the king had flown in to inspect installations there, and as he looked down at the area, he asked what the green spot was in the brown and treeless scene.

"That is the United Mission Engineering Institute," he was informed.

"Then make the rest of the town green also," he ordered.

His Majesty was especially impressed by the hydroelectric system, which had been created with equipment brought from Norway. I was impressed, too, and by the *gobar-gas* project, whereby village folks could cook all their food on methane gas created from cow and buffalo dung mixed with water. I saw that the United Mission was making a great contribution to the life of the Nepali people.

We visited Pokara and various mission stations, as Bob wanted to say goodbye to his missionary friends. Then we went to Delhi where, again, some of his old students had a luncheon for us and, in spite of the lumps of salt in the cake, it was a festive and happy occasion. Our visit to Bombay was special because the Vakil Press, publishers of his book *Birds of Nepal* took care to make our visit a memorable one. They presented each of us with a book especially bound in silk and lovingly inscribed. We would never forget them.

After all of the goodbye visits, we were ready to enjoy our honeymoon. The Seychelles were interesting and we had days of rest watching the waves roll in from the sea and watching the glorious sunsets over the water and the big full moon rising. We then spent time in Nairobi, where from our hotel balcony, we watched strutting black and white crows and scores of superb starlings with their shiny colorful coats, ever so resplendent as they hopped along the parkway lawn.

Kenya was a good central place from which to see the many bird sanctuaries of Lake Nakura, which Bob enjoyed no end. Amboseli with its lions, deer, giraffes, and wildebeasts roaming about free, and its backdrop of Kilimanjaro, was a treat.

---

* The engineer who was showing us around had been sucked accidentally into the flume. But he had held his breath and came out alive at the other end!

A giraffe stepped out from a grove of trees and I called to Bob, "Look, Bob, over there!"

"I think it's a widow bird," he answered.

In his typical way, he saw the bird, not the giraffe!

Bob had some friends, the Hills, in Zambia that he wanted to visit. They were living in Kafue and were helping the fishermen build homes for themselves and secure from the government bits of land left by the white exiles who had fled the country. It was all arranged, until our flight was stepped up by two hours, due to the war in Tanzania, and we missed the flight. The airlines put us up in a hotel for the two days' wait for another plane.

The Hills were glad to see us and took us to their home on Kafue Lake—a camper that had been placed on a raft of oil drums. For a guest house, they had contrived another raft a short distance away in the lake. It was about 6'x8' with an awning and chicken wire around it and sheets put up for privacy. The place had a bunk bed, upper and lower, and one chair and a table made of packing cases. It boasted a candle, matches and a bucket. What a bridal suite!

After depositing us on our raft, they took off for theirs, warning us, "Don't worry about the rocking of the raft, as hippos get under it and rub their backs on the barrels. They won't turn it over; you just think they will."

I was wondering what we would do in the night, if we needed anything. Just wait until dawn, I guessed. Next morning, they came for us for breakfast.

It was great going down to Victoria Falls at Livingstone and watching the great Zambesi River as it rolled off the cliff with a mighty roar.

The deSpindlers, Alf and Margaret, were waiting for us in Wettingen, Switzerland, and what a treat we had there. Looking across the valley, the distant peaks appeared to be only a stone's throw away. The Wetterhorn arose majestically on the horizon. In the clear air; it seemed so close that one could reach out and touch it. The blue gentians covered the mountain slopes and the cow bells tinkled, not in the distance, but right at our gate, as they waited for someone to open it so they could go home.

Then we traveled on to Norway near Oslo where we visited the Bergsakers. He was a silversmith and showed us a lovely tea set he had made for his bride when they were married, and his library boasted fifteen volumes of his writings on mission life and interests. He had trekked with Bob in 1949 in western Nepal on Bob's initial trip into the country to find birds.

In England, we had several places to visit—one of which was the Kew Gardens, where Bob had sent several hundred fern specimens from the Himalayas. These were being classified and studied. While Bob was at the museum, I met my friend, Dr. Neville Everard, for tea, and we had a good time reminiscing until Bob was free to join us. We then visited our Cawnpore friends, Rosalind and Paul Broomhall, at Penhurst, near Battle in Sussex. The couple lived in a 16th century house, which had been lived in throughout its history, although it had been converted, electrified, and refurbished. An old stone church in the neighborhood had been in use since the 14th century. It gave us a sense of antiquity and substance, which we Americans seldom experience.

By the time we arrived in America, we felt like a well-married couple, so it was a surprise when the Millers, who lived in Liverpool, Pennsylvania, had another celebration awaiting us. They deposited us in a motel and told us to rest up. They would send for us for dinner. When dinner time came, they were at our door with a car and took us to their home, which was decorated with flowers, wedding bells and candlelight. As we approached the steps, we heard the piano playing "Here Comes the Bride," and inside a host of friends had gathered. It was a wonderful homecoming; we enjoyed our friends more than I can say—those in India, Nepal, America, England, and all over the world.

After stopping in Chicago to see my sister Bernice, my nephew Ernest Fordham, his wife Betsy, and his three children, Bob and I arrived at our home in Phoenix, which he had never seen. He quickly adjusted to everything, including the church work and many of my friends. We found it was already hot there in June and time to look to the cool northland. We would go to Washington and see his daughter Sally and family. Maybe, if we were lucky, we'd find a house we could rent, or at least some land where we could build a place of our own.

> "We'll build a sweet little nest
> Somewhere in the West

And let the rest of the world go by."

In time, we found a place right on the water, with 272 feet of frontage on the Wenatchee River. The place was delightfully cool and had a backdrop of mountains, remindful of Switzerland. It was surrounded by woods where ponderosa pines and hemlock grew, and the ground was a carpet of blue lupines and bloodroot blossoms. This was it—the most idyllic place, and here we would build our dream cottage. It took the rest of the summer to purchase, make plans and hire a builder. When October came, we left, returning in the spring to construct the house.

Sally Beth and Vern Beieler and their boys Mike and Jimmie were frequent visitors, and the highway from Seattle to Wenatchee passed by our house so more visitors came, and that was joy to our hearts.

Soon as our house was completed, we had many friends drop in. Bob would go to the piano and play—only this time, it was different:

> "We'll build a sweet little nest
> Somewhere in the West
> And let the *best* of the world come by."

And they were the best. The missionary family is a close one, not only because of the places and work they have in common, but also for the wonderful family spirit we've shared.

We spent six months of the year in Phoenix, driving the 1200 or so miles. These trips were some of the most enjoyable days of our lives. Bob got acquainted with the birds of the area, often joining in the bird-watching groups that he already knew, as he had been in Washington on trips home to visit Sally and family.

It was new to me, but I loved it. Even the snakes of the area that we disturbed by our building seemed not to resent us. Bob found a rubber boa under a tree and brought him (or I should say *her*, because we named her Edna) inside. The next day, he found the mate. One morning, Bob was going to the local bank, carrying the snake in his hands.

"Honey," I pointed out, "you'd better leave that snake at home. People will wonder what kind of folks have moved into town, you with your Nepali *topi* and carrying a snake."

Can't you just see the picture?

He just put it inside his shirt and we went on to the bank. While he was transacting business, I could see the snake making its way up to the neck of his shirt. I started getting nervous and said, "Come on, let's hurry."

He had just finished his business when the head of the snake appeared at his neck line. We got out of the bank before anyone noticed.

There was also a larger blue racer which he caught and put in a box in his office. We had just gotten into bed that night when I thought of the snake.

"Bob, did you put that snake outside? I'm afraid it might get out of the box, and I wouldn't want it crawling around inside the house."

He went out to look and was gone a long time. When he came back, I said, "Did you take care of the snake?"

"Yes, I took care of it," he answered and we went to bed.

The next day I was dusting and sweeping the living room when I lifted up a cushion on the settee and there was the snake. I screamed for Bob to come, but as he was on the phone long distance, he took his time. I still screamed. He finally came, caught the snake, and took it outside. I wondered what the telephone caller thought of Bob's new bride!

Bob and I both felt we were retired and free and we should take advantage of this freedom and travel. One of his favorite piano pieces increased our desire to go and see for ourselves:

"Those far away places, with strange sounding names
They're calling, calling to me."

"How about the Galapagos Islands? You've always wanted to see new birds and animals," I asked Bob.

We flew to Iquitos in Peru and took a river boat up the waters of the Amazon.

"It's too dark in there," observed Bob as he strained to see forms to go along with the birdsong he heard in the jungle, but try as he might, no forms came to view. The trees were just too thick. "Tomorrow we're going to another spot a little more open."

At the other spot, according to a brochure, the hoatzins—primitive birds that climbed trees, walked on all fours and swam underwater—were basking in the sun, their webbed feet helpful in the swampy soil. (I later learned that only the fledglings have claws on their wings, for climbing, contrary to what the brochure claimed.)

Cuzco and Machu Picchu lay ahead of us on our way back to Lima and from there we continued to Guayaquil, where a boat awaited to take us to the Galapagos Islands.

The Islands were discovered in 1785 by pirates. Darwin came a hundred years later and the world learned about the place.* There were birds there so tame you could hold them in your hand —blue-footed booby birds and red and black frigate birds with their throats all puffed up.

I walked ahead of the group, watching a blue-footed booby who stood on the path before me. As I approached, he first looked at my feet very intently; then as I stood in front of him, he looked up a little higher at my knees, then still higher at my body, then up into my face. As our eyes met, he never blinked, just stared into my eyes. Such a knowing, intelligent look he had.

We were just about two feet apart, but he never moved. We just stared at each other to get better acquainted and then, as the crowd was coming up behind me, I started to move on. He never changed his position, but stared at each one in turn. I felt I had a real friend in that bird. I wanted to hold him close and tell him so, but we were not allowed. They had absolutely no fear of people, just a trusting acceptance.

Brown penguins and reptiles of huge dimensions just lay in the sand and sunned themselves, the sleeping marine iguanas would let people just step over them. The tortoises didn't open their eyes.

Coming back through Guayaquil, on our way to the airport to get our plane for Quito, we saw the five-story building Clarence had built for the American Consulate. Our good friends, Ruth

---

* In 1959 the Charles Darwin Foundation was established and Ecuador made the islands into a National Park. The park covers 3,000 miles of land mass and 30,000 sq. miles of ocean. Giant turtles weigh up to 500 pounds. (See Eric Hoffman in the *Rotarian*, March 1987, P. 19).

and Neil Weibe, were waiting for us at the airport. They are with the Wycliff Bible Translators and have been living down in the jungles of Ecuador for most of their time there. They now live in an apartment in Quito, so their two little girls can go to school. While we were visiting them, the girls asked us to talk to the 6th grade class. I told them I had taught their grandmother when she was in the third grade in India. What fun! (She was Agnes Kelly in the Mission at Siwait.)

From there we headed south to Chile. It was already getting cold and we knew that the pass over the Andes would soon be covered with snow—and perhaps be impossible to cross. As we started climbing, the snow came. We were in a Mercedes bus and made the grade, but small cars slipped on the icy road and had to be pushed back onto the road, while the midsized ones simply sat there until they could be towed out. As we descended the eastern slopes of the mountains, the sun began to shine and we came down into the most heavenly valley. It was studded with deep blue lakes surrounded by soft purple mountains. Bariloche. What a paradise!

One of the sights I had always wanted to see was Iguassu Falls, which lies between Brazil, Uruguay and Paraguay—a massive cloverleaf of falls impossible to take in from any one place. We rented a helicopter and drank in the beauty while suspended over the whole. It made God and nature so close as to be almost overpowering. We had seen Niagara, Victoria Falls, and Angel Falls, and now Iguassu Falls. It was a glorious sight that will always remain with me.

I once gave a travel talk at Phoenix College and began with the story of an elderly man, with one foot in the grave, who announced to his neighbors that he was going around the world.

"What, an old man like you, going around the world?" they said.

"Yes, I haven't got long for this world and when I get to the pearly gates and the Lord asks me, 'Well, how did you like that world I made for you down there?' I would have to answer, 'Sorry, Lord, but I didn't see much of the place,' and He would be so disappointed that He had made such a beautiful world and I didn't take the trouble to go and see it."

Bob had been on several treks with Dr. Albertson,* from the University of Puget Sound, and now he was being invited for another trip to Nepal. Bob Jr. would take half of the students and his father and Dr. Albertson would take the other half, and they would meet at Lang Tang. It was an exciting prospect, and he accepted.

On our arrival in Kathmandu, we were presented with a copy of the *Rising Nepal* with a picture on the front page of tour guide Madan Gurung holding a copy of Bob's the *Birds of Nepal* with the caption, "Bird Book Saves Life of Guide."

It seems the guide was escorting a group of tourists through the Terai when a female rhino with its young was disturbed and charged at the group. The brave guide stepped out in front and the rhino bit him just where his bird book was in his hip pocket. The teeth marks went in to page 200!

Among the group were the Schneebecks, a couple who were interested in the trip, but who were not up to trekking. We decided to take a tour of our own, while the students were off on their trek, and Ailene Albertson, the Schneebecks and I visited the tourist spots in India: Agra, Fatehpur Sikri, the Red Fort, the Taj Mahal, Itmad-ud-daula, and a new tomb just outside Agra at Dayal Bagh. Here members of a religious sect were building a monument to their departed leader who had died many years ago. The edifice was being built entirely of marble, exquisitely designed with carvings of flowers and vegetables over its arches. Quotations from their sacred writings were cut out of semi-precious stones and inserted around the base.

I had first visited Dayal Bagh in 1927 when it was being built, and after nearly sixty years, it was still in the process of construction. It took one month for a father and son to slice a slab of marble one inch thick. No sound of hammer or chisel was to be heard; all work was done silently. There were signs up saying, "Do not talk to the workmen as they are meditating while they work." The beauty of the whole was breathtaking, even in its unfinished state.

We also visited the Ellora caves, which took one back in time

* Voted University Professor of the Year for 1986 in the U.S.

to antiquity, and we got out our history books to learn about them. They covered such a long period, and each new ruler left his imprint on the caves.

One of the loveliest spots in India is in the middle of an artificial lake—Udaipur, summer palace of Rajput kings—surrounded by blue waters and lily pads and rising in the center an edifice made of concrete lace. From every angle, one looks through arches and sees minarets and balconies draped with flowering vines. One can sit and relax and drink in the ethereal beauty, unperturbed by anything more than the soft patter of bare feet stopping by to attend to your wants.

Sitting in the sparsely occupied dining room with my back to a table where animated conversation was going on, I thought one voice sounded familiar. Just a fortnight before I had heard it, arguing with William Buckley in a heated debate. It was John Kenneth Galbraith—telling how his wife, who was seated next to him, would not consent to marry him until he took out papers and became an American citizen. When he arose, I shook his hand and reminded him of the debate.

"Buckley was an ass, wasn't he?" he remarked.

Jaipur, the pink city, rises on a hill with the beautiful old palace at the top. It was too steep to walk, so we took an elephant up the dusty cobblestone roadway. We were entertained the whole length of the road by an old man playing a fiddle comprised of only two strings, and making them sound like music from heaven—so soft, quaint and sweet.

When we arrived back in Kathmandu, I had just enough time to plan a surprise for Bob on his birthday, which was March 22nd. He was still up in Lang Tang, which was accessible only by helicopter, so I booked a flight for the next morning. Then I went home and baked two large cakes.

Unfortunately, about nine that night, the travel agency called to say that the king had commandeered the helicopter for the day and we would not be going after all. Later when the trekking party returned home, we learned that on his 77th birthday,* Bob

---

* In Nepal, the 77th birthday is a propitious time, and the honoree is festooned and paraded through the streets with the greatest respect and honor.

was carried around the camp on the shoulders of some of the students in true Nepalese fashion.

In the fall of 1983, I had to have surgery and so we were quiet for a while, then we decided to look for a retirement home. Our house in Phoenix was too big for me to keep up alone. I had a good housekeeper, but she was getting on in years, too. We searched several places in the Phoenix area, then went farther afield to California. We found a place in Claremont which, it seemed, was the answer.

By 1984, we had completed the room on our cottage home and had moved to Claremont hoping still to do some traveling and spend the summers in Washington State. It was a big job, moving a house filled with the accumulation of so many years.

We got settled and I went back to Phoenix to wind up our affairs—and it turned out to be too much for me. I had a heart attack and ended up in the hospital for a few weeks. Then it was back to Claremont to recuperate, followed by more surgery. When the weather got hot, Bob prepared to leave for Wenatchee, but the doctor would not let me go with him. So Bob left for our home in Leavenworth which, by then, was complete and beautifully furnished with piano, our Persian rugs and Bob's paintings. He would have to go alone and enlist the help of his sister, Helen, who lived in Washington, and Sally Beth, who would come by and assist her when necessary.

That fall, Bob Jr. and Linda came up to use the house, and that was the last time we ever saw our "sweet little nest." I was not able to go up and take care of closing it up, and that December, it caught fire and burned. It had gone through three winters and everything worked out fine, but not so this time.

I was devastated, and still too ill to fully deal with our loss. Bob had returned to Claremont and we began to plan our lives around our new retirement center. Gone was the lovely dream of woods and river and birds and flowers. But we would survive.

Bob was having fevers and a recurrence of his old malaria from Nepal. I had come into Bob's life at a time when he needed me. I would nurse, support and care for him, as I had for Howard, Clarence, and Don. I enjoyed making him happy, preparing the tea for our friends who stopped by, and our other house guests. I enjoyed putting his songs into print and making them available to old students and friends. I enjoyed his birds and the snakes (at a distance) he enjoyed, and even the lapses of memory when I was ignored, knowing all the while that he cared much for me and loved me. His eyes, so expressive, would look up at me and he would say, "I love you, my sweetheart, and my Jo." *

When we met back in Kathmandu in the Crystal Palace tea room, eight years before, it was indeed a meeting of our minds and hearts. We two were one. As Bob expressed it, we were yoked together with the Lord and with each other. We *had* to succeed with Him holding our hands.

In the summer of 1985, WOSA** planned a reunion, along with alumni of Kodaikanal School in Washington, D.C., and asked Bob to attend. It seemed an impossibility at first, but when I saw his health improve and his eyes sparkle at the thought of it, I made up my mind to do all in my power to see that he got there, and I made reservations. The affair was a celebration in honor of Senator Fulbright and Bob—Senator Fulbright being the choice of Kodaikanal School in South India and Bob the one chosen by Woodstock School to honor.

They were both on the platform in the ballroom of the Cosmos Club and Senator Fulbright was the first to speak. He told of how, in the post-World War II period, he had sought for six years to get through Congress a bill authorizing scholarships for students to study abroad, and got nowhere with the pleading and badgering of fellow senators. Then, a letter came from India, from a nurse, asking Congress to stop the destruction and discarding of surplus war goods—chiefly medical supplies, surgical instruments, x-ray machines, and dental equipment, left from the war effort and not now needed.

He knew this would appeal to the Congress, so he attached his bill on as a rider and presented it to Congress. It passed, as he assumed it would.

As he told this story, there in the presence of a couple hun-

---

* Jo is a Scottish word for sweetheart, also my initials.

** Woodstock Old Students Association.

dred people—Ambassadors, Congressmen, and many others—I began to get goose pimples. I was the nurse who had written the letter! I was in Bombay and saw perfectly good new equipment destroyed and discarded. I had telegraphed to Mrs. Bolton, my friend from Cleveland days who was on the Foreign Affairs Committee of Congress, and told her what was happening. She wired back that if I could get letters from three eyewitnesses as to what was going on, she would take it up with the Committee, of which Senator Fulbright was chairman. I got letters from boys who had been given brand new *kukris** to slash *new* mosquito nets, so they could be destroyed as damaged material! She took my letter to the committee and it was quickly expedited.

I went over to Senator Fulbright and shook his hand, saying what pleasure it gave me after all these years to thank him. Little did I realize until then that I had helped him get his bill through Congress.** What an ovation!

Bob's speech was like a soft touch of love you could almost feel. He spoke affectionately of a trip to Dhanaulti when he took a group of Boy Scouts to camp out under the stars one night. As it grew dark, and the night sounds of the forest became audible, he knew the fears that the younger boys would be experiencing, so he said to one, "Stanley, if you're afraid, you can bring your bed in closer."

"Oh, Mr. Fleming, I'm not afraid."

But he did come a little closer, and then after it grew even darker, a little closer still. And he related how, in the middle of the night, he felt two little knees poking in his ribs. This brought the house down. It was typical of Bob's concern and why he is remembered so lovingly by his students at Woodstock.

Bob was wheeled around Washington in a wheelchair, but it was well worth the effort. The Smithsonian was having an exhibition of village life in India and had brought in villagers with skills in various phases of Indian lore, weavers, carpenters, sweet-mak-

---

*Native Nepali knives.

** In the forty years since his bill passed in the Congress, 60,000 American Fulbright scholars have studied abroad and 100,000 foreign scholars have studied in the U.S. "costing maybe half as much as a Trident submarine." They form a nucleus of world leaders in all walks of life. (*L.A. Times*, 16 Oct. 1987)

ers, *chappati* makers, jewelry artisans, painters, all the trades one finds in rural India. Bob was entranced to see how accurately and realistically they could transport the life of the Indian villager to the modern life of Washington, D.C. We talked with the ones who spoke Hindi or Urdu, and all of them said this was their first sight of a big city. They had not even been to Delhi or Bombay!

Bob was in the hospital for the best part of the next year. Even though I was not able to care for him at home, we enjoyed each other's company, playing Scrabble in the evenings in his hospital room, playing music on our recording machines, or writing to friends, and having our evening devotions together. But it was hard to watch him grow weaker as the days went by. Whenever I looked into his eyes in the days of his long illness, he always came back with, "I love you, my sweetheart."

During Bob's illness, our faithful friends Sam and Mary Esther Burgoyne, who were with me in language school in India sixty years before, came and ministered to him. They lived just over the way in Pilgrim Place in Claremont and added so much to Bob's peace and comfort. Friends from Westminster Gardens in Duarte also came, as well as Woodstock students from all over. He remembered their names and where their families lived, even their class years.

I sat with him all day on the last day, as I somehow knew he soon would be leaving me. He was conscious right up to the last few moments, and then slipped quietly away. I sat there alone with him for a while praying. Prayer was like breathing. Bob was in God's care and I was content. I would go on. I would complete the story of my life which he had started and which I give to you now, wondering about God's purpose in it all.

One of Bob's students spoke of his many-faceted character. His patience in teaching, his inspiration to achieve, his love of nature, birds, ferns, flowers, and trees, his love of music and the songs he inspired. Another student wrote the following,* which was inscribed on the award presented to him at the ceremony:

"For teaching us to look with careful eyes; urging us to

---

* Wayne Wardwell, *Quadrangle*, Woodstock School Alumni Magazine, Summer, 1987, Issue 2, p. 12.

see both bird and beetle, as well as flower and fern—tracking them, recognizing them, saving them and valuing them.

"For showing us how to appreciate and explore the magnificent world of man and nature around us . . . from the lovely shapes of our beloved mountains and valleys to the minivets going north in April . . . from watching the monsoon mists closing in, or feeling the sweet susurration of the wind in the pines, to hearing the pygmy owlet calling from the deep valley at night.

"For seeking out the pathways to distant places, showing us the trails to special spots, bringing us this sense of great excitement, and encouraging us to climb to where the view is worthy of our lives . . .

"For opening to the world of wonder of Nepal; being "Silent Samaritan" there to mountain folk; hosting there the climber, the king, the writer, the wanderer; and publishing there his discoveries on the printed page.

"For sharing with us then his feel for song; telling that we must learn to sing; composing then the words of schooltime memory; and enlisting then the love of Woodstock 'til the day we die . . .

"We his loyal students salute him on this day of note, grateful that he taught us where to go, and pledging now to walk the road, 'rugged and steep,' for 'palms come from striving' we know."

We had a lovely memorial service for Bob and these were the words on the program expressing how we all felt:

"If I should ever leave you grieve not,
Nor speak of me with tears; but laugh and talk
Of me as if I were beside you there.
And when you hear a song or see a bird
I loved, please do not let the thought of me
Be sad . . . For I am loving you just as I always have.* "

As I look back over a long life, I see God's hand moving and working for my best all along. When, up in my room at the Fountain House, overlooking the park sparkling with moonbeams, it

* From a poem by Isla Paschal Richardson.

seemed that God was calling me to give up everything I held dear —that I would bury myself in a lonely village in India, with never a chance to travel or see anything of this world. How far from the life I have actually lived! I have seen a great many more places than the average person, and I have enjoyed every bit of it, knowing it was all a part of His plan for my life.

I come to the close of my days with a very great sense of gratitude. I think of all the people who have given me inspiration, love and affection throughout the years. Each time the door seemed to close on my dreams, another would open. God was very real to me and He would whisper that He had a plan He was working out in my life. He was holding me in His hands. Now that I come to the end and the shadows are gathering, I know that there will be a tomorrow. I will awake to find Him still there.

Bibliography

Beatter & Millard. *Beautiful Indian Trees.* London: Bale & Curnow, 1937.

The Burning Bush. The Metropolitan Church Association. Vol. 4, 27 April 1905: 1, 4, 5.

The Burning Bush. Vol. 27, 24 March 1927: 10

Candlin, Enid Saunders. *A Traveler's Tale.* New York: MacMillan Co., 1974.

Clarke, Arthur C. *Spring, 1984.* New York: Ballantine Books, 1983.

———. *1984: Spring—A Choice of Futures.* New York: Ballantine Books, 1984.

Collins, Larry and Dominique Lapierre. *Freedom at Midnight.* New York: Avon, 1975.

Cooke, Alistair. *America.* New York: Alfred A. Knopf, 1976.

Corbett, Jim. *Man-eaters of Kumaon.* New York: Oxford University Press, 1946.

Eichler, Arthur. *Ecuador.* New York: Thomas Y. Crowell Co., 1966.

Elliott, Elizabeth. *Thru Gates of Splendor.* New York: Harper & Co., 1957.

Fleming, Robert L. Sr., Bangdel & Fleming, Robert L. Jr. *Birds of Nepal.* Bombay, India: Vakil Press, 1976.

Fletcher, Grace Niles. *The Fabulous Flemings of Kathmandu.* New

York: E.P. Dutton, 1964.

Fletcher, Knebel. *The Zin-Zin Road.* Garden City: Doubleday, 1966.

Gunther, John. *Inside Africa.* New York: Harper & Row, 1955.

Harrer, Heinrich. *Seven Years in Tibet.* Translated by Richard Graves. New York: E.P. Dutton, 1953.

Hartley, Cecil B. *The Three Mrs. Judsons.* Philadelphia: Keystone Publishing, (before) 1920.

Harvey, Henry. *Howard B. Bitzer.* Siwait, India: Metropolitan Church Assn., 1936.

Hawkins, R.E. *Jim Corbett's India* ("The Muktesar Maneater"). New York: Oxford University Press, 1978.

Higginbottom, Sam. *Christ and the Plough.*

Jawaharlal Nehru, An Autobiography. London: Lowe & Briden, 1936.

Jeal, Tom. *David Livingstone.* New York: G.P. Putnam & Sons, 1973.

Johnson, Osa. *I Married Adventure.* New York: J.B. Lippincott, 1940.

Journal of the A.C.O.G. Nursing. Vol. 1, No. 2 (1972): 38-40.

Journal of the Bombay Natural History Society. Vol. 83, No. 2 (August 1986).

Kippling, Rudyard. *Something of Myself.*

Koenig, G.H. *Once Upon A Prairie.* Waukesha, WI: Waukesha Freeman, 1984: 65, 136-139, 140, 141.

Liberian Age (newspaper). C.C. Dennis, ed. Monrovia, Liberia, 1954.

Marks, John D. and Victor Marchetti. *C.I.A. and the Cult of Intelligence.* New York: Dell Press, 1983.

McCann, Charles. *Trees of India.* Bombay: D.B. Taraporevala Sons & Co.

Meyer, Karl E. "Did the Asians Beat Columbus Here By 1500 Years?" *The Washington Post,* 4 Dec. 1960.

Moore, Clark D. and David Eldredge, Ed. *India Yesterday & Today.* The George School Readings on Developing Lands. New York: Bantam Books, 1970.

Muirhead, Desmond. *Palms.* Phoenix: Ampco, 1961.

Nayantara Sahgal. *Prison and Chocolate Cake.* London: Heinenann, 1985.

Owen, Juanita. *Where Flows the Ganges.* Brainerd: Mi: Lakeland Color Press, 1978.

Palmer, Flora Lucas. *Message of Victory.* Waukesha, WI: Metropolitan Church Assn.

The Quadrangle. Atlanta, GA: KWF Alumni Office. Vol. 2, Summer, 1985.

Schweitzer, Albert. *Mysticism of Paul the Apostle.* New York: MacMillan, 1955.

Thomas, Lowell, Jr. *Out of this World.* New York: Greystone Press, 1950.

Wallis, Ethel Emily. *The Dayuma Story.* New York: Harper & Brothers, 1960.

Washington, Doris V. *Yulan.* New York: Carlton Press, 1964.

Young, Desmond. *Rommel, the Desert Fox.* New York: Harper, 1950.

Young, James C. *Liberia Rediscovered.* Garden City: Doubleday, Doran & Co., 1934.